D1617312

# GREAT
# POLICIES

# GREAT
# POLICIES

## STRATEGIC INNOVATIONS
## IN ASIA AND THE PACIFIC BASIN

*EDITED BY*
*John D. Montgomery*
*and Dennis A. Rondinelli*

H
97
.G74
1995
West

Under the auspices of the Pacific Basin Research Center

**Westport, Connecticut**
**London**

**Library of Congress Cataloging-in-Publication Data**

Great policies  :  strategic innovations in Asia and the Pacific Basin  /
  edited by John D. Montgomery and Dennis A. Rondinelli  ;  under the
  auspices of the Pacific Basin Research Center.
      p.    cm.
    Includes bibliographical references and index.
    ISBN  0–275–95050–6 (alk. paper).—ISBN  0–275–95398–X (pbk.)
    1. Policy sciences.  2. Policy sciences—Case studies.
3. Marshall Plan.  4. Land reform—Taiwan.  5. China—Economic
policy.  6. Korea—Economic policy.  7. Education and state—Japan.
8. Economic assistance, Japanese—China.  I. Montgomery, John
Dickey.  II. Rondinelli, Dennis A.  III. John F. Kennedy
School of Government.  Pacific Basin Research Center.
H97.G74  1995
320′.6′095—dc20        95–13915

British Library Cataloguing in Publication Data is available.

Copyright © 1995 by John D. Montgomery

All rights reserved. No portion of this book may
be reproduced, by any process or technique, without the
express written consent of the publisher.

Library of Congress Catalog Card Number: 95–13915
ISBN: 0–275–95050–6
      0–275–95398–X (pbk.)

First published in 1995

Praeger Publishers, 88 Post Road West, Westport, CT 06881
An imprint of Greenwood Publishing Group, Inc.

Printed in the United States of America

The paper used in this book complies with the
Permanent Paper Standard issued by the National
Information Standards Organization (Z39.48–1984).

10  9  8  7  6  5  4  3  2  1

In honor of
Daisaku Ikeda
who made it all possible

# CONTENTS

# ILLUSTRATIONS

# ACKNOWLEDGMENTS

The editors are grateful to our contributing authors for their patience with our heavy hand on their good work. Patricia Harrison performed admirably as copy editor and formatter-in-chief during the editorial process, and we are grateful to her for cheerful services that went far beyond the call of duty.

Nearly all the original papers, which were prepared under postdoctoral fellowships at the Pacific Basin Research Center (PBRC), were two to three times as long as the space we were able to allot to them. We had to be ruthless in cutting and rewriting, but we believe that our stern resolve in doing so has represented the best interests of our readers as well as the publisher. In addition, several papers of excellent quality had to be omitted altogether from this collection because they overlapped with other chapters or because they did not add to our cumulative understanding of megapolicies. They are being published as PBRC discussion papers and are available upon request.

The Pacific Basin Research Center was created by Soka University of America in 1991 and is currently functioning as a part of the Center for Science and International Affairs (CSIA) at the John F. Kennedy School of Government, Harvard University. The support of these two institutions has been indispensable to our work. The original PBRC concept and unwavering loyalty of Daisaku Ikeda has given focus to our efforts and encouraged us to expand our activities over the past three years. In addition to the postdoctoral program on megapolicies, PBRC has conducted programs in trade and in the environment in such fields as solid and toxic waste management and small-scale energy systems in Asia and the Pacific. In all of these enterprises, PBRC has enjoyed a creative and symbiotic relationship with its colleagues at Harvard, especially the

CSIA. We hope that this relationship will continue as we move into additional fields of research.

# ABBREVIATIONS

AET      assistant English teacher
AID      Agency for International Development
ALT      assistant language teacher
ARD      Accelerated Rural Development
BET      British English Teaching
*BR*      *Beijing Review*
BSTC      Bureau of S&T Cadres
CARD      Committee for Accelerated Rural Development
CAS      Chinese Academy of Science
CCOP      Committee for Coordination and Operational Planning
*CD*      *China Daily*
*CE*      *Chinese Education*
CEEC      Committee of European Economic Cooperation
*CEN*      *China Exchange Newsletter*
CFM      Council of Foreign Ministers
CGIAR      Consultative Group on International Agricultural Research
CGP      Clean Government Party
CIR      coordinators of international relations
CLAIR      Council of Local Authorities for International Relations
CPCC      Communist Party Central Committee
CSIA      Center for Science and International Affairs
CSS      Chinese students and scholars
CST      China Science and Technology
DAC      Development Assistance Committee

| | |
|---|---|
| DOLA | Department of Local Administration |
| DSP | Democratic Socialist Party |
| ECA | Economic Cooperation Administration |
| ECSC | European Coal and Steel Community |
| EEC | European Economic Community |
| ERIC | Educational Resources Information Center |
| ERP | European Recovery Plan |
| ESL | English as a second language |
| FAs | Farmers' Associations |
| FAO | Food and Agriculture Organization |
| FAPATUX | Fábricas de Papel Tuxtepec (a foreign-owned logging firm) |
| FBIS | Foreign Broadcast Information Service |
| FOA | Foreign Operations Administration |
| *FRUS* | *Foreign Relations of the United States* |
| GDP | gross domestic product |
| GEF | Global Environment Facility |
| GNP | gross national product |
| ICA | International Cooperation Administration |
| IDC | Industrial Development Commission |
| IFCSS | Independent Federation of Chinese Students and Scholars |
| INCORA | Colombian Land Reform Institute |
| INSEAD | Institut Européen d'Administration des Affaires (European Institute of Business Administration) |
| JCP | Japanese Communist Party |
| JCRR | Joint Commission on Rural Reconstruction |
| JET | Japan Exchange and Teaching |
| JFQ | complete laws and regulations for education |
| JPRS | Joint Publications Research Service |
| JSP | Japanese Socialist Party |
| KMT | Kuomintang (Chinese Nationalist Party) |
| LDCs | less developed countries |
| LDP | Liberal Democratic Party |
| MEF | Mombusho English Fellow |
| MFN | most favored nation |
| MFR | Ministry of Foreign Relations |
| MIQRO | Maderas Industrializados de Quintana Roo (a state timber company) |
| MOE | Ministry of Education |
| MOF | Ministry of Finance |
| MOFA | Ministry of Foreign Affairs |
| MOFERT | Ministry of Foreign Economic Relations and Trade |
| MOHA | Ministry of Home Affairs |
| MOI | Ministry of Interior |
| MOP | Ministry of Personnel |

| MSA | Mutual Security Agency |
| NAFSA | National Association of Foreign Student Affairs |
| NBER | National Bureau of Economic Research |
| NEPA | National Environmental Protection Agency |
| NGOs | nongovernmental organizations |
| NRCSTD | National Research Center for Science and Technology for Development |
| NSC | National Security Command |
| NT$ | New Taiwan dollar |
| ODA | official development assistance |
| OECD | Organization for Economic Cooperation and Development |
| OEEC | Organization for European Economic Cooperation |
| PBRC | Pacific Basin Research Center |
| PRC | People's Republic of China |
| PRI | Partido Revolucionario Institucional |
| PTA | Parent Teacher Association |
| R&D | research and development |
| RGWX | Selected documents on personnel work |
| *RMRB* | *Renmin ribao* (*People's Daily*) |
| ROC | Republic of China |
| RTG | Royal Thai Government |
| S&T | science and technology |
| SC | State Council |
| SEC | State Economic Commission |
| SEdC | State Education Commission |
| SETC | State Economic and Trade Commission |
| SEZ | special economic zone |
| SMEs | small- and medium-scale enterprises |
| SPC | State Planning Commission |
| SST | supersonic transport |
| SSTC | State Science and Technology Commission |
| STAPRC | Science and Technology Association of the People's Republic of China |
| SWNCC | State-War-Navy Coordinating Committee |
| UN | United Nations |
| UNCED | United Nations Center for Environment and Development |
| UNDP | United Nations Development Programme |
| UNEP | United Nations Environmental Programme |
| UNRRA | United Nations Relief and Rehabilitation Administration |
| USAID | United States Agency for International Development |
| USOM | United States Operations Mission |
| WHO | World Health Organization |
| ZFZWH | collection of documents on policies towards intellectuals |

# GREAT
# POLICIES

# 1

## BEYOND GOOD POLICIES

*John D. Montgomery*

The opportunity to introduce major policy innovations comes only rarely. Most of the time, well-established routines will suffice, even for meeting new challenges. Governments and other large organizations have to provide the basic services and functions they need without violating conventional procedures. Through routine processes, they set up new budgets and recruit and maintain new types of personnel and procure the improved supplies and equipment they need to produce valued outputs. Standard practices follow the constitutional means by which they perform their essential functions: to provide for the common (including their own) defense and establish enough tranquillity or contentment to justify themselves in the eyes of their constituencies. In short, even the least efficient of them can usually adopt and implement conventional policies as they approach their immediate goals.

Occasionally, however, they face problems of a different order that draw them outside established jurisdictions and procedures. Novel or complex problems can lead them across the frontiers of custom and comfortable institutional conventions. When governments begin to grapple with problems of that order, routines are insufficient and new policies become necessary; some of them are unique enough to be called great.

Such events may be rare, but they occur often enough to invite further inquiry. Current empirical and historical research on routine policies is already an established art form; such studies have progressed far enough to enable analysts to compare sectoral policies and measure their successes as well as to suggest incremental improvements in them that will lead them to higher levels, commonly known as good policies. But great policies are of a different order;

such major innovations require a commitment beyond the standard function-
ally or professionally distinct arenas of activity known as sectors. What common
characteristics do these unconventional, innovative policies share? How can we
identify the range of complex problems that give rise to them? Can these
experiences provide insights into the central nature of such creativity, at whatever level it occurs, and perhaps offer lessons and warnings to decision makers
who find the need to venture into unknown areas of policy making? This book
was conceived to consider these questions.

## HOW GOOD POLICIES ARE MADE

Governments and other large organizations pursue what they conceive as
policies by providing authoritative expressions of purpose, which in turn imply
a sequence of steps needed to pursue them and suggest a basis for appraising
their effectiveness. Thereafter, policy historians can record these implementing
steps by following them through standard organizations (such as ministries and
departments concerned with finance or personnel or procurement), by observing recognized procedures (including budgets and job classification systems),
and, finally, by evaluating the extent to which they have achieved their agreed
objectives (such as generating socially valued products like safety or wealth).[1]
Standard analytical procedures like these make it possible to compare even
different policy initiatives by treating them in terms of their sectoral dimensions, including their organizational and behavioral characteristics. Historical
analyses and comparisons permit some degree of experimentation in the sense
that they can yield predictions and suggest incremental improvements.[2]

When policies take the form of sectoral interventions, they make themselves
more readily capable of incremental change. Comparisons among social policies, for example, have made it possible to build on experience in quite different
situations and to improve the performance of organizations and institutions
that differ widely in their goals, strategies, and procedures.[3] Analysts have
increasingly treated such policies as the outputs or products of government and,
thus, developed insights into politics, structure, and public responses that were
unknown even to the policy makers themselves.[4] The structured (if imaginary)
differentiation by sector and institutional jurisdiction simplifies making decisions and produces warnings and lessons by simple extrapolation from familiar
to unfamiliar settings.

These intellectual achievements are not trivial. Knowledge of experience and
institutional learning and structure has permitted incremental improvements
in performance throughout the world. Even in relatively backward organizations, routine policies have become good policies. Such improvements are
marks of organizational maturity; they have contributed to major advances in
government performance.[5] Many—perhaps most—good policies result from
such incremental change in current practice.[6]

Progress through incremental improvement offers few surprises to historians. Probably most human problems are solved by the familiar plugging-away process, which makes improvements at the margin and produces progress step by step.[7] Policies can evolve in much the same way as technologies do: like cars and televisions, they can get better with each year's model if there is enough challenge to produce the effort required to change. The mounting information about viruses and genes and carcinogenesis has gradually (or, sometimes, jerkily) produced better diagnosis and therapy, which in turn are eventually absorbed in the physician's repertory.[8] Better data about economic and voting behavior have contributed to more accurate and usable forecasts and, sometimes at least, to more effective policies and action programs. Social security benefits, food stamps, and drivers' licenses are delivered more efficiently than they were twenty years ago. The history of science, engineering, medicine, and policy making is full of such incremental improvements, augmented only occasionally by quantum jumps in understanding. Knowledge about such incremental changes creates a reassuring sense of progress.

## TRANSCENDING INCREMENTALISM

Policies that are merely good have their own limits, however. They can achieve their ultimate potential and still not solve some emergent problems. On the contrary, sometimes the successes of good policies create problems caused by their own side effects. When existing policies interact with each other in such a way as to produce conflict or the possibility of synergistic change, incremental improvements—important as they may be—can be insufficient. Innovation of some other kind is required when good policies cannot be improved enough to meet changing demands.

The change from incremental policy improvements to a quantum leap toward greatness is subtle but palpable. The policy equivalent of a new Galilean or Darwinian world view invites the analyst's attention to new problems and new directions. Examples of such changes occur more frequently than convention recognizes, and they range from the trivial to the transcendental. Issues as basic as human rights have taken on new dimensions nationally and internationally. Experimental uses of solar power by local, national, and international actors for rural health facilities or as a potential solution to major energy shortages often demand new organizational approaches and substitutes for the economic and political advantages of conventional power sources. Neighborhood parks are being converted to historic monuments to protect localities against undesirable land uses and to introduce new tourist industries. Instead of command and control mechanisms for protecting air purity by restraining industrial activities, the United States and other countries are experimenting with market-oriented tradable permits that introduce new incentives to self-discipline and at the same time defray some of the costs of regulation.[9] Debt-for-equity swaps are producing a new form of diplomacy, replacing international regimes for recovering loans as well as exhortations against inhumane policies. The World Summit on Environment and Development tried to stimulate innovation by introducing regional sustainable development centers to conduct research on efficient natural resource development and at the same time provide assistance to member governments that lack the technical capacity for change. Policies in aid for education of women are challenging social institutions and developing new sources of talent, as well as contributing to the solution of population problems. Highly effective agricultural stations were created by the Consultative Group on International Agricultural Research (CGIAR) to provide science and technical assistance to developing countries, and they have succeeded as innovations in both technology transfer and diplomacy.[10] That experience is being reviewed now as a model for sociotechnical innovations to deal with global warming. Solving such problems will suggest quantum leaps in the history of policy making. These policies may produce new social insights and new institutional responses as well. That hope was the inspiration for the three years of research that is reported in the chapters that follow.

## INNOVATIVE GREATNESS

Innovative policies can respond to problems that arise out of unexpected side effects or policy interactions without being great. Innovation can appear almost anyplace where policy interactions compel decision makers to act. Policy complexity invites, but does not guarantee, greatness. Sometimes intersectoral complexity can be resolved by conservative, incremental steps. The usual response to conflicting objectives among interacting values is to reduce or restrain one or another of the policies involved or to make modest changes in their direction.[11] The usual response to complementarity among objectives is to increase or accelerate one or both of the policies involved. Great policies emerge when modest, incremental steps seem insufficient or inappropriate.

Innovative greatness is rare enough to deserve recognition as a special policy genre. Our research team has adopted the term "megapolicies" to describe the experiences we regard as prototypical. Our megapolicies could be expected to share certain easily identifiable characteristics: (1) they transcend traditional sectoral and intellectual boundaries and jurisdictions, (2) they require new organizational or procedural devices for their implementation, (3) they generate new expectations that cannot be met by normal programs, and (4) they define new models of policy responses and suggest new paradigms of policy analysis.[12] Such policies do not always succeed, but when they do, they can redefine the potential of government action.[13] Even in failure, they can be inspirational if their moral purposes demonstrate a noble vision of leadership.[14]

Rare though they are, megapolicies are easily recognized in the light of history. In setting forth an agenda for research on these experiences, the Pacific Basin Research Center suggested four prototypical models against which to analyze great policies: (1) the U.S. Marshall Plan of the 1940s, (2) Taiwan's bonds-for-land swap of the 1950s, (3) Chinese and Korean reverse-brain-drain policies beginning in the 1970s, and (4) Japan's recruitment of foreign teachers to internationalize secondary education in the 1980s.[15] These four policies emerged from quite different circumstances: the first case was an unprecedented opportunity arising out of problems that could not be addressed by conventional means; the second came about when it was discovered that surplus resources in one sector could be used to complement efforts in another arena of equal concern; the third was a series of responses to the negative consequences of an ambitious program of human development; and the fourth was an initiative for local action that arose out of international concerns in the prime minister's office and spilled over into the foreign office before reaching the education ministry and the prefectural governments.

The Marshall Plan to offer aid for European reconstruction in the wake of World War II had no real precedents. It was not a military sequel to the war, though it served security objectives; it was not a diplomatic gesture, even though it employed State Department professionals and created a new diplomatic corps; and it was not undertaken as an economic development policy, though its aspirations as well as its consequences for American and European industry were developmental. New organizations had to be created, both in the United States and in Europe, to set conditions and standards and to garner the cooperation of the participating states. It offered hope to Europe and, eventually, to other regions that had suffered heavy losses during the war. And, finally, it produced a cadre of experts in foreign aid and a clutch of theories about development and reconstruction that have been invoked ever since as a solution to chaotic international circumstances.[16]

Taiwan's land reform was conceived out of the Japanese experience in dispossessing absentee landlords and empowering tenants in the process, but it was carried out by an independent state, not in an occupied country.[17] Moreover, it was not merely a replication of the familiar "land to the tiller" doctrine in which landlords would be dispossessed in favor of the peasants who were working on small plots in large estates. Rather, it incorporated an exchange: because Taiwan's new nationalist government had taken title to the industrial resources the Japanese had owned during their decades of occupation, it was possible to offer stock ownership in them as partial compensation for the landlords' losses. This policy simultaneously redistributed land and permitted a subsample of the former landlords to flourish as a new industrial elite and to lead the country in the direction of an export-oriented economy. The innovative character of this policy led the Sino-American Joint Commission on Rural Reconstruction (JCRR) to devise rapid new procedures to bring about the transfers required.

Both the newly independent farmers and the new industrial elites now enjoyed a prosperity that exceeded their previous hopes. Land reforms in other countries have taken the JCRR experience as a model to be emulated when similar opportunities could be identified.[18] Those that followed conventional, good-policy patterns were less successful.[19]

Both China and Korea undertook major programs to develop needed scientists and engineers by sending qualified students abroad. The Chinese program began as part of Deng Xiaoping's modernization drive in 1978 and expanded so rapidly that it turned into a study-abroad craze that propelled both privileged opportunists and eager students to seek financing at universities in the United States, Japan, and Europe. Selecting candidates became an almost feverish activity in central, provincial, and local governments as well as in universities and research institutions and far transcended the capacities and authority of the Ministry of Education.

Study abroad soon turned into a one-way flow, however, when only a third of the 200,000 scholars who left China had returned by the end of 1993: a brain drain of massive proportions that compelled the government to change the incentives and institutional opportunities available to talented individuals. Korea, which had embarked on a similar program in the 1960s, discovered that only 20 percent of its students abroad were returning, and it, too, responded by an extensive round of innovations, setting up a science park, research centers, and high-tech university programs to provide opportunities for the emigrants. By the 1980s, two-thirds were returning home, and more than 90 percent of them were engaged in research and teaching. This return of the natives was induced not by changes in the educational program or by civil service reforms but by a combination of public and private efforts that had no precedent in either China or Korea.[20] New organizations were created in both countries to give stability to the reverse Diasporas; the returnees began to enjoy career expectations that paralleled the hopes of their original sponsors.

Japan, still sensitive to the failure of its defeated imperial ambitions, was becoming increasingly aware in the 1980s of a need to surmount its isolation from world affairs. The Ministry of Education resisted efforts to change the curricula of the secondary schools, which, after all, were managed by the prefectural authorities; under pressure it nevertheless responded to suggestions bubbling up from bureaucrats in the prime minister's office, and later from the foreign ministry, by importing 8,000 Americans and other English speakers and giving them two-year teaching assignments in selected high schools—hoping for a cultural spillover that would encourage international interest among Japanese youth. Some observers liken the experiment to the Peace Corps initiative in the Kennedy Administration, another megapolicy that continues to influence the foreign projections of national aspirations in several other countries.

## RESEARCH ON MEGAPOLICIES

Those four examples of megapolicies share other common features that could illuminate the process by which such complex problems are confronted. Our comparative analysis of selected megapolicies in Asia and the Pacific has provided further insights into their origins, the process by which they rose to become a prescribed course of action, their organizational dimensions, and their outcomes, both in terms of their objectives and of other consequences. These chapters were chosen to illustrate the range of megapolicy experiences in the region and to explore their relevance to other situations.

Although all policies were selected because they shared the four dimensions we have ascribed to megapolicies, they display other common elements as well. First of all, as expected, their origins offered some clues to relationships between the innovations themselves and conventional policies from which they emerged. In all four cases, the political leaders took a problem out of the jaws of the bureaucracy or the legislature and moved it to new levels of administration and public commitment because those responsible for the earlier policies were unable to deal with some of the consequences of their interaction with other policies. These decisions were more than a flashy political bonanza; they emerged out of a recognition that existing policies were no longer adequate for the changed situation. In each case, the context of innovation seemed to begin with a conscious recognition of problems produced by the side effects of previous policies, both good and bad. These side effects took the form of unexpected demands, disappointed beneficiaries, and dissatisfaction among puzzled administrators over the consequences of previous operations. These were problems that could not have yielded solutions by incremental policy improvements; the preliminary consultations that identified them took place across the normal boundaries of bureaucratic and political communication. Contrary to the public vision of the emergent moments of political greatness, megapolicies like these did not spring full-blown from a newly elected leadership but came out of a churning system that was reacting to the puzzle of sectoral problems that it could not resolve by conventional approaches.

Second, the issues that surrounded these megapolicies expanded the range of activity normally accepted as the responsibility of the innovating government. Neither the U.S. War Department nor its State Department was positioned to deal with the mixed fruits of victory and defeat after World War II; the conflicting demands of the peasants and the landlords did not fit the missions and jurisdictions of the agencies charged with land reform and with reorganizing the parastatal corporations in Taiwan; the loss of technical and scientific manpower produced by foreign training was not the responsibility of the Ministries of Education alone in China or Korea; and preparation for national citizenship as perceived by Japan's Ministry of Education did not accommodate its new international needs. Seemingly irrelevant contradictions among traditional public programs—education for national citizenship versus creation of a favorable international environment, in the case of Japan, for example—could provoke complex interventions that transcended the responsibilities of either sector. In each case, the previous policies (waging war and occupying conquered territory as opposed to introducing conditions favorable to peace and prosperity; or the conventions of educational and agricultural programs versus producing a more viable national presence) continued to prevail even while new, more pervasive policies were introduced.

Third, these unconventional responses have transcended not only organizational sectors but also basic constitutive systems and have extended their reach to intergovernmental or even international institutions. The Marshall Plan invited the European partners of the United States to create new planning and coordinating resources, and each of the other megapolicies in our sample required cooperation among several ministries and different levels of government and eventually inspired experimentation by other nations. The achievements of these policies stimulated innovations in new settings that were sometimes quite dissimilar to their own origins. The Marshall Plan created a new cadre of committed Americans who provided the core of the venturesome diplomacy of foreign aid. Its tactics provided a model for postwar aid to Greece and Turkey and, later, to Latin America and Asia and finally reached its most ambitious pretension when it seemed to call for the virtual recolonization of Viet Nam. The other megapolicies studied thus far, though less dramatic, also produced spin-offs for new situations.

The effects of such afterthoughts were not always salutary. The Vietnamese adventure of the United States is sometimes regarded as a deranged aftermath of the Marshall Plan because its early phases made use of veterans of European reconstruction. No one would argue today that it delivered equivalent benefits to U.S. foreign objectives or even to the intended beneficiaries. Nor has the export of techniques for an industrial renaissance in Korea and Taiwan prospered as impressively abroad as it did at home. Japan, too, has found it wise to proceed cautiously in expanding the introduction of foreign personnel to offset its parochial traditions.

Finally, these megapolicies have shown that they could follow unpredictable trajectories as they served new values. If they have enabled governments to resolve conflicts without sacrificing one set of values in order to achieve another, they have demanded rising levels of political commitment as they have persisted. If they have generated new political coalitions, they have bypassed negotiations among conflicting groups or goals.[21] And, finally, where they have required active participation from their beneficiaries, from collaborating agencies and levels of government, and from the private sector, they have added to the normal confusions of policy implementation.

All four of these megapolicies were announced with great fanfare, a step that gave the operating bureaucracies a sense of commitment to objectives that lay beyond their technical responsibilities and provided guidance in the interpretation of operating procedures. But in the process, they had to cater to rising expectations in order to avoid political, popular, and administrative fatigue. They had to proceed in advance of a coherent, recognized body of theory or experience even though, in their aftermath, theories and explanations have abounded. Yet, this very uncertainty has favored continuing experimentation and a high degree of concurrent appraisal.

## LEARNING FROM MEGAPOLICIES

The possibility that governments will learn from these experiences should not be taken for granted. Governments have enough trouble learning from their conventional policy experience.[22] There is undoubtedly a stubborn, almost universal resistance to experiential learning, whether caused by reluctance to abandon obsolete intellectual habits or by complacence and satisfaction with prevailing good policies. Failures of imagination also explain the persistence of mediocre solutions to growing problems. Perhaps an acquaintanceship with the experience of innovation itself can help governments think afresh about complex problems whose solutions lie beyond current traditions of policy making. Innovation, wherever it occurs, is always worth studying.

All four of the prototype policies described in this chapter were national, but the research that followed was not limited to central authorities and national issues. The expectation was that such events can occur at any level of government. Even provincial or municipal units may encounter such interactions and can experiment with such megapolicies: cities move in that direction, for example, when they develop alternatives to burdensome directives from national laws that conflict with local standards, perhaps using their political resources to create new programs in order to escape restrictions on their prerogatives.[23] Like nations, states and local governments are constantly experimenting with megapolicies, such as novel forms of privatization, citizen voluntarism, and civic rewards for socially desirable public behavior. Private corporations working in a multinational context have been known to reconfigure themselves and their mission when they have run out of conventional solutions. Even apparently dormant international agencies like the United Nations have shown they can rise to the occasion in order to deal with unexpected environment-development or sovereignty-peacemaking interactions.

Recognizing these possibilities, the Pacific Basin Research Center began its research on megapolicies with a closer examination of some of the four prototype policies and proceeded to other experiences that might display the same characteristics. The search for examples included the merger of agricultural and industrial policies in Taiwan and Thailand; various combinations of high-tech industrial support policies as they emerged in Japan, the United States, and Korea; the introduction of environment-saving goals at some cost to developmental goals in Mexican electric utilities; processes by which the private sector has introduced toxic waste programs in Asia; measures taken to mitigate unfavorable environmental consequences of international trade agreements; recent policies to link industrial development to regional concerns in the Pacific Basin; and several locally based experiments with township industries and municipal public works programs in the People's Republic of China. The chapters that follow present some results of this research.

We had expected to find that megapolicies would arise out of interactions among existing policies, and our case studies illustrated both conflicts and synergies that encouraged innovation. We began by speculating on known consequences of interactions among security, environmental, educational or cultural, and economic development policies, and we reviewed examples of each to explore the extent to which recognition of these interactions spawned innovation. The cases we decided to pursue included conflicts between agricultural and industrial development priorities, economic and security policies, social and infrastructure investments, and local and central preeminence, as well as private and public purposes. Such interactions appeared recognizably as an impetus to innovation. Our studies confirmed the fact that these policy originators were fully aware of the contradictions and symbioses with which they were dealing.

Although all of these chapters describe cases that were originally selected as illustrative examples of megapolicies, their range extends beyond even our fondest expectations. Some involved economic growth strategies (Chapters 3, 4, 8, and 12), some were social policy initiatives that had unexpected repercussions (Chapter 7), some dealt with local government problems (Chapter 10), while others were international (Chapters 2, 5, and 11) or even global; and some were primarily scientific or technological innovations in the private sector (Chapters 6 and 9). We had expected to find some transforming vision or coherent strategic ambition as the origin of these innovations, and so we did, but there were also exceptional cases when the original intention was moderately incremental until the accumulated changes overtook policy conventions and emerged from the chrysalis of tradition. As expected, however, all of the cases can be explained as responses to interacting values or policy dilemmas, and all had their beginnings in a recognition somewhere in the bureaucracy before they became politicized. None were free of at least some bureaucratic turf warfare, but all demanded administrative changes. None were expressions of abstract political ideology, but all were bold ventures. In calling attention to the rewards of intellectual boldness in addressing complex problems, we do not intend to ignore the more familiar lessons of policy implementation, even in the case of megapolicies. Boldness can be overdone. But so can incrementalism, and, even more, so can ill-considered use of analogies. Megapolicies can be seductive: there are technical advisors waiting in the wings of public office who are all too ready to transfer knowledge derived from one set of experiences to another setting. The analogies that appear in the headlines today offer misleading suggestions of innovation-made-routine, and they need to be considered carefully in context: Is the Marshall Plan really a prototype for the reconstruction of eastern Europe? Can land reform in Latin America encourage an industrial class by buying off displaced landlords? What resources would other governments require to replicate the Chinese or Korean reverse brain drain in an era of greater international competitiveness in science and technology? Can the importation of language teachers have the same internationalizing impact in a multicultural society as it did in Japan?

The usual problems of implementation will persist even in appropriate sites for transferring a megapolicy experience. There is no immunity from administrative misadventure. Even if innovations are not undertaken on a large scale, they are likely to require special resources that can inspire managerial carelessness and external suspicion. Megapolicy solutions, like good policy successes, can be oversold and overprotected.

Almost certainly the application of a megapolicy paradigm will be riskier than the transfer of more routine policy and administrative operations through the conventions of technical assistance. But surely it will offer more guidance for innovation than the bureaucratic models and static formulas that dominate many current studies of public policy in this era of rapid change.

## NOTES

1. For example, see Richard E. Neustadt and Harvey Fineberg, *The Epidemic That Never Was: Policy-making and the Swine Flu Affair* (New York: Vintage Books, 1983).

2. A suggested methodology for conducting these analyses appears in Chapter 2 of this book.

3. For examples of this style of analysis, see John D. Montgomery, Harold D. Lasswell, and Joel S. Migdal, *Patterns of Policy: Comparative and Longitudinal Studies of Population Events* (New Brunswick, N.J.: Transaction Books, 1979).

4. Mark H. Moore, "Creating Public Value, Strategic Management in Transfer of Government Benefits," *Federal Reserve Bulletin* 77 (April 1991): 203–17; and Mark H. Moore, *Creating Public Value: Strategic Management in the Public Sector* (Cambridge: Harvard University Press, forthcoming).

5. A well-documented example is described in John D. Wood and Dolores S. Smith, "Electronic Transfer of Government Benefits," *Federal Reserve Bulletin* 77 (April 1991): 203–17.

6. Adding or subtracting resources, the usual definition of incrementalism, comprise "first-order policies," according to Peter Hall. His "second-order policies" involve changes in the organization or administrative structure. Innovation, for him, means paradigm changes, such as a transition from Keynesianism to monetarism in economic policy. Such innovations do not constitute megapolicies in our definition, however, unless they are intersectoral. A well-documented discussion with examples appears in Peter A. Hall, "Policy Paradigms, Social Learning, and the State," *Comparative Politics* 25, no. 3 (1993): 275–96.

7. A justifiably famous study of such an experience is Martha Derthick, *Agency Under Stress: Security Administration in American Government* (Washington, D.C.: The Brookings Institution, 1990).

8. The 1991 Nobel Prize in medicine was awarded for discoveries regarding ion exchange on the cellular level, a megadiscovery that was the product of years of research by others.

9. See Robert N. Stavins, "Toward a New Era of Environmental Policy," in *Regulating the Future: The Creative Balance*, ed. Carol Tucker Foreman (Washington, D.C.: Center for National Policy Press, 1991).

10. Warren C. Bau, *Partners Against Hunger: Consultative Group on International Agricultural Research* (Washington, D.C.: The World Bank, 1986).

11. Some policies cannot be terminated or even reduced, regardless of their external costs, but usually some modifications are possible. There are few absolutely irreducible policies in the hierarchy of public values, no "lexicographic" priorities that must always be observed. See Robert E. Goodin, *Political Theory and Public Policy* (Chicago: University of Chicago Press, 1982). A familiar example of philosophical objections to such compromise opposed the banning of the Concorde aircraft while permitting the use of defense-related versions of the supersonic transport (SST), which were thought to have similar environmental consequences. The argument was that neither was essential, whether to commercial development or national defense; but for political reasons, termination was impossible.

12. Many, but not all, large-scale policies fit this definition even though they may share certain characteristics (such as, going beyond incremental change, requiring special resources, being indivisible in terms of task separation, and their relative insusceptibility to trial or pilot project forms of experimentation). Moreover, not all great policies are necessarily large-scale. The lessons that large-scale policies might impart to administrators, however, resonate with those we are encountering in our study of these policies: the easy access to resources; the reinforced obligations on managers to find solutions to unexpected problems; the psychological burdens posed by the politician's tendency to oversell the product; the risk of over-protecting the policy itself; increased possibilities for political interference or micromanagement; vulnerability to influence by heterogeneous interest groups; and the risk of political, public, and administrative fatigue as the operation progresses. Many of these conditions are described by Paul R. Schulman in *Large-Scale Policy Making* (New York: Elsevier, 1980), which examines such activities as the space program, the war on poverty, and the war on cancer.

13. In his comment on an early draft of this chapter, my colleague Harvey Brooks remarked that private sector megapolicies deserve similar attention, citing the work of Frederick Winslow Taylor as the antecedent to Ford's production line along with the prehistory of Japanese industrial management innovations that could be traced back to Walter Shewman, Demint, and others. Great achievements do not always constitute megapolicies, however. There may be an equivalent for these policies in the private sector, but their distinguishing characteristics would obviously be somewhat different from those described here.

14. Failure, like success, lies somewhere behind the eyes of the observer. Some megapolicy successes can have disappointing, even catastrophic, consequences. For example, Mao's cultural revolution, Khrushchev's virgin land program, Diem's agrovilles, Nyerere's *ujaama* (freedom) villages, Johnson's "maximum feasible participation," and others that were aimed at a moral purpose were generally pronounced failures. Hitler's Final Solution might once have seemed a megapolicy, but to the degree that it succeeded, it was a catastrophe. My colleague Milton J. Esman believes that a moral purpose should be an explicit dimension of megapolicies.

15. This organization was established in 1991 by Soka University of America, located in Los Angeles. It is currently operating as a unit in the Center for Science and International Affairs at the Kennedy School of Government, Harvard University. During its first three years, it devoted most of its resources to postdoctoral fellowships to study megapolicies.

16. Robert Donovan, *The Second Victory* (New York: Madison, 1987), 27–28.

17. Some interpretations of the Taiwan experience suggest that the Kuomintang (KMT) government of that island was itself a kind of occupation. Its remoteness from responsibility to local landlords certainly contributed to its vigorous policies. Critics should be reminded, however, that KMT had begun an ambitious land reform (too late) on the mainland.

18. Neil Jacoby, *U.S. Aid to Taiwan* (New York: Praeger, 1966), 62–63, 82, 171–72; T. H. Shen, *The Sino-American Joint Commission on Rural Reconstruction* (Ithaca, N.Y.: Cornell University Press, 1970), 52, 71–76; Hui-Sun Tang, *Land Reform in Free China* (Taipei: China Engraving, 1954), 20–21; John D. Montgomery, Rufus B. Hughes, and Raymond H. Davis, *Rural Improvement and Political Development* (Washington, D.C.: American Society for Public Administration, 1966); Cal Clark, *Taiwan's Development: Implications for Contending Political Economy Paradigms* (Westport, Conn.: Greenwood, 1987); Michael Hsin-huang Hsiao, *Government Agricultural Strategies in Taiwan and North Korea* (Taipei: Academia Sinica, 1981); Joseph Yager, *Transforming Agriculture in Taiwan: The Experience of the Joint Commission on Rural Reconstruction* (Ithaca, N.Y.: Cornell University Press, 1988).

19. See John D. Montgomery, "Allocation of Authority in Land Reform Programs: A Comparative Study of Administrative Processes and Outputs," *Administrative Science Quarterly* 17, no. 1 (1972).

20. For a study of the consequences of these policies, see Ha-Jung Sung, *Who Stays? Who Returns? The Choice of Korean Scientists and Engineers*, doctoral dissertation, Harvard University, May 1991, especially pp. 20, 203.

21. A recent example is an agreement between oil industry representatives and national environmental groups to supply cleaner-burning gasoline to the smoggiest cities beginning in 1995, a step that is expected to reduce tailpipe pollution emissions by 15 percent. The agreement was consistent with the 1990 Clean Air Act but not required by it. This "regulatory negotiation" agreement stipulated that the parties would not litigate or lobby against regulations to implement the compromise.

22. Lloyd Etheredge, *Can Governments Learn? American Foreign Policy and Central American Revolutions* (New York: Pergamon Press, 1985).

23. There is a Chinese saying describing this phenomenon: "Higher authorities have policies, lower levels have countermeasures."

# 2

# THE ORIGINAL MEGAPOLICY: AMERICA'S MARSHALL PLAN

*John Orme*

The Marshall Plan of 1947–1952 surely ranks as one of the most original and successful foreign policy initiatives of the twentieth century, by the United States or any other power. The program's originality was twofold. Unlike previous efforts, the European Recovery Plan (ERP) aimed not just at short-term relief but rather at a long-term solution to Europe's economic difficulties to be achieved by an increase in production, which was seen as "the touchstone of economic recovery."[1] Second, the program envisioned the integration of Europe as the primary means of fostering both greater prosperity and international stability. Hence, it placed particular emphasis on the liberalization of trade restrictions among the European countries and on the development of international institutions to coordinate policy between them.[2]

The effects of the Marshall Plan, though in some respects falling short of its designers' initial hopes, were impressive and far-reaching. Three stand out. First, through the provision of both material and intangible support, it stimulated a rapid expansion of Europe's economy and made possible the attainment by 1952 of production levels 35 percent higher than before the war in industry and 10 percent greater in agriculture, as well as a 70 percent increase in trade.[3] The transfer of $13.3 billion in U.S. aid over four years (hitting a peak of 2.4 percent of gross national product [GNP] in 1949) made it possible for friendly governments to maintain the high rates of investment that fueled economic growth without politically dangerous cuts in living standards. Although the tangible contribution this made was very important, the psychological impact may have been even greater.[4] The offer of assistance was, in the words of Britain's foreign secretary, Ernest Bevin, "a lifeline to sinking men. It seemed to bring hope where there was none." Within months, it had begun to restore confidence in the ability of democratic societies to deal with the enormous problems confronting them.[5]

Second, the ERP led to the development of new organizations on both continents and gave a small but crucial impetus to efforts at enhancing international integration and cooperation among European nations and between Europe and the United States. In the United States, a new agency outside the jurisdiction of existing departments, the Economic Cooperation Administration, was created to administer the program. It evolved subsequently through several stages into a permanent bureau for the disbursement of economic assistance (the present day U.S. Agency for International Development).[6] In Europe, the program not only revived the economies but also helped to heal the wounds of war and foster habits of cooperation. It gave rise to one of the first and most influential organizations for international economic collaboration, the Organization for European Economic Cooperation (OEEC), (later the Organization for Economic Cooperation and Development, or OECD), and laid the foundation for other instruments of international diplomacy such as the European Coal and Steel Community (ECSC), the North Atlantic Treaty Organization, and eventually the European Community.

Through participation in deliberations over the Marshall Plan, habits of cooperation were established that prepared the way for more intensive collaboration later in other settings. Under its auspices, the European Payments Union, established in 1950, made great strides in eliminating trade barriers and reversing the partitioning of Europe into autarkic units. In 1950, France proposed the Schuman Plan to create the ECSC, which placed French and German industries (along with those of the four other signatories) under supranational authority. It seems unlikely that this remarkable effort, in the words of Jean Monnet, to "exorcise history" would have come about without the prior and continuing efforts of the United States. Although the Treaty of Rome was not signed until 1957, the ECSC was a crucial first step towards the founding of the European Community.[7] The Truman administration fell far short of the ambitious objective of a complete integration of the European economies, but in the judgment of Michael Hogan, "it seems clear that American recovery policy helped to set the Europeans on a road that led from the economic autarky of the 1930s to the Common Market of the 1960s."[8]

Finally, the undoubted success of the ERP made it a model and an inspiration in many future situations, from the efforts at Third World development during the cold war years to the travails of postcommunist societies in the present day. Whether the comparisons drawn are entirely appropriate or not, the repeated calls for a new Marshall Plan in settings as diverse as Latin America and Eastern Europe are indirect tribute to the continuing influence of the original conception of George Marshall and his colleagues.

How and why, then, did this unique initiative come about? Why did the United States decide to commit resources on such a scale to Europe in 1947?

Why did the program take the form that it did? In order to address these questions, this chapter will first recount the process by which the Truman administration conceived the plan and persuaded Europe and Congress to act on it, then focus more closely on these key points of interpretation.

## ORIGINS OF THE POLICY

The concepts that inspired the Marshall Plan developed first not in the minds of the top leadership of the Truman administration but rather among junior officials in the State Department's economic bureaus. Drawing on their experience with United Nations' agencies in Europe during 1945–1946, officials in the U.S. Economic Mission in London, the German and Austrian Economic Division, and the Division of Investments and Economic Development opposed a reconstitution of independent national economies, which in their view retarded production in Europe and proposed, instead, regional coordination and liberalization of trade restrictions in the hope of forestalling the division of Europe and promoting economic recovery.[9] The most significant of these efforts was a plan submitted by W. W. Rostow of the State Department's German and Austrian Economic Division on February 25, 1946. In essence, it called for the U.S. to propose a general political settlement in Europe, including Germany, along with the creation of an all-European economic organization to promote recovery which the United States would then be prepared to support with substantial levels of economic aid. Rostow's proposal won the backing of two influential undersecretaries, Will Clayton and Dean Acheson (both key proponents of the Marshall Plan a year later), who suggested the idea to Secretary of State James Byrnes in April. Byrnes was not persuaded, however, and the proposal was never presented to the Russians. The most important reasons for its failure, Rostow suggests, were that the sense of crisis necessary to force a shift in policy of this magnitude was not yet present and that Byrnes, a man jealous of his authority and autonomy, hesitated to embark on a policy that could only have succeeded with the full involvement of the president.[10] As a result, the birth of the Marshall Plan was delayed for several months.

On January 20, 1947, after three weeks of the harshest winter weather in living memory, the British government issued a white paper that characterized the state of the economy as "very serious." Britain now faced, in the phrase of one Member of Parliament, "an economic Dunkirk."[11] The clear implication was that the Labour government would have no choice but to reduce Britain's overseas commitments. A month later, the cabinet informed Washington that despite the imminent danger of communist takeovers in Greece and Turkey, Britain would be compelled to cease her financial assistance to them. On March 12, President Truman appealed to the Congress to take up this burden, asserting that "it must be the policy of the United States to support free peoples who are resisting attempted subjugation by armed minorities or by outside pressures."[12]

During the deliberations leading to President Truman's request for aid to Greece and Turkey and his simultaneous declaration of the Truman Doctrine, Secretary of the Navy James Forrestal, General Eisenhower, and others came to believe that the crisis in the eastern Mediterranean was only part of the larger problem of Britain's exhaustion from war. Forrestal pressed the cabinet to investigate further, and Secretary of State George Marshall concurred. On March 5, 1947, the State-War-Navy Coordinating Committee (SWNCC) was directed to examine other situations in the world where U.S. aid might be required and to report as soon as possible. The SWNCC study, completed on April 14, recommended the integration of Germany into a comprehensive recovery program as well as greater integration of the European economies. The committee's work later became a key building block for U.S. policy.[13]

During March, leading American journalists began discussing the need for additional aid to Europe and the necessity of a large U.S. aid program. The most striking and influential was an April 5 column by Walter Lippmann entitled "Cassandra Speaking" in which he asserted that Europe was on the brink of economic collapse and predicted that to avert "the crisis which will otherwise engulf Europe and spread chaos throughout the world the measures will have to be very large—in Europe no less than an economic union and over here no less than the equivalent to a revival of Lend-Lease." Although these thoughts did not come as news to State Department officials, Lippmann's column prepared the public for the demands to follow and also challenged the department's officials to proceed expeditiously.[14]

A second spur to activity came in early March in the form of a report on the German economy presented by former president Herbert Hoover. To grasp its importance, we need to consider briefly the situation in Germany and the sorts of political conflicts surrounding it. By this time, Britain and the U.S. army of occupation in Germany were chafing under the restrictions on production and reparations required under the agreement of March 1946. Steel production was limited to 7.5 million tons per year, a level that inhibited the economic recovery of the defeated Reich and greatly added to the costs of occupation to Britain and the United States. To ease this burden and promote recovery in Europe, the British had sought to raise the production level to 11 million. France, on the other hand, remained committed to the Monnet Plan, which aimed at a 50 percent increase of France's industrial production and a doubling of prewar steel production (12 million tons); this could be achieved only by replacing German production. Hence, France demanded cession of the Saar (a major coal producing area), heavy exports of German coal (at the expense of German domestic use), and detachment of the Ruhr and Rhineland from Germany leading to some form of economic association of these vital industrial areas with France. The State Department, mindful of the intensity of feeling in Paris and the domestic dangers to the French government if they abandoned these objectives, had consistently fought the army's efforts to ease the burden on Germany, with much success.[15]

Hoover's report recommended lifting the existing limits on the level of production, ending the removal of industrial plants, and preventing the transfer of the Ruhr and Rhineland (as France had demanded). These steps would allow Germany to recover, and thus contribute to the European economy as well as saving U.S. taxpayers' money, but they also implied an abandonment of the State Department's previous policy of balanced recovery (between Germany and the rest of Europe) and seriously risked antagonizing France. The proposal touched off a heated debate inside the administration, with the army and several cabinet officers endorsing Hoover's recommendations and the State Department in staunch opposition. But Marshall and other officials recognized that Congress, as well as their British allies, would probably not tolerate an indefinite continuation of the status quo in Germany. If the administration did not produce a proposal of its own, there was considerable danger that Congress would force the Hoover recommendations on them with potentially disastrous results for U.S. relations with France.[16]

On April 7, President Truman asked Acheson to deliver a speech to the Delta Council at Cleveland, Mississippi. Acheson, already convinced of the seriousness of the problems facing Europe, wanted to make the speech a vehicle "not to put forward a solution or a plan, but to state the problem and the facts," which, he expected, would "shock the country." Acheson told the president that "he wanted it clearly understood that the administration would have to catch the ball that he was going to throw out." Truman gave his assent, and Joseph Jones was selected to compose the speech. Jones, who had been sitting in on the SWNCC meetings, drew on the committee's work for the substance of the talk. The first draft was completed on April 23, and the speech was delivered by Acheson in Cleveland on May 8.

Acheson's prescriptions for policy were much less detailed than his analysis of the problems, but one sentence toward the end revealed a great deal about the direction of the administration's thinking: "European recovery cannot be complete until the various parts of Europe's economy are working together in a harmonious whole." That is, early German recovery was seen as essential for the economic recovery of Europe as a whole. Furthermore, "the achievement of a coordinated European economy remains a fundamental objective of our foreign policy." Press coverage of the speech was spotty, but within the State Department it "acted as a powerful stimulus and instruction to staff work and discussions already in progress."[17]

Meanwhile, the secretary of state was attending the meeting of the Council of Foreign Ministers (CFM) in Moscow, where the principal topic was the future of Germany. Ernest Bevin and Marshall agreed on the need to increase production in Germany in order to reduce the costs of occupation and stimulate the European economy. Georges Bidault, representing France, insisted that the four powers pledge to meet France's demands for German coal before he would commit himself to the economic unification of Germany or a change in production levels. Soviet Foreign Minister Vyacheslav Molotov was willing to increase production provided that the Western powers accept his demands for $10 billion in reparations as well as a centralized government for Germany. Marshall refused to accede to these conditions and argued that the reparations would amount in effect to U.S. aid to Russia and that a centralized government would be vulnerable to takeover by totalitarian forces (more likely communist than Nazi).

## EMERGENCE OF THE MARSHALL PLAN

After several weeks of fruitless exchanges, Marshall began to suspect that Molotov was engaged in a calculated effort to delay any progress in the negotiations and sought a direct meeting with Stalin in hopes of breaking the impasse. The Soviet dictator's nonchalance over the conference deadlock convinced Marshall, according to Charles Bohlen, that "Stalin, looking over Europe, saw the best way to advance Soviet interests was to let matters drift." Hence, "to deal with the problem of Germany it was necessary to deal with the problem of Europe." [18] In order to induce Stalin to negotiate seriously over Germany, the United States first would have to convince him that his interests would not be served by delay because Washington was not going to stand aside and watch the economies of the western European nations collapse.

In absence of Soviet cooperation, the administration then would have to take steps promptly to arrest the economic deterioration and promote recovery. On April 8, Marshall accepted, with some qualifications, a bilateral plan suggested by the British representative to increase production in their occupation zones (which had been fused to form "Bizonia" at the beginning of the year). But, mindful of the enormous controversy this might generate, Marshall delayed its implementation. "All the way back to Washington," Bohlen recalls, "Marshall talked of the importance of finding some initiative to prevent the complete breakdown of Western Europe." In the radio address delivered upon his return on April 28 Marshall left no doubt as to the urgency of the situation. "The patient is sinking," he told the American public, "while the doctors deliberate." The following day, Marshall instructed George Kennan to have the newly formed Policy Planning Staff produce a report on the question of Europe's economy within two weeks. When Kennan—daunted by the magnitude of the problem in relation to the time frame in which it was to be addressed—asked for clarification as to how to proceed, the laconic general answered simply, "avoid trivia." [19]

Will Clayton returned from Europe in mid-May, greatly distressed by what he had seen there. His memo, which reached Marshall on May 27, made a persuasive and powerful call for immediate action, and his oral testimony to top State Department officials was even more compelling. Clayton reported that the damage done by the war to the economies of Europe had been "grossly underestimated." "Millions of people," he asserted, "are slowly starving" as a result of a near breakdown in relations between the cities and the countryside. Because of the necessity to import coal and food, Britain, France, and Italy all faced the danger of a complete depletion of their foreign exchange reserves within a few months. "The facts are known," he concluded, and prompt action was imperative. The American public and Congress must be apprised of the seriousness of the situation and be prepared to shoulder the burden of $6–7 billion in aid for the next three years. The aid would be utilized most effectively, he suggested, if Europe were no longer "divided into small watertight compartments" but reorganized into a "European economic federation."[20]

The Policy Planning Staff's report, which drew heavily from the previous work of SWNCC, was also completed at this time. Kennan and his colleagues perceived two problems, one short term and one longer term. The immediate problem, as they saw it, was to overcome the despair and demoralization that threatened to paralyze the Europeans. For this purpose, short-term actions were essential, and the best choice seemed to be an effort to break one of the most important bottlenecks to recovery—the shortage of coal—by means of a plan to increase production in the Rhineland. The longer-term problem was, of course, the economic recovery of Europe. Kennan himself had adopted the views of the SWNCC committee and favored drawing "the maximum contribution" from Germany to Europe's economy and the formation of "some form of regional political association of western European states." One may infer from this that Kennan was beginning to see economic and even political integration of Europe as a solution for the dilemma of how to reconcile the revival of Germany with the security of her neighbors. Even so, Kennan and his colleagues advised Marshall not to present an American plan to Europe but rather to leave the formal initiative to the Europeans. "The role of this country," they concluded, "should consist of friendly aid in the drafting of a European program and of the later support of such a program, by financial and other means, at European request."[21]

On May 28, Kennan, Clayton, and other top officials met with Marshall to discuss the two reports. Acheson remembers being impressed with both Clayton's "command of the subject and the depth of his conviction." After hearing Clayton's presentation, he recalls, Marshall remarked that "it would be folly to sit back and do nothing." This sentiment was unanimous.[22] A consensus quickly formed that the United States ought to aim at achieving "closer European economic cooperation" that would "break down existing economic barriers" and lead eventually to an "economic federation." The main points in dispute were whether to present an American plan or leave the initiative to Europe and whether to invite the Soviet Union and eastern European nations to participate. On the first, Charles Bohlen's suggestion that Europeans would understand that the aid plan was politically feasible only if they demonstrated the ability to cooperate together won wide support. On the second, Marshall accepted Kennan's advice to play it straight and extend the offer to the Soviets, most likely with the expectation that Stalin would refuse and assume the onus of dividing the continent.[23]

## TRANSFORMING AN IDEA INTO ACTION

After this discussion, Secretary Marshall confirmed his acceptance of an offer from Harvard University to present an address at the commencement exercises of June 5. Against the advice of Acheson, who believed that a commencement speech would be ignored by the media, Marshall decided to use the occasion to broach the department's thinking regarding U.S. aid and European recovery and charged his aide Charles Bohlen with the task of drafting the speech. Bohlen drew primarily on the recent memoranda of Clayton and Kennan, and their influence on the speech is clear. Apparently to avoid the controversies that had followed the Truman Doctrine speech, Marshall stated that "our policy is directed not against any country or doctrine but against hunger, poverty, desperation and chaos." Furthermore, "any government that is willing to assist in the task of recovery will find full cooperation . . . on the part of the United States government." Following the advice (and also borrowing the phrasing) of the Policy Planning Staff, Marshall left the planning and initiative for the program to the Europeans. "It would be neither fitting nor efficacious," he said, "for the Government to undertake to draw up unilaterally a program designed to place Europe on its feet economically. This is the business of the Europeans. . . . The role of this country should consist of friendly aid in the drafting of a European program and of later support of such a program so far as it may be practical for us to do so." Marshall set only one condition for this assistance: "The program should be a joint one, agreed to by a number, if not all, European nations." [24]

The response from Europe was prompt and enthusiastic. According to one British official, Ernest Bevin, the corpulent foreign secretary, "heard of it in bed and got in touch with the Foreign Office immediately. It was astonishing the way in which he, with his elephantine frame, sprang into action." France's foreign minister, Georges Bidault, was equally decisive; on June 13 he invited Bevin to Paris for consultations and extended his offer to Molotov of the Soviet Union as well. Molotov arrived on June 27 but withdrew and returned home after Britain and France made clear their insistence on a cooperative approach. On July 3, Bevin and Bidault issued invitations to twenty-two nations to discuss a common recovery plan in Paris. Moscow retaliated by announcing the formation of the Cominform on July 6 and a series of barter agreements between her eastern European satellites, which came to be known as the Molotov Plan six days later.[25]

Sixteen of the invitations were accepted, and the representatives of these nations convened in Paris on July 12. The conference's first step was to form the Committee of European Economic Cooperation (CEEC) to assess the economic capabilities of the participating nations, that is, what each could accomplish and what assistance it might require. Four technical subcommittees were also established for the sectors of food and agriculture, iron and steel, fuel and power, and transport.[26] Early on, U.S. officials were counting on the Europeans to draft a program for recovery and initially did not envision their role as more than advisory. As the Policy Planning Staff frankly stated in a memorandum of July 21, "We have no plan. Europe must be made to take responsibility."[27] By mid-August, however, the State Department had become "much concerned" about the trend in Paris. "Too little attention is being paid by the participants," Robert Lovett cabled to Ambassador Jefferson Caffery in Paris, "to the elements of self-help and mutual aid. . . . An itemized bill summing up prospective deficits against a background of present policies and arrangements will definitely not be sufficient." A "full collaborative effort" would be required. Writing more bluntly a week later, Lovett said that the Europeans had simply produced "sixteen shopping lists" and that the projected demand of $29.2 billion was "unreasonable." Caffery concurred. In the absence of American intervention, he suggested in early September, the conferees would soon submit a report "which could lead to [the] impression in [the] United States of an inability of [the] sixteen governments to formulate [a] realistic and defensible program." More than any other factor, the immense total of $29 billion convinced U.S. officials that the time had now come for them to offer the friendly aid of which Marshall had spoken.[28] In late August, the Americans communicated to the CEEC Executive Committee the essentials that needed to be adopted to make the plan acceptable in Washington. These included a stabilization of finances, liberalization of trade restrictions, and the establishment of production targets to be overseen by a supranational organization with strong powers of enforcement. The Europeans, however, continued to balk at this potential erosion of their sovereignty.[29]

On September 7, U.S. envoys in the capitals of all countries participating in the conference were instructed to warn the governments that the report, as it was taking shape, would be unacceptable to the United States and would endanger U.S. support. They were advised to delay its promulgation for ten days so that it could be revised substantially. The first reaction of the conference's Executive Committee to this friendly aid was that the Americans were hoping for too much; a completely new report could not be written so swiftly, and there was no chance of achieving an integrated plan as Washington seemed to favor.[30] On the following day, the American representatives received a cable enumerating six precise changes that Washington would like to see adopted. They were somewhat less demanding than those presented in late August:

1. Statement that individual countries should obligate themselves to the group to attain the production targets they had set for key commodities;

2. Revision of financial section removing thought [*sic*] that effective stabilization measures could only be adopted after external aid commenced and production substantially increased;

3. Greater emphasis on and sharpening of principles, including commitment to reduce and eventually to eliminate trade barriers among the participating countries;

4. Segregation of capital equipment (agricultural and mining excepted) with clear indication that conference will look to International Bank and other lending agencies for financing these items;

5. (a) Agreement to "recess" rather than "adjourn" the conference, (b) postponement of formal conference session to September 20; and

6. Firm commitment by participating countries that, if assistance is assured, they would form a multilateral organization with powers to review performance of each country.[31]

By September 17, Ambassador Caffery had assurances that the conference would meet points one through five without qualification and point six in a weaker form, though only after much grumbling about U.S. pressure from Bevin. German recovery was seen as essential to that of Europe as a whole but was to be controlled with vigilance to forestall the rise of a new threat to the security or prosperity of other states. As production increased, "all possible steps" would be taken to hold down inflation and reduce tariffs and other trade barriers. The conferees revised the report's preamble to include promises of "concerted action" to bring about "a new era of European cooperation" and also committed themselves, once the program was under way, to form a new international organization (which became the OEEC), but with none of the powers of enforcement foreseen by Robert Lovett.[32] These declarations of principle, without strong guarantees of implementation, fell far short of Washington's initial objectives, but the CEEC's endorsement of American aims and reduction of their claim to $19.3 billion at least presented the Truman administration with a more defensible position before Congress and set the stage for immediate passage of the coming request for emergency assistance.[33] U.S. officials, more confident now that they had a plan that would stand up to Congressional scrutiny, passed the completed report to the president on September 24. Truman called Congress into special session to act on his request for $597 million in emergency assistance to France, Italy, and Austria in November and submitted the complete ERP program, requesting $17 billion through mid-1952, to Congress on December 19.[34]

Initially, the plan met with considerable skepticism both in Congress and with the public at large and led to deep concern on the part of the administration over their ability to win support for the program, especially in the Midwest. President Truman found the Congressional leaders he met in September unenthusiastic about the interim aid package he intended to propose to a special session. Polls taken in mid-October 1947 showed that only 46 percent had heard of Marshall's proposal; less than 50 percent favored it if it were to involve sacrifices for Americans, such as shortages or higher prices; and nearly 60 percent thought that Europeans were not working hard enough on their own recovery. Soundings by the conservative Committee for Constitutional Government claimed that large majorities opposed both the concept and proposed amounts of assistance.[35]

## MOBILIZING SUPPORT

In order to build public support for the program, President Truman appointed two governmental committees (headed by Julius Krug and Edwin Nourse) and a third composed of nineteen distinguished Americans from all segments of society and led by Secretary of Commerce Averell Harriman. The Harriman committee's report, submitted November 7, concluded that the United States "has a vital interest" in European recovery, the achievement of which "will impose definite sacrifices on Americans." They recommended the disbursement of $12.7–17.2 billion in aid, to be administered by a new government agency. Expenditures of this magnitude would be justified, they argued, in part because of the economic interest the United States had in the prosperity of Europe, which provided an outlet for U.S. exports at a time when the United States might slide into recession. The Committee for the Marshall Plan, an umbrella organization of groups backing the proposal, was also formed in late 1947 on the initiative of two former cabinet officers, Henry Stimson and Robert Patterson. It strove with much success to build support for the ERP at the grass roots but limited its role to defense of the basic principles rather than trying to contribute specific proposals.[36]

These efforts bore fruit. By mid-December, the percentage of those who had not heard of the plan had fallen to 36 percent, and those approving of it now outnumbered those opposed by 56 percent to 17 percent (with 27 percent having no opinion). The ERP had also picked up endorsements from the leading organizations in all sectors of the economy, including business, industry, labor, and agriculture. By early 1948, the enactment of some sort of program was a foregone conclusion. The only questions were how large the allocations would be and how the program would be administered.[37]

Opponents now concentrated their efforts not on blocking an aid program but rather on reducing the expenditure. The threat this posed to ERP was potentially serious. Critics as diverse as Robert Taft, Henry Wallace, and former president Herbert Hoover recommended reductions; there was considerable sympathy for Taft's position among the isolationists of the middle western and mountain states. The administration countered them by appealing to Americans' economic self-interest, their fear of communism, and their generosity.[38] Economic arguments, however, were something of a double-edged sword. To the contention, made first in the SWNCC report and repeated by the Harriman committee, that a continuation of the high level of exports was necessary to avert a recession (of which there were growing fears in 1947), Senator Taft responded that the program would create a "false prosperity which [could] not be permanently maintained" and would lead to shortages of goods, higher taxes, and "coercive" controls of the U.S. economy. Administration lobbyists found that their warnings of communist advances in Europe generated much more enthusiasm on Capitol Hill than the discussions about markets. To fiscal conservatives worried about the costs of the ERP, they pointed to a Defense Department study that predicted a 25 percent increase in military spending should the program fail to pass. To the public at large, the humanitarian arguments appeared to be the most successful: 56 percent of those polled said it was best seen as "an act of charity" while only 8 percent believed it would "curb communism" (35 percent cited other motives).[39] This debate came to an abrupt halt in February 1948 when the communists seized power in Czechoslovakia through a coup supported by Moscow. In Charles Kindleberger's judgment, "it is quite uncertain that ERP would have been enacted had it not been converted from a pro-European measure to an anti-Soviet one."[40]

Controversy arose not only regarding the levels of funding but also on the question of how and by whom the program would be administered. There was strong opposition in Congress to giving responsibility to the State Department. Many Republicans were upset at what they believed to be the inefficiency of previous programs, were suspicious of the State Department's policy in China, and were eager to reclaim for the legislative branch some of the authority over foreign affairs that had shifted to the executive during the war years. In addition, some interest groups felt that State Department officials lacked the professional competence to make decisions regarding the domestic implications of the program. These concerns, if unaddressed, threatened seriously to undermine budgetary support for the ERP.[41] In response to these pressures, a special committee chaired by Lincoln Gordon to draft a plan for the program's administration, was appointed in the State Department. In late October, this committee recommended the creation of a new agency, the Economic Cooperation Administration (ECA), to be headed by a director in Washington and to be represented in Europe by a special envoy of ambassadorial rank who would be responsible to the State Department. The agency's powers were to be narrowly defined: all decisions relating to foreign policy were to be made by the Department of State, and the power to allocate exports would remain with Commerce and Agriculture Departments.[42]

## ENACTMENT INTO LAW

After some intraexecutive skirmishes, the Gordon report won Truman's endorsement. In presenting the plan to Congress, officials stressed that the State

Department would retain direction and control over matters of foreign policy. This led critics such as Senator Arthur Vandenberg to fear that the agency would lose its independence and become subject to interference from Foggy Bottom. Vandenberg asked the Brookings Institution to prepare an alternative report and this became the basis of legislation passed by Congress. The ECA was to be staffed primarily by experts recruited from the private sector. Its director, who was to be appointed by the president and confirmed by Congress, was to have equal standing with cabinet secretaries; any disputes between the director and the secretary of state would be resolved by the president. Unlike the State Department's plan, the special representative in Europe was to report to the ECA chief, not the secretary of state. The ECA administrator would take counsel in matters of policy from a Public Advisory Board which was explicitly required to be nonpartisan in composition. In deference to Congress, Truman passed over his preferred candidate Dean Acheson and named Paul Hoffman, the president of Studebaker and (most importantly) a prominent Republican, as the first incumbent.[43] Regarding the form in which ECA finally emerged, Michael Hogan comments:

> They sought to substitute for the State Department's political control a bipartisan public-private partnership in which essentially private leaders would make operational decisions and collaborate with their public counterparts in the formulation of policy. . . . The administrative structure adopted was one that deliberately dissolved the distinction between the public and private spheres and did so as part of a strategy for advancing the goals of American public policy.[44]

After these Congressional emendations, the Economic Cooperation Act passed by a wide margin in both houses of Congress and was signed by President Truman on April 3, 1948. The subsequent history of the implementation of the ERP is too complex to be considered here in its entirety. In view of their long-range importance, two steps by the United States to implement the original design bear mentioning. On June 5, 1948, the U.S. special representative, Averell Harriman, informed the OEEC that the United States would insist that they take responsibility for the allocation of aid between countries. The primary motive was to strengthen OEEC, but U.S. officials also hoped to curb the incessant lobbying efforts by European representatives in Washington. OEEC's first effort to execute these responsibilities nearly ended in disaster. Experts from four different countries received proposals from all sixteen participants and then repaired in July to Chantilly to prepare their recommendations. Upon the presentation of their report, as one eyewitness recalls, "pandemonium broke loose." By mid-August 1949, only Belgium was content with her portion, and U.S. General Lucius Clay was demanding a substantial increase in the outlay for occupied Germany. The differences among the Europeans were composed in frenetic last-minute efforts by OEEC Secretary General Robert Marjolin and Baron Snoy, his colleague on the executive committee. Clay was appeased through the intervention of ECA in the proceedings, which secured for him a larger allocation without undermining the independence of the organization. Through this harrowing but fruitful exercise the practices of mutual scrutiny and supervision by a supranational authority were much more firmly established. As a result of this, in the judgment of Ernst Van Der Beugel, "Intra-European economic cooperation [was brought] to an unprecedented level in an extremely short time."[45]

## IMPLEMENTATION

Despite this achievement, by 1949 Congress was impatient with the slow progress toward integration in Europe. Agreement was reached regarding the size of the appropriation only after protracted argument. The ECA became concerned, as a result, that it would face serious problems in obtaining additional funding unless it could point to some tangible signs of movement toward greater integration and cooperation. With a view to encouraging this outcome, Paul Hoffman, in his address to the OEEC on October 31, 1949, called for the creation of a large single market by removal of all barriers to trade and suggested that Congress and the American public would more likely continue assistance at a high level if Europeans could give evidence of tangible progress in this direction. In the year preceding Hoffman's speech, there had been virtually no increase in the volume of trade in Europe and no visible progress toward convertibility of currencies. In November, the ECA presented its own proposal for the reform of the system of international payments. Three months later, Hoffman made the disbursement of $.6 billion of his authorization contingent upon the pursuit of a program of liberalization of trade and payments. This pressure, along with the active role played by Harriman in Europe, was an instrumental factor in overcoming resistance, particularly from Britain, and in persuading ERP recipients to adopt the European Payments Union on July 7, 1950. Although this reform fell far short of achieving the full convertibility of currencies, it eliminated the need for a country to balance its accounts with each of its trading partners bilaterally through the creation of a multilateral clearing mechanism and thus opened the way for a rapid expansion of trade and further liberalization.[46]

With this achievement, the period of greatest American influence came to a close. Although the ERP continued officially until 1952, the outbreak of the Korean War in June 1950 altered its focus from recovery to rearmament.[47] By this time, the ECA's geographical jurisdiction had widened, for it had been assigned the responsibility of administering aid programs to China, Korea, and Southeast Asia. In accordance with the new military emphasis, the ECA was transformed by Congress in 1951 into the Mutual Security Agency (MSA), which was charged with the supervision of all foreign aid programs, military as well as economic and technical. The MSA was required under the Mutual Security Act to work more closely with the State and Defense Departments and thus lost some of its former independence. Although in the last phase of the Marshall Plan nearly all U.S. aid to Europe was military assistance, it was through this process that the provision of economic aid became institutionalized as a permanent part of U.S. foreign policy.[48]

## CONCLUSIONS

By the time of its completion, the ERP had transferred some $13 billion from a people who had borne heavy sacrifices through a decade and a half of depression and war. Why did the American leadership decide to commit resources of this magnitude to Europe in 1947, and how were they able to persuade the public and its representatives to do so?

The reader will recall that W. W. Rostow submitted a proposal that bore some similarities to the Marshall Plan in early 1946, but without success. Rostow attributed this failure to the absence of a sense of economic crisis at that time as well to the opposition of Secretary Byrnes. Both those conditions had changed a year later. The failure of the Rostow-Clayton-Acheson proposal to win acceptance, like the "dog that did not bark" for Sherlock Holmes in the Conan Doyle story "Silver Blaze," provides us with some indication of what had to change before something like the Marshall Plan could become U.S. policy. In brief, the key factors appear to be the deterioration of the European economies resulting from the harsh winter weather of 1946–1947; the outcome of the Council of Foreign Ministers conference of March–April 1947 and the inferences drawn from it by Secretary Marshall; a change of leadership in the State Department; and, perhaps, in the eyes of more recent writers, the growing problems posed by the U.S. occupation of Germany.[49]

Prior to the winter storms of early 1947, Europe, with the important exception of Germany, appeared to be on the road to recovery. If one excludes from the total the U.S. and British occupation zones in the defeated Reich, where output in the spring of 1947 was only one-third of that of 1938, total industrial production for the countries participating in the Marshall Plan had reached the prewar level by the second quarter of 1947. Growth stalled in France, Belgium, and Italy in the third quarter, but expansion remained robust in Britain after the weather eased and then resumed in France and Belgium by the fall.[50] It is doubtful, however, whether this recovery could have continued in the absence of U.S. intervention. The European economies were being sustained by huge balance-of-payments deficits. The SWNCC study calculated that the United States would export some $16 billion and import only $8 billion in 1947. U.S. aid programs covered $5 billion of this, but the remainder was being funded by liquidation of the reserves of the Europeans. "Under present programs and policies," the SWNCC study concluded that "the world will not be able to continue to buy U.S. exports at the 1946–1947 rate beyond another 12–18 months." Clayton estimated that Britain and France would deplete their foreign exchange reserves before the end of the year, and Italy even sooner.[51]

The underlying causes of the balance-of-payments crisis were a shortfall of production that had led to an abnormal dependence on U.S. exports as well as a weakness in Europe's ability to export. The most significant production problems were with two key commodities, coal and food. The coal shortage acted as a bottleneck to expansion because of its role as a critical input in industry. War damage, a shortage of skilled workers, and obsolescent equipment all contributed to this problem, and the severe weather certainly exacerbated it, but the delay in bringing German facilities back into full production was especially important.[52] In general, the availability of food was improving between 1946 and 1947, but caloric intake was not yet sufficient to maintain good health in Italy, Germany, or Austria. In France, the severe winter, which had disrupted agriculture as well as industry, was followed by a summer drought, producing the worst harvest of the century.[53]

The political consequences of these economic problems were potentially very serious. Consider the situation in France where the Communist Party had received some five million votes in the 1945 elections, more than any other party.[54] The freezing winter weather and shortages of consumer goods led the peasants to hoard wheat, which created a food shortage in the cities and accelerated inflation. On May 1, the bread ration was reduced from 300 grams to 250 grams. Food riots followed in several places. In Lyons, crowds stormed into the Prefecture, screaming "du pain, du pain!" On May 15, President Auriol appealed to the farmers to deliver all of their wheat at once. The Minister of Agriculture reported in September that the harvest would be less than half of normal. The woes of the agriculture sector alone were serious enough, but, in addition, the encouraging expansion of French industrial production that had begun in 1946 halted abruptly during the spring of 1947, primarily because of a shortage of coal. As a consequence, wages were depressed, and this, in combination with the shortages of food, led to restiveness among the working class. On April 30, 20,000 Renault employees struck in protest of these conditions, thus seriously endangering the government's efforts to stabilize the economy by means of a freeze on wages and prices. France's communists endorsed the strike and were dismissed from the cabinet by Prime Minister Ramadier. The government was soon faced with additional strikes in automobile factories, coal mines, electrical plants, the oil industry, the retail sector, and the railways, which threatened collectively to so disrupt the economy that the gates to power would be opened to the communists. "By the time that the Marshall Plan had been developed," states one historian, "there was a great question as to whether an economy so debilitated and upset . . . could resist the appeals of Communism."[55] The situation facing Italy was equally grim.[56]

In these circumstances, U.S. officials came to realize that the economic and political challenges they faced were closely interrelated and required a common approach. Containment of communist expansion could only be achieved if the conditions conducive to the growth of communist influence were ameliorated.[57] Although the facts, as Clayton maintained, admitted no other conclusion, one can still concur with Louis Halle's observation:

> The threat of an imminent collapse in western Europe had drawn the United States across the Atlantic in 1917 and again in 1940–1941. It was, I think, a foregone conclusion that the same threat would draw it again in 1947. Circumstances dictated this, and the statesmen merely gave expression to it. Much depended, however, on the shrewdness, the intelligence, the very style of the expression. Statesmanship might have faltered and fumbled. Confusion might not have been avoided—and, in fact, it was not altogether avoided in the initial move to assist Greece and Turkey. The fact that this was not now the case is attributable to the statesmanship of a few men, with whatever reservation one may wish to make in favor of luck or providence.[58]

Of these men, two merit particular commendation. The first is the president himself. Facing a Congress controlled by the opposition, low popularity in public opinion polls and an election in the following year, Harry Truman, in the words of Joseph Jones, "without considering its possible effect upon his personal popularity or re-election prospects . . . made his decision on the basis of what the security of the nation seemed to require and boldly confronted Congress and the people with their responsibilities. . . . There is no substitute," Jones concludes, "for this kind of courageous leadership."[59]

The accession of Marshall to the office of secretary of state in January 1947 may have been critical, not because of the eponymous one's intellectual contribution to the development of policy, which was admittedly slight, but because he was able to reorganize the department, restore morale, and generate bold ideas. Byrnes, who had spent the better part of his term in office abroad, had done little to revitalize a bureau dispirited by President Roosevelt's habits of circumventing those whom he dismissed as "striped pants boys," a practice the department itself encouraged by adhering rigidly to stifling bureaucratic routines. Marshall, with the assistance of Acheson, implemented reforms in the structure of the department early in his tenure that gave freer vent to creative thinking, with impressive results.[60]

It was Marshall's experience in Moscow that provided the third stimulant to action in 1947. Historians are in agreement on the importance of the meeting, but interpretations have diverged on the more specific question of what precisely led the secretary to the conclusions he reached. Earlier accounts stressed Marshall's disillusionment with the Soviet Union and his growing conviction that progress toward economic recovery, even if it came through unilateral action, was a precondition to success in negotiation with the communists. John Gimbel's account, on the other hand, attributes the deadlock at Moscow to U.S. and British disagreements with France over policy toward Germany and suggests that Marshall's need to find political cover for the deal he struck with Bevin to raise the German level of industry was the key factor. A thorough discussion of this issue would take us beyond the scope of this chapter, but a few remarks on the controversy may not be out of place.

Like earlier historians, Gimbel believes that the events at the CFM conference in Moscow provided the crucial impetus for the development of the Marshall Plan. He differs from them, however, in his explanation of why this was the case. In his view, the four powers deadlocked not, as U.S. officials later said, because of Soviet intransigence, but because the French continued to demand sweeping concessions from Germany and vetoed an increase in the level of industry in Germany (which would permit increased production) proposed by Britain.[61] This contention is not persuasive. According to Charles Kindleberger, Gimbel makes too much of French obstruction at Moscow. "The French were not taken seriously," he remembers, because "Bidault was conspicuously drunk on occasion and once leaned on Secretary Marshall for physical as well as moral and economic support." The conference broke down without an agreement to unify Germany because the Soviets demanded reparations in quantities that could not be met without continued injections of U.S. and British support for Germany even if the level of industry were increased. "The French," he asserts, "made no contribution to the level of industry debate." Although the political bureaus of the State Department may have seen the matter differently, in his office the French were considered "a nuisance but were not of consequence."[62]

Furthermore, if one reconsiders the chronological sequence of events, Gimbel's thesis appears to be somewhat overstated. Specifically, two important facts are overlooked. First, the initiative to begin the SWNCC study, which grew out of the concerns of military leaders and the Cabinet over Britain's exhaustion (not, as far as one can tell, over German issues), was made *before* the Hoover report touched off an intragovernmental row over Germany. And, second, the Truman administration's commitment to a large-scale aid program came *before* the Moscow conference concluded. It was on April 7, the day before Marshall began his talks with Bevin, that Truman cleared Acheson to give the Delta speech. For these reasons, it would be a mistake to attribute the birth of the Marshall Plan solely to the need to deal with the German dilemma; other issues—especially the economic distress of the rest of western Europe and the communist danger—were clearly important as well.[63]

Three general factors explain why officials in the Truman administration made the momentous decision to request from Congress a vast program of economic assistance in 1947 after a similar scheme was suggested only a few months before. The origins of the Marshall Plan can be traced to the manifold economic crisis in Europe (which was simultaneously a crisis of production, both of food and commodities, and a crisis of payments); the complex outcome of the Moscow summit (both in its implications for relations with the Soviet Union and for the German problem); and to the change of leadership in the State Department, which brought into office a man with the wisdom and organizational ability to act decisively and effectively in response to these problems. As we have seen, the economic and political crises threatening Europe in 1947 convinced American officials that *something* had to be done. Contrary to what some revisionists have alleged, these men were neither alarmists nor cynics; their concerns were genuine and well founded. But the specific form of the U.S. response was by no means predetermined; other approaches were conceivable. In the absence of initiative from the administration, Congress might have adopted the Hoover recommendations for Germany, and in the absence of pressure from Congress, the administration might have continued piecemeal assistance through the United Nations Relief and Rehabilitation Administration (UNRRA) or other channels.

As we noted at the outset and emphasized throughout, the answer they hit upon was distinctive in at least two aspects: it aimed not just at relief but at a lasting economic recovery by supporting high levels of investment to expand production and by encouraging the integration of European economies through a reduction in barriers to trade and an intensification of international cooperation. Why, then, did the Marshall Plan take this particular form?

No doubt part of the answer, as Michael Hogan has said, is that the United States arrived at these solutions by projecting onto Europe its experience of economic expansion made possible by the construction of a large market free of barriers to trade.[64] But a more complete answer must take into account the domestic and international political difficulties faced by the administration. It was their need to cope with these dilemmas that inspired U.S. officials to conceive the particular solution that was to become the Marshall Plan.

The first political problem was winning support for the program in Congress. Prior to 1947, most U.S. officials assumed that relief assistance through UNRRA, supplemented by loans from such sources as the International Monetary Fund or the International Bank for Reconstruction and Development, would permit Europe to recover. The recurrence of economic crisis in Europe in 1947 completely discredited this optimistic view.[65] Intense effort by the administration had been required to secure a loan for Britain in 1946, and influential legislators had made plain after the passage of the aid bills to Greece and Turkey that they would look askance at additional piecemeal requests or programs in which aid was used at the discretion of the recipients. The United States had already spent some $9 billion on relief for Europe.[66] An increasingly skeptical Congress had to be persuaded that the Europeans were doing all they could to promote their own recovery and that the demands for assistance would not continue endlessly.

"We ought to do all we possibly can," said Congressman Lawrence Smith of Wisconsin, "but . . . can we expect from these nations any more in the future than we have in the past so long as we give and give and give?" Marshall recalled later that he feared that "any new proposal for more funds to be appropriated would be ruthlessly repulsed."[67]

These sentiments compelled the administration to present a more convincing rationale for the provision of additional assistance, particularly in the sums contemplated. As we noted at the outset, the ERP differed from these programs both in its emphasis on European integration and its emphasis on increased production, which was seen as "the touchstone of economic recovery." Greater coordination between the Europeans promised to bring more effective results with U.S. aid than a continuation of piecemeal aid to individual countries, while an expansion of capacity would permit them to meet domestic demand out of their own production and to increase their exports.[68] Both would bring their imports and exports back into line and thus resolve the balance-of-payments crisis. But the increase in production required to bring this about could only be achieved by a very high rate of capital formation—the target rate was 20 percent; and, in the absence of foreign assistance, this would not be possible without drastic reductions in consumption—sacrifices that were probably not politically feasible for unstable or beleaguered governments in many countries. The ERP was, in essence, a program to boost investment in order to stimulate economic expansion and wean Europe permanently from U.S. aid. Although U.S. assistance was only 4 percent of Europe's GNP in 1948–1949, it was, nevertheless, crucial because it provided essential inputs that, due to the dollar shortage, Europe could not otherwise have procured and, more importantly, it made possible the high rates of investment that drove the rapid expansion forward.[69] "The necessities of politics," journalist James Reston reflected, "may produce some very imaginative things. . . . The exigencies of the time forced people into new fields of inquiry."[70]

The second political problem facing the Truman administration was the dilemma of German recovery. After the promulgation of the Hoover report the administration was facing growing pressure from Congress, the public, and the British to do something to ease the burdens of occupation. But the French had steadfastly refused to consider an increase in the level of industry set earlier. If the administration failed to come up with its own plan, it was expected that Congress would insist on the Hoover proposal, which would probably set off a diplomatic firestorm in Paris. The proclamation of a recovery plan based on integration of the European economies promised to ease this dilemma in several ways. First, German economic reconstruction could take place under multilateral controls and in the context of growing economic interdependence, which would reassure the French and others who feared a revival of German aggression that Germany's industrial might would not be used again to create a military threat.[71] The plan also addressed France's primary economic concern, for U.S.

aid promised to make available enough coal to France to fuel a vigorous expansion of her own industry without inhibiting German growth.[72] Finally, if persuasion failed, the offer of aid and the threat to withhold it could be used, as Kennan suggested in one memorandum, to induce Paris to acquiesce to an increase in German production.[73]

European unity within the context of a comprehensive aid program thus promised to provide a politically acceptable framework for German recovery.[74] Faced with the nasty dilemma of how to revive the defeated Reich without antagonizing and perhaps destabilizing an important ally, U.S. officials devised a creative solution which, though not immediately successful in achieving its maximal aims, nonetheless exercised considerable influence over the future evolution of Europe.

The Marshall Plan can be said to have emerged out of the efforts of U.S. officials to achieve four goals simultaneously: the continuation of postwar prosperity in the United States; the relief of distress abroad; the containment of communism; and the reconstruction of Germany at an acceptable cost to U.S. taxpayers. The first three of these were largely synergistic, and the happy coincidence of these objectives strengthened the hands of the program's sponsors against opponents and skeptics of all political hues. Although concerns over a looming recession and the need to sustain U.S. exports may have been convincing to many businessmen or labor leaders, warnings about the communist danger were more effective in persuading the fiscally conservative Republicans of the 80th Congress to support the ERP. On the other hand, U.S. liberals and Europeans on the moderate left had criticized the Truman Doctrine on the grounds that it put too much emphasis on military solutions, neglected Europe's most pressing problems, and might undermine the political position of friendly governments dependent on left-wing support. The humanitarian and economic emphasis of Marshall's speech reassured those of this opinion, at least in Europe and, as the polls cited above indicate, made a favorable impression on the American public as well.[75] But as we have seen, the fourth goal conflicted with the others, especially the third: German rehabilitation was extraordinarily difficult to reconcile with the continuation of cooperative relations with France, not to say her political stability. The interaction of these four goals thus played an important part in the genesis and enactment of the Marshall Plan. The synergism eased the administration's problems in persuading a somewhat reluctant Congress to authorize the vast sums that were required; while the contradiction provided an important spur to creative thinking in the U.S. bureaucracy and Congress.

The solution that was adopted—economic recovery by means of increased production and European integration—even if less than entirely successful in attaining its objectives during the years of its operation, nonetheless served the U.S. aims that gave rise to it remarkably well and in doing so exercised profound influence on the future evolution of Europe, if not the world beyond.

36                                    *Great Policies*

## NOTES

1. Harry Price, *The Marshall Plan and Its Meaning*, (Ithaca, N.Y.: Cornell University Press, 1955), 92–94, 98, 299, 329–30; Charles Mee, *The Marshall Plan: The Launching of the Pax Americana* (New York: Simon & Schuster, 1984), 90, 172; Imanuel Wexler, *The Marshall Plan Revisited* (Westport, Conn.: Greenwood, 1983), 71. I describe the concept of recovery in greater detail in note 4 below.

2. Michael Hogan, *The Marshall Plan: America, Britain and the Reconstruction of Western Europe, 1947–1952* (Cambridge: Cambridge University Press, 1987), 27, 35, 53.

3. Price, *Marshall Plan and Its Meaning*, 399.

4. More recently, revisionist authors have questioned the necessity of the ERP for either the purpose of reviving Europe economically or arresting the spread of communism. Charles Maier, for one, has asserted that communism would not have been adopted by or forced on western Europe if the United States had not acted, whereas Alan Milward, author of a lengthy study of the economic effects of the Marshall Plan, believes that Europe would have recovered without it. Charles Maier adds that the contribution of the United States to capital formation during the period of the ERP was only 10 to 20 percent of the total in the first two years and less than 10 percent later. See Alan Milward, *The Reconstruction of Western Europe 1945–51* (Berkeley: University of California Press, 1984), 4–5, 54, 469–70; and Charles Maier, "The Two Postwar Eras and the Conditions for Stability," *American Historical Review* 86 (April 1981), 341–43. There is not room for a complete discussion of these points here, but perhaps some brief remarks would not be out of place.

Milward argues that Europe would have recovered without it, noting that economic growth resumed before European Recovery Plan (ERP) aid arrived in the fall of 1947 (*Reconstruction,* 7–8, 465). European governments faced only a balance-of-payments crisis, which they could have solved on their own by deflating their economies (*Reconstruction,* 48–50, 54). His argument is unpersuasive for three reasons: (1) deflation would have been politically dangerous (Hogan, *Marshall Plan,* 431–32; Charles Kindleberger, *Marshall Plan Days* [Boston: Allen & Unwin, 1987], 261–62); (2) the balance-of-payments crisis could have led to depression if individual countries had tried to curb their deficits by the use of import controls, as in the 1930s, and this had degenerated into a vicious circle of protection and unemployment (*Foreign Relations of the United States 1947* [hereafter *FRUS*] III: 362); (3) he ignores the psychological importance of Marshall's speech. In the absence of decisive action by Washington, business confidence might have continued to erode, thus creating the vicious circle of investor pessimism and economic stagnation described by Keynes (Maier, "Two Post War Eras," 343; Scott Jackson, "Prologue to the Marshall Plan," *Journal of American History* 65 (March 1979): 1046; Robert Donovan, *The Second Victory* (New York: Madison, 1987), 19–20). Maier's view is misleading because it neglects the importance of the U.S. contribution *at the margin.* Wexler's conclusion is closer to the truth: "Such high rates of investment in all probability could not have been sustained, especially during the early years of the program, without the financial resources provided through ERP aid." (Hogan, *Marshall Plan,* 431–32; Wexler, *Marshall Plan Revisited,* 251)

5. Quoted in Theodore Wilson, *The Marshall Plan: An Atlantic Venture of 1947–1951 and How It Shaped the World* (New York: Foreign Policy Association, 1977), 47–48; Wilson develops these thoughts on pp. 47–48, 53.

6. Wilson, *Marshall Plan,* 46–47.

7. Price, *Marshall Plan and Its Meaning,* 293–94, 297–98, 347, 355–56, 399; Donovan, *Second Victory,* 47, 59–60, 68, 103–6, 120; Joseph Jones, *The Fifteen Weeks* (New York: Harcourt, Brace and World, 1955), 99, 244; Hogan, *Marshall Plan,* 54; *FRUS,* 221–22, 317; Milward, *Reconstruction,* 94; Ernst Van Der Beugel, *From Marshall Plan Aid to Atlantic Partnership* (Amsterdam: Elsevier, 1966), 56.

8. Hogan, *Marshall Plan*, 438.

9. Hogan, *Marshall Plan*, 35-39; Kindleberger, *Marshall Plan Days*, 156–57.

10. W. W. Rostow, *The Division of Europe after World War II* (Austin: University of Texas Press, 1981), 3–8, 74–75, 80–83.

11. Donovan, *Second Victory*, 20–22.

12. Donovan, *Second Victory*, 19–26.

13. Jones, *Fifteen Weeks*, 199–201; Jackson, "Prologue," 1050; Hogan, *Marshall Plan*, 40–41; *FRUS*, 214–15.

14. Jones, *Fifteen Weeks*, 227–29.

15. John Gimbel, *The Origins of the Marshall Plan* (Stanford, Calif.: Stanford University Press, 1976), 38–40, 62, 156–58, 186–87, 232–33, 252.

16. Gimbel, *Origins of Marshall Plan*, 183–86; Hogan, *Marshall Plan*, 33–35.

17. Max Beloff, *The United States and the Unity of Europe* (Washington, D.C.: Brookings, 1963), 18–19; Acheson, *Present at the Creation* (New York: Norton, 1969), 227–30; Jones, *Fifteen Weeks*, 206–13, quotations from 280.

18. Forrest Pogue, *George C. Marshall: Statesman 1945–1950* (New York: Viking, 1987), 177–81, 185–91, 195–96; Jones, *Fifteen Weeks*, 218, 222–24; Rostow, *Division of Europe*, 74; Gimbel, *Origins of Marshall Plan*, 188–98, 275–76.

19. Jones, *Fifteen Weeks*, 224.

20. Hogan, *Marshall Plan*, 42–43; Jones, *Fifteen Weeks*, 246–48; Beloff, *United States and Unity*, 19–20; *FRUS*, 230–32.

21. Jones, *Fifteen Weeks*, 241, 249–50; *FRUS*, 221–22, 224–29; Hogan, *Marshall Plan*, 41–42.

22. *FRUS*, 230; Jones, *Fifteen Weeks*, 248; Acheson, *Present at Creation*, 231–32.

23. Hogan, *Marshall Plan*, 43–45; George Kennan, *Memoirs—1925–1950* (Boston: Little Brown, 1967), 360; *FRUS*, 234–35.

24. Jones, *Fifteen Weeks*, 254–56, quotations from the speech, 283–84.

25. Price, *Marshall Plan and Its Meaning*, 27–29.

26. Price, *Marshall Plan and Its Meaning*, 36–37. Those participating were Austria, Belgium, Denmark, France, Greece, Great Britain, Iceland, Ireland, Italy, Luxembourg, the Netherlands, Norway, Portugal, Sweden, Switzerland, and Turkey (Donovan, *Second Victory*, 38).

27. *FRUS*, 335.

28. Hogan, *Marshall Plan*, 72–73; *FRUS*, 356–57, 363, 372–74, 391–92, 407; also 364–65, 367–68.

29. Hogan, *Marshall Plan*, 74–75.

30. *FRUS*, 412–13, 421–23, 425.

31. *FRUS*, 426; characterization from Hogan, *Marshall Plan*, 78.

32. Hogan, *Marshall Plan*, 78–82.

33. Ibid., 79.

34. Price, *Marshall Plan and Its Meaning*, 47; Donovan, *Second Victory*, 41 47; *FRUS*, 434, 436, 438.

35. Wexler, *Marshall Plan Revisited*, 26, 261; Price, *Marshall Plan and Its Meaning*, 58–60; Mee, *Marshall Plan*, 97–98, 216–17.

36. Van Der Beugel, *Marshall Plan Aid*, 89–90; Wexler, *Marshall Plan Revisited*, 27, 31, 35; Price, *Marshall Plan and Its Meaning*, 55–57; Donovan, *Second Victory*, 42–50; Mee, *Marshall Plan*, 217–18.

37. Price, *Marshall Plan and Its Meaning*, 59–60; Wexler, *Marshall Plan Revisited*, 39–41.

38. These three goals were stated clearly in the report of the Harriman Committee. See Price, *Marshall Plan and Its Meaning*, 305–6. They may have been successful in convincing peak business organizations, but the evidence I have come across is not very specific on this point. See Hogan, *Marshall Plan*, 97; Mee, *Marshall Plan*, 98.

39. Hogan, *Marshall Plan*, 95–96; Mee, *Marshall Plan*, 230, 239–41; Price, *Marshall Plan and Its Meaning*, 52–53; Jones, *Fifteen Weeks*, 262–63; Wilson, *Marshall Plan*, 14; Donovan, *Second Victory*, 42–43; Jackson, "Prologue," 1054–56.

40. Donovan, *Second Victory*, 42–50; Kindleberger, *Marshall Plan Days*, 192–93; Mee, *Marshall Plan*, 245.

41. Hadley Arkes, *Bureaucracy, the Marshall Plan, and the National Interest* (Princeton, N.J.: Princeton University Press, 1972), 64, 91–96, 103; Hogan, *Marshall Plan*, 104–5; Price, *Marshall Plan and Its Meaning*, 68.

42. Hogan, *Marshall Plan*, 103–5.

43. Hogan, *Marshall Plan*, 105–8; Price, *Marshall Plan and Its Meaning*, 69–71; Mee, *Marshall Plan*, 247–48.

44. Hogan, *Marshall Plan*, 108–9.

45. Richard Mayne, *The Recovery of Europe 1945–1973* (Garden City, N.Y.: Anchor, 1973), 146–47; Van Der Beugel, *Marshall Plan Aid*, 161–65, quotation on 221; Hogan, *Marshall Plan*, 161–65.

46. Van Der Beugel, *Marshall Plan Aid*, 177–87, 192–203; Beloff, *United States and Unity in Europe*, 42–46; Price, *Marshall Plan and Its Meaning*, 122–27, 143–44.

47. Van Der Beugel, *Marshall Plan Aid*, 137–43.

48. Price, *Marshall Plan and Its Meaning*, 165–66, 184, 195, 203; Wilson, *Marshall Plan*, 46–47. The Mutual Security Agency (MSA) in turn begat the Foreign Operations Administration (FOA), which became the International Cooperation Administration (ICA), which eventually evolved into the Agency for International Development (AID).

49. Rostow, *Division of Europe*, 73–74.

50. Milward, *Reconstruction*, 7–13, 465.

51. Jones, *Fifteen Weeks*, 207; *FRUS*, 210, 230–31.

52. Price, *Marshall Plan and Its Meaning*, 30.

53. Kindleberger, *Marshall Plan Days*, 251–52; Milward, *Reconstruction*, 8–9, 12, 17–19; Donovan, *Second Victory*, 43.

54. Price, *Marshall Plan and Its Meaning*, 33.

55. Herbert Feis, *From Trust to Terror: The Onset of the Cold War 1945–50* (New York: Norton, 1970), 233–36; Alexander Werth, *France 1940–1955* (New York: Henry Holt, 1956), 353–54, 359, 362–64.

56. Price, *Marshall Plan and Its Meaning*, 33–34.

57. Price, *Marshall Plan and Its Meaning*, 6; *FRUS*, 224–25.

58. Louis Halle, *The Cold War as History* (New York: Harper, 1967), 129.

59. Jones, *Fifteen Weeks*, 260.

60. Wilson, *Marshall Plan*, 15–16.

61. Gimbel, *Origins of Marshall Plan*, 187–89.

62. Kindleberger, *Marshall Plan Days*, 157, 186–87, 191.

63. Jackson, "Prologue," 1056–58.

64. Hogan, *Marshall Plan*, 27–28, 427; also Price, *Marshall Plan and Its Meaning*, 287.

65. Price, *Marshall Plan and Its Meaning*, 258–59; Wilson, *Marshall Plan*, 12; Hogan, *Marshall Plan*, 35.

66. Wilson, *Marshall Plan*, 7–8; and Mee, *Marshall Plan*, 172 give conflicting estimates as to the amount of aid the United States had given. I have used Hogan's figure, *Marshall Plan*, 30.

67. Mee, *Marshall Plan*, 90, 172; Jones, *Fifteen Weeks*, 89–90; *FRUS*, 240; Hogan, *Marshall Plan*, 33; Price, *Marshall Plan and Its Meaning*, 258–59; Rostow, *Division of Europe*, 56; Wexler, *Marshall Plan Revisited*, 9; Wilson, *Marshall Plan*, 7–8, 13; Marshall quotation from Price, *Marshall Plan and Its Meaning*, 25; and Smith quotation from Price, *Marshall Plan and Its Meaning*, 53.

68. Price, *Marshall Plan and Its Meaning*, 287.

69. Wexler, *Marshall Plan Revisited*, 71–74, 86; Hogan, *Marshall Plan*, 431–32; Donovan, *Second Victory*, 60; Price, *Marshall Plan and Its Meaning*, 92–94, 116, 329–30. This is the point missed by Maier, who has pointed out that ERP assistance probably amounted to no more than 20 percent of Europe's capital formation in the first two years and 10 percent thereafter (Maier, "Two Post War Eras," 341–42.) He forgets that the United States might have been and probably was crucial at the margin. See on this point Hogan, *Marshall Plan*, 189–90; Price, *Marshall Plan and Its Meaning*, 329; and Wexler, *Marshall Plan Revisited*, 251.

70. Quoted in Price, *Marshall Plan and its Meaning*, 258.

71. Hogan, *Marshall Plan*, 429; Beloff, *United States and Unity in Europe*, 45.

72. Gimbel, *Origins of Marshall Plan*, 173–75, 196–99.

73. *FRUS*, 332.

74. Gimbel, *Origins of Marshall Plan*, 254.

75. Jones, *Fifteen Weeks*, 208–9. Kennan addresses the problems the Truman Doctrine speech gave rise to in *FRUS*, 224–25.

# 3

# GROWTH WITH EQUITY MEGAPOLICIES IN TAIWAN: LAND REFORM AND EXPORT-LED GROWTH

*John Orme*

After its disastrous rule on the mainland, its retreat to Formosa, and a series of blunders in the first two years of what was to become a permanent exile, the Chinese Nationalist Party (Kuomintang, or KMT) defied expectations and implemented two policies in Taiwan that were among the most impressive and successful government initiatives in the developing world. Both the land reform policy that was implemented from 1949 to 1953 and the shift to an export-led strategy of economic development from 1958 to 1962 had widespread and beneficial effects in Taiwan, while simultaneously promoting economic growth with social equity and political stability. Because of its impressive success with economic development, the Republic of China (ROC) has much to teach other countries about how innovative government policies can be designed and implemented effectively. The experience in Taiwan also provides valuable insights into the evolution of megapolicies. This chapter will describe land reform as well as export-oriented economic growth policies and their effects and explain how and why these decisions were made.

## LAND REFORM ON TAIWAN

Between 1949 and 1953, the KMT implemented a sweeping agrarian reform on Taiwan that created the foundation for both economic growth and an equitable distribution of income and wealth. The land reforms undertaken during this period eventually increased the portion of Taiwan's farmland worked by the owner from about 50 percent to 75 percent and reduced tenant-cultivated land from nearly 42 percent to 16 percent. The landlords' 25 percent of rural income in the 1930s fell to just 6 percent by the late 1950s.[1]

The reform proceeded in three stages. First, in 1948, the government disposed of the territory confiscated from the Japanese at the end of World War II, which amounted to one-fifth of the island's arable land. The cultivators were given the first option to buy at a price 2.5 times the annual yield of the main crop. Second, in 1949, the rents that sharecroppers paid to their landlords—previously averaging 50 percent of the crop and reaching as high as 70 percent among some groups—were limited to 37.5 percent. The third and most ambitious phase of the reform was enacted and implemented in 1953 and compelled landlords to sell all holdings in excess of 7.5 acres of rice land (there was some allowance for the quality of the land) at a price 2.5 times the annual value of the main crop, a price well below market value. Compensation to the landlords was made primarily in commodity bonds (about 70 percent) and in shares of public corporations (about 30 percent). The land was then resold at the same price to tenants, who paid twenty installments in rice or cash over ten years at 4 percent interest. These payments were usually smaller than the 37.5 percent rental payments.[2]

### Impacts of the Reforms

Land reform policies in Taiwan were extraordinarily successful. Phases one and three together redistributed 13 percent of the country's 1952 gross national product (GNP).[3] Prior to the reform, an American observed of tenants that "what they have most are children; what they have least are the things that spell material well-being. Tenants' huts, so-called barnyards, equipment and livestock as well as their health point to nothing but poverty."[4] By the late 1950s, after the beneficiaries had paid off the land, their income increased by about 67 percent. The gratitude this created in the countryside not only reduced communism's potential appeal to Taiwan's farmers but also gave the government confidence to implement a sharp "price twist" that later extracted large amounts of capital from agriculture to finance industrialization.[5] The land reform contributed to the island's development in many other ways as well: by diminishing the attractiveness of land investment; by shifting capital to industry; by stimulating the development of food processing; by increasing rural incomes and strengthening the domestic demand for consumer goods; and by privatizing public corporations that funded the third phase of the program.[6]

How and why was it possible to achieve these results? Conditions were unusually, perhaps uniquely, favorable for the implementation of land reform in two fundamental ways. First, the political obstacles to reform were extremely weak. In Asia, national legislatures have been more responsive typically to the demands of the landed classes than to peasants. In Taiwan, however, the unusual structure of the government limited the landlords' influence. Taiwan, by virtue of its role as host to a government in exile, had two governments—a provincial one for the island itself and a national one for all of China dominated by mainland Nationalists. The latter had been elected previously on the mainland, so the local landlords had almost no representation in it. They had much more influence in the provincial assembly, but it was subordinate to the national government, and its role was merely advisory and consultative. Second, in both governments, the executive was far more powerful than the legislative branch and took the initiative in all phases of the reform. Both rent reduction and sale of public lands were enacted by executive decree and met no effective opposition.[7]

### The Evolution of Land Reform Policies

In order to understand why the KMT seized this opportunity, one must appreciate the history of KMT rule on the mainland that preceded it. In his 1924 publication, "Three Principles of the People," which was the basic ideological inspiration for the KMT, Sun Yat-sen asserted that tenancy was the root of China's agrarian problems and that the problems of poverty among the peasants could not be solved until all farmers owned their own land and could earn a livelihood from it. At the First National Congress of the KMT in the same year, the KMT pledged to provide land to tenants.

In 1930, five years after Sun's death, the Nationalist government enacted the Land Law, that promised to reduce rents and eliminate ownership by absentee landlords. In practice, however, for the next fifteen years, the KMT sided primarily with landlords. Chiang Kai-shek, who inherited the mantle of leadership from Sun, rejected agrarian reform as a way of dealing with the plight of rural Chinese and preferred instead to rely on technological improvements. The 1930 decree, for the most part, was enforced half-heartedly and brought significant improvement to the peasants' lot only in Hupeh Province, where Chen Cheng was governor. Tenants continued to pay as much as 60 to 70 percent of their crops as rents. In areas taken back from the communists, Nationalist armies relied on former landlords as guides. In return for their assistance, the KMT restored their ownership of lands expropriated by the communists and allowed them to use KMT forces to inflict revenge. At the Sixth Kuomintang Party Congress in May 1945, a group of reformers pushed successfully for a resolution calling for the redistribution of landlord property. After the end of World War II, the government also decreed a 25 percent reduction in rents. But these measures brought no significant change.

When the KMT arrived on Formosa, there was no outward sign of peasant dissatisfaction on the land issue. As nearly every commentator on the agrarian reform has noted, the KMT was not an indigenous political force but a regime analogous to colonizers or an army of occupation. As such, it had no ties to the local landlord class and no specific class interest to defend. In the language of contemporary social science, the KMT was "autonomous" from society. Furthermore, General Chiang's ability to control the party and the army had greatly increased as a result of the flight from the mainland, which became the functional equivalent of a purge. The most corrupt or disloyal officials went elsewhere, to Hong Kong or the United States. The majority of those who crossed the strait were either loyal to Chiang personally or had no alternative. There were no longer independent warlords to challenge his control over the armed forces.

In March 1947, conservatives in the KMT persuaded the Central Executive Committee to drop the party's position in favor of early redistribution, and, at the local level, landlords effectively thwarted all efforts to reduce rents or limit their powers. As the KMT's fortunes continued to ebb in the civil war with the communists, interest in land reform intensified. Opposition of any kind was poorly organized in Taiwan at the outset because the Japanese had tolerated no such activity. But when protests against the misrule of Chen Yi, the first KMT governor, reached a dangerous level in 1947, the army unleashed brutal repression by killing between 10,000 and 20,000 Taiwanese and decimating their landowning elite. It is true that the land reform was accomplished later without violence, but by then the landlords were so completely intimidated that no further repression was necessary. Even if the presence of an army of 630,000 in a country of 6 million had not been sufficient to overawe the inhabitants, this massacre surely ended any hope of violent resistance.[8]

The events of 1947 had provided the KMT not only with an opportunity but also, in the eyes of some observers, with a motive. The landlord class had provided much of the leadership for the rebellion of 1947, and some speculate that the KMT may have concluded that its interests would be best served by eliminating the landed elite as a potential rallying point for opposition. Once their land was expropriated, there would be no immediate threat from the elite or rival to the KMT's authority on Taiwan.[9] The only likely source of opposition was from within the Nationalist Party itself.

There are few occasions in history where leaders have been given a second chance after initial failures of the scope that befell the KMT on the mainland. But by the time they had reached Taiwan, the Chinese Nationalists, unlike the restored Bourbons of France, had forgotten something and learned something. In September 1948, eighty-six members submitted a bill to the Legislative Yuan calling for the abolition of tenancy, while the government ordered a reduction in rents of one-third and began plans for the nationalization of all land. Several provincial governments also implemented agrarian reforms in mid-1948. Even at this late date, these proposals were controversial and touched off heated debate. The regime was collapsing, but the Legislative Yuan continued its futile debate.[10]

Late in 1948, Chiang appointed as governor of Taiwan a man who enjoyed Chiang's complete confidence and who had long been committed strongly to reform.[11] Chen Cheng explicitly attributed the Nationalists' defeat to their failure to carry out land reform on the mainland, which had allowed the communists to seize the issue and mobilize the peasants against them. He was determined to prevent them from doing so again.[12] Chen was ably assisted by an unusual joint agency composed of officials from both the Nationalist Chinese and the American governments. In October 1948, the Sino-American Joint Commission on Rural Reconstruction (JCRR) was established. The JCRR's chairman, Chiang Monlin, soon thereafter persuaded Chiang to implement a trial land reform near Nanking. In Kwantung in December, the JCRR offered financial help to rebuild dikes on the condition that local landlords decrease rents 25 percent.

In late June 1949, two months after the communist army had crossed the Yangtze, the JCRR declared publicly its support for rent reduction. Beginning in August, the governor of Szechuan Province implemented, with technical assistance from the JCRR, a 25 percent rent reduction. In March 1949, Chiang Monlin and two other commissioners came to Taiwan to advise the provincial government in devising the plan to limit rents to 37.5 percent.[13]

Japanese cadastral surveys undertaken from 1898 to 1925 already provided extensive data on the productivity of various categories of land. This information was very useful, perhaps invaluable, to the government in designing the first phase of the reform—the rent ceilings—in that it allowed the government to estimate the standard yield of a parcel for the main crop. These records told the government who owned which piece of land but did not indicate the total amount of land any individual held. Hence, Chen concluded, it would be difficult or impossible to proceed with a redistribution of property without a new cadastral survey.

In July 1950, Chiang Kai-shek established a Central Reform Committee, staffed primarily by younger and less corrupt members of the KMT, and gave it the task of purging the party. Under its auspices, men like the reactionary Chen brothers were retired over the next two years.[14] Finally, although the KMT's policies on the mainland were conservative, the original ideological inspiration of the party was reformist, even socialist. Agrarian reform had been part of Sun Yat-sen's basic party principles enunciated many years before. To Chen Cheng, who considered himself "a faithful disciple of Sun," the KMT's failure to implement reform was a cause for deep regret.[15] Further, since the KMT's domination of Taiwan was based in part on its claim to Sun's legacy, implementation of the three principles could bolster their fragile legitimacy.

The violence in 1947 occurred exclusively in urban areas, and the communists, as yet, had what U.S. intelligence considered to be a negligible presence on the island. Hence, there was no need for immediate action. At the time the first stage was implemented, the civil war was still being fought on the mainland, resistance from the landlords could not be excluded, and the KMT lacked the administrative experience necessary to carry through a program on this scale.

With the help of the JCRR, which provided technical assistance and training and paid 82 percent of the cost, a cadastration of the entire island was begun in

January 1951 and completed by April 1952. This procedure gave a much clearer picture of patterns of land utilization and ownership and thus permitted the government to proceed with the drafting of legislation. The JCRR also played a significant role in the enactment of the legislation and administration of the program.

Beginning in 1951, the JCRR also encouraged and supported the transformation of the Farmers' Associations (FAs) that had been inherited from the Japanese and that had functioned previously as an instrument of colonial control over Taiwan's agricultural sector. Acting on the recommendations of a study sponsored by the JCRR, Taiwan's provincial government reorganized the FAs and introduced elections for such key positions as the chairmanship of local councils. The JCRR also helped finance the reconstruction of the FAs' facilities damaged in the war and provided training for more than 10,000 FA officers and staff. The reformed associations provided an impressive array of services to Taiwan's farmers, including disseminating new agricultural techniques (such as introducing new strains of rice and more frequent application of pesticides and fertilizers) as well as creating marketing, milling, and credit cooperatives—all of which played an important role in bringing about a 12 percent improvement in productivity between 1953 and 1960.[16]

The importance of JCRR's role in the land reform is conveyed in a memorandum written in 1952 by its first chairman, Chiang Monlin, in which he pointed out that the land reform program was entirely indigenous and came from the Chinese government. JCRR provided advice, technical services, and administrative expenses, but its contribution to the success of the land reform was crucial. The reforms may not have succeeded without JCRR's technical assistance.[17] Because of the cadastral records, the 1951 legislation allowed the government to fix rents at a maximum of 37.5 percent of the standard annual yield of the main crop rather than at a percentage of the total harvest and, thereby, offered additional protection to the tenants. By mid-1952, Farm Tenancy Committees (composed of two government officials and elected representatives of landlords, owner-operators, and tenants) were in place at both the county and village levels to implement the regulations, estimate the annual yield, and resolve disputes between landowners and tenants.

The first draft of the Land to the Tiller legislation prepared by the provincial government contained the proposal to compensate landlords in part with stocks in government-held firms, and the provincial assembly actually requested that the percentage of total compensation made in this manner be increased to 40 percent.[18] Nationalist officials supported the stock distribution for a number of reasons, most of them straightforward and unsurprising: (1) to ease opposition from the landlords, (2) to strengthen the private sector, (3) to avoid the potential inflationary effects of payment in currency that Japan had experienced during its land reform, and (4) to buffer the provincial Land Bank (which was responsible both for collecting payments from the tenants and paying interest to the landlords on the commodity bonds) from default should large numbers of the peasants fall into arrears (although in practice, few did). If the version of events presented by Dennis Fred Simon is to be credited, support also came from an unexpected source—the opponents of privatization.[19]

Prior to the third phase of the land reform, 55 percent of Taiwan's industry was in public hands, and the government had made no serious effort to sell off public corporations to the diminutive private sector. Indeed, the government continued to discriminate against private businesses in the allocation of raw materials and credit. This discrimination was partly a matter of conviction. Many of the leaders had studied in Germany and viewed state control over the economy as more efficient than market forces. Sun had also favored extensive public ownership. As Neil Jacoby explains, "Most Chinese officials were public administrators by training and experience and had strong predilections toward taking over and operating as public enterprises the former Japanese private enterprises. Nothing in their situation—nor in their economic philosophy— motivated Chinese officials to foster the growth of a strong private sector."[20]

In addition, there was a need to find jobs for the large numbers of mainlanders who had fled to the island. The Minister of Economic Affairs, T. K. Chang, was an advocate of both state control over the economy and the subordinate position for private enterprise, and his position enjoyed widespread support.

In mid-1953, however, the position of Chang and the U.S. foreign aid mission was strangely reversed and generated a controversy over the timing of the distribution of shares in public corporations. U.S. officials were concerned about the viability of the four state corporations under private ownership—all faced serious financial problems and were reliant on government support—and suggested delaying the transfer until the companies were in sounder financial condition. It was widely feared that the shares would, in practice, turn out to be nearly worthless. They were not received with great enthusiasm by the landlords, and most of the shares were rapidly resold. Chang, however, was adamant on proceeding quickly with the transfer and led U.S. officials to suspect that he was hoping that the firms would fail under private ownership and thus discredit private enterprise.

At one point, an international land reform expert, Wolf Ladejinsky, was invited to talk to the KMT on the issue of compensation under phase three. According to one account, the KMT leadership was quite irritated by this attempt to bring influence to bear and informed the United States that the decisions would be made without outside interference. Ironically, the privatization that accompanied the land reform, which was so important for the island's future, may have come about in part because of miscalculation by state officials in the ROC government.[21]

Despite the KMT's dominance over the institutions of government, the enactment of the third phase, the Land to the Tiller law, was still a process "marked with strong opposition from conservative forces . . . and heated debates between the policymakers and economic experts."[22] In its original version—drafted by the provincial Land Bureau in consultation with the JCRR and other ROC agencies— the legislation made available for transfer 83 percent of the tenanted land, or 215,000 hectares. Although the provincial assembly's assent was not required by the constitution, Governor K. C. Wu opted in 1952 to submit it for the body's consideration. When the assembly balked, the KMT's Central Reform Committee declared on July 24 (presumably at the behest of Chiang Kai-shek) that the legislation must be adopted by the first of the year and stated that all KMT members would be expected to comply. After this proclamation, the provincial assembly was compelled to accept the inevitability of land reform of some sort but began to work to minimize its effects by introducing amendments. The most damaging of these would have permitted landlords to circumvent expropriation by transferring land as gifts to family members.

Although they were not entirely effective in amending the legislation, the landlords were encouraged to press their claims more forcefully on the executive branch, and there they met with considerable success initially. The Executive Yuan referred the issue to several ministries for additional study, and the plan the ministries subsequently drafted would have reduced the amount of land available for transfer to only 60,000 hectares. On October 17, 1952, the chairman of the JCRR weighed in with a counterproposal that restored most of the original provisions. Although it is not clear how effective this appeal was, the issue was decided in a meeting of KMT leadership on January 13, 1953. Acting on their recommendation, the Legislative Yuan passed legislation a week later claiming 170,000 hectares for redistribution.

### Factors Affecting the Success of Land Reform

Compared to that of other developing countries at the time, the situation in Taiwan in the late 1940s and early 1950s was unusually propitious for reform. Most governments are not as insulated from the political power of landlords as the KMT regime was, and most leaders have not received both the harsh lesson history taught Chiang and his colleagues and the opportunity to apply that lesson in new circumstances. Even so, it would still be a mistake to assume that the adoption of land reform was a foregone conclusion in 1949. Opportunities are not transformed into results, after all, unless someone has the wisdom to do so. The success of the land reform program in Taiwan can be attributed in part to committed political leadership, to the characteristics of the policies that they fashioned, and to the critical role of the JCRR and U.S. aid.

#### Political Leadership

The circumstances may appear favorable for reform from hindsight, but no doubt the situation was less clear in the late 1940s. Chen Cheng was by no means hesitant to use harsh methods in pursuit of internal security. He and the generalissimo's son, Chiang Ching-kuo, arrested thousands of suspected communists and sympathizers and by 1952 were still holding several thousand political prisoners, many without trial.[23] But Chen had understood that repression alone was not a reliable guarantor of stability. As Wolf Ladejinsky concludes, "None of these other factors might have sufficed were it not for the fact that General Chen Cheng, then governor of Taiwan and an influential member of the Nationalist Party, had resolved that rural Taiwan was to undergo a thorough change."[24] For these reasons then, Hung-chao Tai has concluded that "[Chen's] demonstrated commitment to reform and the tight control of the island by the army were conditions sufficient for the rapid conclusion of the program."[25] Tai's assessment is fundamentally right but may obscure some important matters of detail.

## Characteristics of the Policies

Given the extent of control exercised by the KMT and the strength of Chen's motivation, land reform of some kind was going to be implemented. But it remained to be seen what kind of reform would be enacted, how well it would be implemented, and what its long-run effects would be. The Taiwan program was notable in all three of these respects. First, despite the complexity and scope of the endeavor (half the country's rural households were involved, requiring "a staggering amount of paper work and field investigation"), the reform was carried out expeditiously and with a minimum of disruption.[26] Second, unlike many land reforms elsewhere, this program not only increased peasant incomes but also stimulated a steady expansion in agricultural production. Even without a large increase in inputs of land and labor, the strengthening of the peasants' incentive to work led to a doubling of agricultural output from 1952 to 1972.

Finally, one of the most singular and controversial aspects of the land reform was the method of compensation for the third phase. To reiterate, 30 percent of the landlords' compensation was given in the form of shares in four public corporations. Two possible consequences of this method bear consideration. First, one might suppose that the general orderliness of the process might owe something to the fact that the land was not simply expropriated but that the government made some effort to soften the blow to the landlords. If so, then the key to success may not have been the KMT's autonomy, commitment, and degree of control, as stressed earlier, but rather its generosity. A closer look at the compensation, however, shows that this is the wrong lesson: the compensation was a good deal less generous in practice than in theory. The landlords were paid a price approximately two and one-half times the value of the land's annual yield, but studies have found that land was selling for four to eight times the annual yield prior to the war. The imposition of rent ceilings would, of course, have depressed the price of land, but the landlords were probably not wrong in assuming that they were being paid much less than market value for their land. Moreover, the return on the bonds was well below the market rate of interest, and, with the exception of Taiwan Cement Corporation, the shares were over-valued by the government and maintained only one-third to one-half of their face value on the stock market.[27] Martin Yang found in a survey of 575 landlords (500 smaller holders and 75 larger holders) that 98 percent of the smaller holders and 91 percent of the larger ones sold off their shares.[28]

The exchange of "land to the peasant" for "stock to the landlord" was significant not only as a means of carrying out land reform in a manner that was not wholly confiscatory—which may have facilitated its implementation—but also in the long-term effects it had on Taiwan's economy. Because most of the landlords sold off their stocks in the four corporations, within a few years three of the four were primarily in the hands of former KMT officials and Taiwanese businessmen, many of whom got their start working for Japanese companies during the colonial period. Relatively few of the landlords used the capital thus derived to enter business. In Yang's survey of 575 former landlords, only 10 percent of the smaller landlords and 17 percent of the larger landlords used the capital from the sale of their stocks to start up businesses.[29]

According to a smaller survey done in 1959, these landlords invested approximately 40 percent of their total compensation in business and industry. If that sample was representative, then one can reasonably conclude that the stock transfer did shift some capital from agriculture into industry, even though the sale of shares did not alter the balance between the public and private sectors decisively in the short run. The percentage of the government sector of manufacturing fell only about 6 percent as a result of the distribution of shares. Hence, the contribution of the stock distribution to Taiwan's industrial development was probably less than that of other factors, such as the price twist in agriculture and the weakening of the incentive to invest in land caused by the fall in land prices.[30] Some of the larger landowners did make the transition to business and finance successfully. These landlord-financiers bought up stocks from smaller landlords—in this way gaining control of Taiwan Cement Corporation—and acted as intermediaries for the mainlanders.

Still, this privatization through compensation helped lay the foundation for the growth of a private sector, which had expanded to 56.3 percent of total industrial production by 1964. In the view of one scholar, "the key elements of Taiwan's emerging pattern of industrial development were decided during the latter stages of the land reform process."[31]

### Role of the JCRR and U.S. Aid

The JCRR's basic responsibility was to administer U.S. aid first to rural China and later to Taiwan. According to one study of its operations, it was effective not only because of the high caliber of its leaders and staff but also because of its unusual structure and position. Three Chinese and two U.S. commissioners were appointed and granted extensive authority, thus making the JCRR a de facto ministry of agriculture for the ROC as well as the agricultural division of the U.S. aid mission with "virtually plenary powers with respect to the rural development of Taiwan."[32] This arrangement was not uncontroversial. U.S. documents show that the commission's independence was sometimes resented by others in the ROC government and the U.S. aid mission.

But this unusual composition insulated the JCRR from political pressures, allowed it to respond more directly to requests from the grass roots without going through cumbersome bureaucratic channels, and permitted decisions to be made on their technical or economic merits rather than on the basis of political influence. Further, the close and continuing cooperation among national representatives prevented the inevitable differences in national perceptions and interests from hardening into intransigent positions. This facilitated compromise and the resolution of disagreements.[33] The circumstances that made its success possible—the relative restraint of other ministries, the high quality of the staff, the confidence of the Chinese, and their willingness to accept the U.S. role and presence—may be unique to Taiwan at that time.

There are three fundamental questions one ought to ask in thinking about a prospective land reform: Will it be enacted? Will it be implemented? And if so, how well will it be carried out and what will be its long-run consequences? In these respects, Taiwan is close to a best-case scenario, which makes it useful as a point of comparison but which also makes the drawing of lessons and application of them elsewhere somewhat problematic.

Governments often have difficulty promoting land reform because the land classes either have control over the legislature or the sympathy of the army and bureaucracy, or both. In Taiwan, as a result of unusual historical circumstances, they had neither. The KMT was consequently quite autonomous from local social forces and also had a strong grip on the island, so forceful resistance was dangerous and probably futile in any case. These factors made land reform possible, and the ability of KMT leadership to learn, albeit belatedly, from the experience on the mainland made it inevitable. None of this, however, guaranteed that the reform would be carried out with the efficiency, relative lack of disorder and confusion, and, ultimately, the many beneficial long-term effects that it achieved. Much of the credit for this must go to the JCRR, but even here, luck played a role. The U.S. commissioners were reluctant to proceed quickly with privatization, which provided a significant stimulus for the growth of private enterprise on Taiwan, and the government apparently undertook it for the purpose of thwarting that very development. On the mainland, the KMT's errors were exacerbated by ill fortune; on the island, the KMT not only learned from its past mistakes but also prospered from its new ones.

## TAIWAN'S EXPORT-LED GROWTH POLICY

Between 1958 and 1962, the government of the ROC adopted and implemented a series of policy changes that broke decisively from the prevailing import substitution model of economic development and set Taiwan on the path toward export-led growth. Two key decisions initiated these changes. The first, taken by the top leadership on April 9, 1958, was to replace the existing multiple exchange rate system with a unitary (and considerably devalued) exchange rate. The second, reached on March 23, 1960, by the KMT's Central Standing Committee, was to adopt the Nineteen Point Program of Economic and Financial Reform drawn up in the previous months by K. Y. Yin.[34] Over the next two years, the government reduced tariffs and other import controls, particularly those on raw materials and other inputs used in the production of manufactured goods, and also granted rebates on these imports if the goods were exported. Because material inputs constituted such a large percentage of the value of the outputs of Taiwan's businesses (70 percent or more on average), reduction of these costs was a crucial step in enhancing the competitiveness of Taiwan's exports.

The effect of the change in policy was to bring prices into line with those of the world market and, thus, to allow Taiwan's manufacturers to exploit their comparative advantage of low labor costs and thereby to shift successfully to production for export. Later, the government added several measures to attract foreign investment, including the establishment of duty-free and tax-free zones. The results were nothing less than spectacular. In 1957 and 1958, Taiwan's GNP grew at an annual rate of 6.6 percent and her industrial exports at a rate of 14.5 percent, certainly respectable figures. But from 1963 to 1969, after the changes were adopted, these rates rose to an astonishing 10.2 percent and 33.6 percent per year respectively.[35]

### The Origins of Export-Led Growth

The liberalization of Taiwan's economy implemented between 1958 and 1962 was indisputably a success, but it hardly appeared so at the time. The policy involved substantial risks for the ruling elite both immediately and in the long run and promised somewhat uncertain rewards. There were, at this time, few precedents for a strategy of export-led growth. Many doubted that Taiwan's industries could compete effectively in world markets and feared that inflation and balance-of-payments deficits would ensue if tariffs were reduced. The domestic firms that benefited from protectionism could be expected to oppose its elimination, but their influence with the KMT was relatively weak.

Powerful interests within the ruling elite stood to lose a great deal from the policy. The military—concerned primarily with defense—strongly preferred to emphasize heavy, not light, industry. In addition, the extensive government controls over foreign exchange and trade had led to the expansion of bureaucracies to enforce them. Liberalization would endanger not just the power and job security of the incumbents in these positions but the opportunities for corruption that the system afforded them as well. Finally, there was the long-term risk that the development of a vigorous private sector would lead to the rise of a competing Taiwanese business elite that might eventually challenge the mainlanders' monopoly of power—which was, indeed, what more or less happened.[36] Despite these risks, the KMT regime moved again and moved decisively to implement a program that brought immense long-run benefits to Taiwan.

How and why was this possible? In the late 1940s, the ROC adopted an economic policy of import substitution by raising tariffs, setting quotas on imports, and establishing multiple and considerably overvalued exchange rates in an effort to protect and stimulate domestic industry.[37] In the following years, two factions contended for influence over economic policy. The division was roughly, though not completely, along bureaucratic lines. One coalition, led by O. K. Yui, was based in the financial agencies; the other, headed by Chen Cheng, dominated the industrial agencies. Yui's group favored monetary stability, avoidance of a trade deficit, and greater control by the public sector over the economy. Through the mechanism of multiple exchange rates, they attempted to discourage most imports, especially capital goods, while allowing some consumer necessities in order to hold down prices. They argued against devaluation of the currency on the grounds that it would increase the cost of imports and fuel inflation without doing much to stimulate exports since demand for the island's main exports at the time (sugar and rice) was inelastic, and they were skeptical of the ability of Taiwan's textile or other industries to compete. Hence, this approach did not aim at and was not likely to generate large-scale industrialization, particularly through an expansion of the private sector, and thus left ample resources for the military. Because of this as well as Yui's support of the public sector, the armed forces and the KMT conservatives, who were intent on a return to the mainland, were quite comfortable with these policies.

Chen and his followers also supported a return to the mainland but argued that it could only be achieved after the construction of an industrial economy. To foster this process, Chen's principal advisor, K. Y. Yin, advocated a diminished government role in foreign trade, a larger private sector, and an end to the system of multiple exchange rates. Chen himself may not have had a strong personal commitment to this strategy, but it was politically necessary to have an alternative program to that of his rival.

Prior to 1958, Yin enjoyed occasional success as chairman of the Industrial Development Commission (IDC) but, for the most part, had difficulty enlisting entrepreneurs in the projects he deemed most important. The monetarist group remained predominant through most of the 1950s. As a result, the restrictions on imports and controls of foreign exchange transactions implemented in the late 1940s to control inflation remained in effect, thus raising the cost of inputs for manufactured goods well above world market prices and considerably overvaluing the currency (New Taiwan dollars, or NT$). The combination of these factors made it very difficult for Taiwan's industries to compete in export markets, and few tried. Moreover, the banking system failed to encourage private business (two-thirds of all loans went to government-owned firms), and Yin's IDC remained dependent on the Economic Stabilization Board for its own funds.[38]

### Changing Circumstances and Opportunities for Policy Innovation

By late 1957, the import-substitution strategy, which had enjoyed some initial success, was creating serious difficulties. The domestic market was reaching the saturation point; as a consequence, GNP growth rates were declining (and had been every year since 1952) and investment was lagging, particularly from the private sector. In addition, because the 50 percent rise in imports resulting from the increased demand for capital goods was not offset by any improvement in exports, the ROC was running a persistent and worsening trade deficit. This situation was clearly not tenable over the long run without injections of U.S. economic aid. Late in the year, Chiang Kai-shek appointed a nine-man committee headed by Chen Cheng to investigate the last of these problems. K. Y. Yin argued persuasively before the committee that the existing multiple exchange rate system fostered corruption and inefficiency and exacerbated the balance-of-payments problems it was intended to prevent. Several conservatives resigned from the committee, but the KMT top leadership was convinced, although only after the reformers were able to persuade them, that devaluation would not be inflationary. On April 9, the Central Standing Committee gave its approval to a reform program of phased devaluation and simplification of the exchange rate system. The first step was taken immediately, but the consolidation into a single, devalued exchange rate was not completed until October 1963.

On June 30, O. K. Yui resigned as premier and was replaced by Chen Cheng, who removed monetarist officials from nearly all the key positions and filled them with men advocating industrialization. For the first time, the development-oriented faction was in total control of policy making, and this was undoubtedly a precondition for the continuation of the trends underway. Chiang's decision to change prime ministers, then, was crucial in the development of an outward-oriented strategy.

Why was the change made? The most straightforward explanation is that the change of personnel and policy was a rational response to the economic situation facing the regime, but it may not have been the correct one. It is not clear that Chen's support for the reformers was a matter of deep conviction; he may have only desired to present an alternative program to that of his rival. For his part, Chiang's motives may also have been more connected with current political matters. Yui had suffered several recent defeats in the legislature, and Chiang had reproached him in February for waste and irregularities in his government. In May, three members of the cabinet had been dismissed on charges of graft. Furthermore, despite Yui's favorable treatment of the military, he was seen as a less "martial" figure than the highly esteemed former general, Chen Cheng. In view of the continuing tensions across the Taiwan Strait, he may have wanted to strengthen the image of the Nationalists in the eyes of their adversary. For these reasons, Robert Wade concludes that "the president accepted the strategy mainly because he wanted to change his leading personnel for reasons not closely connected with economics, and the change in strategy came along with the new personnel."[39]

Two more developments were significant in convincing the government to proceed with reform. First, by the late 1950s, the more sensible officials among the KMT leadership must have begun to accept that they had no realistic chance of returning to the mainland in the foreseeable future. But the events of the early fall drove this message home in a manner so compelling it could not be ignored. On August 23, 1958, the Chinese communists initiated the second crisis over the Taiwan Strait by bombarding the islands of Quemoy and Matsu. The United States extended strong support to the ROC and once again deterred attacks by the People's Republic of China (PRC), not only on Taiwan itself but also on most of the smaller islands close to the mainland. After the crisis was past, however, U.S. Secretary of State John Foster Dulles visited the island and requested Chiang to sign a communique stating that unification was to be achieved only by peaceful means. This declaration greatly strengthened the hand of those who had argued that the wisest course for the KMT would be to attempt to legitimize its rule, not by exclusive emphasis on and preparation for an increasingly unlikely return to the mainland but rather by encouraging economic development of Taiwan as a means of winning the confidence of the local population. The selection of Chen may have been made in part because Chiang may have been concerned with maintaining an image of militancy, not just to deter the communists from aggression but also to assuage the KMT conservatives for changes that he anticipated even before the strait crisis and the American response.[40]

The policy of the United States was of decisive importance in one other sense. On a visit to Taiwan in October 1959, Undersecretary of State Douglas Dillon told the KMT that the United States would be willing to increase economic aid if the government were to adopt a program to accelerate economic growth. On December 20, 1959, the United States Agency for International Development (USAID) presented the government with a specific list of eight steps the ROC could take to improve its economic performance—stressing privatization, continuation of the liberalization of exchange controls, and reductions in military spending. The U.S. government promised Chiang an increase in assistance of $20 million to $30 million if the program was accepted and threatened to reduce assistance if it was not. USAID urged a quick response in order to persuade the U.S. Congress to authorize the assistance in 1961. K. Y. Yin, who was charged with drafting the government's response, added several points, including proposals to liberalize trade. The resulting Nineteen Point Program was then adopted by the KMT's Central Standing Committee on March 23. Because the leadership balked at the proposed cuts in defense expenditure, $20 million in assistance was granted.

In the view of several scholars, the U.S. role in these events was decisive.[41] These inducements were credible, in the view of Neil Jacoby, because the United States was not threatening an ally with punishment so severe that it could be pushed over the abyss. The U.S. aid program was large enough to allow marginal increases and decreases that could affect Taiwan's growth rate significantly without putting the regime's survival at risk. U.S. pressure was effective because in a situation where "there [were] conflicting political groups . . . some of whom support desirable economic reforms and others of which seek to block them," USAID was able to "strengthen the influence of the former groups and . . . tip the political scales in their favor." "Without the intervention of [US]AID," he concludes, "private enterprise would not have become, by 1965, the mainspring of Taiwan's economy."[42]

The balance-of-payments problems facing the regime also strengthened the hand of both the United States and the advocates of reform in the bureaucracy in more than one sense. Without some improvement in economic performance, the ROC would be dependent on the United States indefinitely for economic support; the United States, because of budgetary constraints as well as a shift in perspective, was now warning that Taiwan should expect a long-term decline in aid levels. To help wean the ROC from dependence on the United States, however, the USAID mission was willing to increase assistance in the short run. Paradoxically, K. T. Li recalls, Chiang was convinced to support reforms that increased the island's dependence on the international market by the argument that they would ultimately reinforce Taiwan's independence—a process that his American allies not only tolerated but fostered.[43]

The adoption of the exchange rate reform and the export promoting liberalization of the Nineteen Point Program was a remarkable achievement, not only because of its subsequent brilliant success but also because there were so few precedents for such an approach in the postwar world. The successful application of export-oriented strategies by Taiwan undoubtedly qualifies as a paradigm shift in the field of economic policy.

This reorientation came about through a combination of several factors. By late 1957, the economy was beginning to experience many of the problems typical of an import substitution policy. Unlike Latin America, however, the government was not prevented from dealing with them by the strength of a populist political movement, for none existed in Taiwan. Indeed, the regime, insulated as it was from both landed elites and local business, was subject to virtually no effective constraints—or assistance for that matter—by social forces outside the government. The main obstacle to reform was the loose coalition of all those inside the bureaucracy, party, and military who, by conviction or interest, favored a continuation of state controls over the economy. The defeat of this coalition owed much to the persuasiveness of reform advocates, in particular K. Y. Yin, but also to the friendly but effective pressure applied by the United States. The shift in emphasis from security to growth, perhaps inevitable in the long run, was catalyzed by the dramatic events in the Taiwan Strait. Finally, the rise to power of Chen's reform faction, though amply justified on economic merits, may well have taken place for short-term tactical political reasons having little to do with economics.

## CONCLUSIONS: LESSONS FROM TAIWAN'S MEGAPOLICIES

On two occasions since their flight from the mainland, the KMT implemented policies that not only initiated an unprecedented economic expansion on Taiwan but also distributed the fruits of that development broadly and equitably. This is, indisputably, a remarkable achievement. Assuming that this is a fair characterization, one is left then with the question: What were the sources of Taiwan's success?

In Taiwan, the development of great policies has been associated with the presence of four factors: (1) strong political and bureaucratic leadership, (2) an autonomous regime able to overcome resistance, (3) synergies among policies, and (4) the importance of catalytic events.

### Strong Political and Bureaucratic Leadership

Clear from the outset is the importance of the role of able statesmen and officials in conceiving, promoting, or implementing changes in policy. Without Chen Cheng's determination to avoid a repetition of the mistakes on the mainland, the favorable opportunity for land reform facing the KMT in rural Taiwan in the late 1940s might never have been seized. Without the persuasiveness and autocratic methods of K. Y. Yin, the top KMT politicians might never have been convinced to depart from the cautious but constraining economic programs pursued through the 1950s.

The impetus for land reform came from the political leadership, but the design and implementation was carried out by the provincial Land Bureau with the assistance and support of the JCRR. That the program was accomplished with such speed and so little disruption, particularly in view of the complexity and scale of the task, speaks well for the capabilities of personnel of both bodies. The economic liberalization, on the other hand, came about on the initiative of economic technocrats advising K. Y. Yin. Although Chen's role was again important, economic reform was much less a matter of conviction with him than was the redistribution of land. At least some of the opposition to these steps was overcome during 1957–1960 period when proponents of the change were able to make convincing arguments on economic grounds that devaluation would not be inflationary and would bring about an improvement in the balance of payments.[44]

One explanation for the ROC's success with land reform and export-oriented growth policies, then, is the quality of its personnel at the upper and middle levels in the government. The KMT was fortunate to inherit a large number of able officials trained under the Japanese. Another important injection of experience and talent came with the flight of the KMT from the mainland. The population of Taiwan was thus unusually well trained for a developing country; it was probably the best educated in Asia after Japan's.

These assets might have been wasted, however, had Chiang not shown the capacity to learn from his mistakes on the mainland. The importance of this for the enactment of land reform has already been emphasized. It was important in his choice of personnel as well. Before the retreat to Formosa, Chiang had tended to favor the loyal over the able. Here, with the advantage of this large pool of talent, he could select officials who were both, and, with his support, men such as Chen Cheng and K. Y. Yin rose to positions of power and contributed much to the island's development.[45]

### An Autonomous Regime Able to Overcome Resistance

Important though the vision and competence of the regime's politicians and officials were to the success of policy, it would distort the record to suggest that this in itself was the whole story. A fundamental rule of politics is that any policy that seeks to influence society on a large scale is bound to generate strong political opposition from forces who, whether from conviction or interest, fear change and its consequences. If a reform is to be enacted and implemented, those promoting it must defeat the forces of resistance and opposition.

The ability of Taiwan's government to overcome resistance varied over time but prevailed in the debates over land reform and export-oriented growth policies. In the late 1940s, the regime was unusually autonomous from the society it was governing; its officials had virtually no vested interests to protect. The society had been so thoroughly intimidated by the repression of 1947 and the size of the army's presence that resistance to the policy would have been futile. Moreover, land reform was the sort of policy initiative that could be implemented effectively, if need be, by the use of force. The government, in other words, was powerful and autonomous, and these strengths were directly applicable to the issue at hand.

By the end of the 1950s, the KMT was still highly autonomous from societal forces. In encouraging economic development through an export-led strategy, the KMT was not so much allying with local capitalists as conjuring them into existence. The only serious opposition was within the regime itself, and that was overcome by effective pressure from the United States.

## Synergies among Policies

These two policy successes were attributable partly to the way in which their diverse goals impinged on each other. Both megapolicies were characterized by interactions between different policy sectors—security, agricultural progress, and commercial development in the land reform on the one hand, and international and domestic security and economic development in the export-led growth policy on the other. The perception of interactions among elements of these policies did not encourage policy makers to tinker with piecemeal adjustments in policy and focus on goals of the moment. Reliance on such incremental shifts in policy simply would not have fostered a burst of creativity, and there would have been no great policy.

The synergistic relationships that were perceived by policy makers in these two cases allowed megapolicies to emerge. In the land reform case, favorable circumstances made it possible for the KMT to strengthen its political position against the communists, to increase agricultural productivity, and to give a boost to the incipient industrial economy—all with one stroke. Several goals could be achieved at once provided the government had the courage and will to attempt it.

The origins of export-led growth are somewhat more complex. In this instance, officials long assumed that attempts to accelerate growth through exports could undermine the security and independence of the regime. After the strait crisis of 1958, some of them came to believe that the regime's security could actually be enhanced by what had previously been viewed as measures that might increase wealth at the expense of military power. But this conclusion required a modification in the regime's concept of security. In this case, the latent synergy between development and security was only grasped in the midst of crisis. It was discovered, one might say, through the prodding of necessity.

## The Importance of Catalytic Events

The last point raises another important characteristic of Taiwan's megapolicies. The rethinking that led to the adoption of a strategy of export-led growth came about only after a catalytic event, the strait crisis of 1958. Although the regime survived, the outcome made it clear that the previous hopes and methods of legitimation could not be continued. The realization that no return to the mainland was in the offing compelled the regime's leadership to reassess their situation.

Crisis was also a strong stimulus to creativity in land reform. Reformist circles in the KMT had long advocated such measures. But only after the loss of the mainland did Chiang commit himself to rapid reform. An overwhelming failure again provided the incentive to reexamine past policies and practices.

In brief, the emergence of great policies in Taiwan's economic development resulted from circumstance and creativity and depended in large measure on four factors: (1) courageous, sensible, or technically competent leadership—either intellectual or political; (2) the existence of a powerful government autonomous from social forces; (3) the perception or discovery of synergistic relationships between two or more goals pursued by the government; and (4) the occurrence of a catalytic event that compelled the leadership to reassess and reconsider its past policies.

## NOTES

1. Hui-Sun Tang, *Land Reform in Free China* (Taipei: Joint Commission on Rural Reconstruction, 1954); Russell King, *Land Reform: A World Survey* (Boulder, Colo.: Westview Press, 1977).

2. Tang, *Land Reform in Free China*, 13; King, *Land Reform*, 212.

3. Samuel Ho, *Economic Development in Taiwan 1860–1970* (New Haven, Conn.: Yale University Press, 1978).

4. American land reform advisor Wolf Ladejinsky, quoted in Joseph Yager, *Transforming Agriculture in Taiwan: The Experience of the Joint Commission on Rural Reconstruction* (Ithaca, N.Y.: Cornell University Press, 1988), 101.

5. Michael Hsin-huang Hsiao, *Government Agricultural Strategies in Taiwan and South Korea* (Taipei: Academia Sinica, 1981), 62–63, 121–24.

6. T. H. Shen, *The Sino-American Joint Commission on Rural Reconstruction* (Ithaca, N.Y.: Cornell University Press, 1970), 67; Cal Clark, *Taiwan's Development: Implications for Contending Political Economy Paradigms* (Westport, Conn.: Greenwood, 1987), 160–61; Yager, *Transforming Agriculture*, 122–23.

7. Ralph Clough, *Island China* (Cambridge, Mass.: Harvard University Press, 1978), 35–36; Dennis Fred Simon, "External Incorporation and Internal Reform," in *Contending Approaches to the Political Economy of Taiwan*, ed. Edwin Winkler and Susan Greenlalgh (Armonk, N.Y.: East Gate, 1988), 147; Hung-chao Tai, *Land Reform and Politics: A Comparative Analysis* (Berkeley: University of California Press, 1974), 118–20; Wolf Ladejinsky, "Agrarian Reform in Asia," *Foreign Affairs* 42 (April 1964): 455–56; Thomas Gold, *State and Society in the Taiwan Miracle* (Armonk, N.Y.: East Gate, 1986), 60–62.

8. George Kerr, *Formosa Betrayed* (Boston: Houghton Mifflin, 1965), 297–310; Thomas Gold, *State and Society*, 51–52; King, *Land Reform*, 209; Clough, *Island China*, 38–39, 69–70.

9. John Israel, "Politics on Formosa," in *Formosa Today*, ed. Mark Mancall (New York: Praeger, 1964), 59; Clark, *Taiwan's Development*, 124.

10. Lloyd Eastman, *Seeds of Destruction* (Stanford, Calif.: Stanford University Press, 1984), 82–84; Tai, *Land Reform and Politics*, 83–85.

11. Anthony Kubek, *Modernizing China: A Comparative Analysis of the Two Chinas* (Washington, D.C.: Regnery Gateway, 1987), 57–59; Clough, *Island China*, 42–43.

12. Chen Cheng, *Land Reform in Taiwan* (Taipei: China Publishing Company, 1961), 47–48; Clough, *Island China*, 42–43.

13. Tang, *Land Reform in Free China*, 19–20.

14. Robert Wade, *Governing the Market: Economic Theory and the Role of Government in East Asian Industrialization* (Princeton, N.J.: Princeton University Press, 1990), 266–67; Clough, *Island China*, 33–34, 48.

15. Cheng, *Land Reform in Taiwan*, xiii, 19.

16. Neil Jacoby, *U.S. Aid to Taiwan: A Study of Foreign Aid, Self-Help and Development* (New York: Praeger, 1966), 172; Anthony Koo, *The Role of Land Reform in Economic Development: A Case Study of Taiwan* (New York: Praeger, 1968), 65–77; Yager, *Transforming Agriculture*, 128–31; Clark, *Taiwan's Development*, 161–62; King, *Land Reforms*, 214–16; Shen, *Sino-American Joint Commission*, 52, 71–76.

17. Cited in Yager, *Transforming Agriculture*, 102.

18. Tang, *Land Reform in Free China*, 109, 111.

19. Simon, "External Incorporation and Internal Reform," 139–44.

20. Jacoby, *U.S. Aid to Taiwan*, 1367.

21. See Simon, "External Incorporation and Internal Reform," 139–44; Wade, *Governing the Market*, 257; Shen, *Sino-American Joint Commission*, 62.

22. Yager, *Transforming Agriculture*, 111–15.

23. Clough, *Island China*, 42–43.

24. Ladejinsky, "Agrarian Reform in Asia," 457.

25. Tai, *Land Reform*, 276.

26. Samuel Ho, *Economic Development*, 241–43; Jacoby, *U.S. Aid to Taiwan*, 82.

27. Ching-yuan Lin, "The 1949–1953 Land Reform," in *The Taiwan Experience*, ed. James Hsiung (New York: Praeger, 1981), 14–23.

28. Martin M. C. Yang, *Socio-Economic Results of Land Reform in Taiwan* (Honolulu: East-West Center Press, 1970), 232.

29. Ibid., 102–3, 233.

30. See Ladejinsky, "Agrarian Reform in Asia," 451–52; and Shirley Kuo, Gustav Ranis, and John Fei, *The Taiwan Success Story* (Boulder, Colo.: Westview Press, 1981), 60–62.

31. Simon, "External Incorporation and Internal Reform," 140–41.

32. Jacoby, *U.S. Aid to Taiwan*, 62–63.

33. John Montgomery, Rufus Hughes, and Raymond Davis, *Rural Improvement and Political Development: The JCRR Model* (Washington, D.C.: Comparative Administration Group of American Society for Public Administration, 1966), 2, 5–6, 36–37, 57–58, 73; Simon, "External Incorporation and Internal Reform," 139; Jacoby, *U.S. Aid to Taiwan*, 172.

34. Stephen Haggard and Chien-kuo Pang, "The Transition to Export-Led Growth in Taiwan," paper prepared for Conference on the State and Economic Development (Taiwan, Los Angeles: UCLA Center for Pacific Rim Studies, 1989).

35. Samuel Ho, "Economics, Economic Bureaucracy and Taiwan's Economic Development," *Pacific Affairs* 60 (Summer 1987): 237–39; Gold, *State and Society*, 77; Wade, *Governing the Market*, 52–53; Clark, *Taiwan's Development*, 174–75.

36. Stephen Haggard, *Pathways from the Periphery: The Politics of Growth in the Newly Industrializing Countries* (Ithaca, N.Y.: Cornell University Press, 1990), 87–88; Clark, *Taiwan's Development*, 127–28, 147–48, 174; Gold, *State and Society*, 77, 124, 128–29; Ho, "Economics, Economic Bureaucracy," 244; Haggard and Pang, "Transition to Export-Led Growth," 29.

37. Clark, *Taiwan's Development*, 168.

38. Wade, *Governing the Market*, 388–92; Ho, "Economics, Economic Bureaucracy," 237–38; Haggard, *Pathways from the Periphery*, 87–89.

39. Wade, *Governing the Market*, quoted at 391–93; *Facts on File*: 1958, 59E1, 98G2, 215F1.

40. Haggard and Pang, "Transition to Export-Led Growth," 2, 26–27; Wade, *Governing the Market*, 246, 392.

41. See Gold, *State and Society*, 77, 128; and Simon, "External Incorporation and Internal Reform," 149–50.

42. Jacoby, *U.S. Aid to Taiwan*, 131–34.

43. Haggard, *Pathways from the Periphery*, 98; Haggard and Pang, "Transition to Export-Led Growth," 27, 35, 40; quotation by Li in Gold, *State and Society*, 77–78.

44. Ho, "Economics, Economic Bureaucracy," 240–46.

45. Alice Amsden, "The State and Taiwan's Economic Development," in *Bringing the State Back In*, ed. Peter Evans et al. (New York: Cambridge University Press, 1985), 83, 96–97; Jacoby, *U.S. Aid to Taiwan*, 225–26; Clough, *Island China*, 48; Ho, "Economics, Economic Bureaucracy," 246–47.

# 4
# STRATEGIC NOTIONS AND GREAT POLICIES: REFLECTIONS ON TAIWAN'S EXPERIENCE WITH ECONOMIC TRANSFORMATION

*Bruce F. Johnston and Albert Park*

Taiwan's economic progress during the past four decades is a remarkable success story.[1] According to recent estimates, per capita gross national product (GNP) rose from "a wretched $145 in 1951 to $8,800 in 1991."[2] In addition, economic progress was accompanied by widespread economic participation that allowed Taiwan to avoid the severe poverty experienced in many other developing countries as their economies were transformed. Observers attribute Taiwan's economic success to a range of explanations from the allocation of investments between agriculture and industry to the personal motives of political leaders. What these explanations overlook, however, are the unique set of factors that brought these elements together in creating Taiwan's economic development policies.

The argument that will be made here is that after the defeat of the Chinese Nationalist Party (Kuomintang, or KMT) on the mainland, there emerged a vision of a better future on Taiwan that could be achieved by a carefully crafted set of government interventions. Such a vision informed choices and shaped the evolution of Taiwan's economic development policies. That vision was driven by strategic notions of individual leaders in Taiwan and gave direction to decisions that were made at strategic moments in history. To explain these aspects of policy innovation, this chapter contrasts prevailing interpretations of Taiwan's economic achievements with a concept of strategic notions and identifies factors that allowed Taiwan's economic development to occur the way it did.

The two decades that began with the transfer of General Chiang Kai-shek's KMT regime to Taiwan in 1949 were critical in transforming the island's predominantly agrarian economy. In 1960, the midpoint of that period, over half of the country's labor force still depended mainly on agriculture for income and employment. But after 1960, the rate of structural transformation was extraordinarily rapid. There is surprisingly little agreement, however, about how Taiwan's leaders were able to integrate the various elements of economic development policy that were most crucial to its success.

Many agricultural specialists have stressed the decisive importance of the post–World War II land reforms, and some even viewed them as a necessary precondition for Taiwan's economic success.[3] Other economists have focused attention almost exclusively on macroeconomic policies, thereby underestimating the crucial role of agricultural development and the transformation of Taiwan's rural economy. For example, Ian Little and Robert Wade take sharply divergent positions with respect to the nature and impact of the government's macroeconomic policies, but neither gives much attention to those policies that were of central importance in making possible Taiwan's impressive increases in farm productivity and income.[4]

In examining the lessons from Taiwan's experience, it is important to understand that Taiwan's policy makers were guided by an integrated perspective that took account of the related effects of macroeconomic policies, agricultural development, and transformation of the rural economy, including investments in human resources through education, health, and family-planning programs. The considerable attention given to the postwar land reforms may have diverted analysts from exploring other aspects of agricultural and rural economic transformation, including those that encouraged the rapid and geographically dispersed growth of small- and medium-scale enterprises (SMEs).

## THE IMPORTANCE OF STRATEGIC NOTIONS IN POLICY INNOVATION

Agricultural development strategy can be defined as a combination of policies, programs, and projects that jointly influence the rate and pattern of agricultural growth. Beyond this definition lie the forces that determine government decisions and actions. It is individuals, not governments, who have the notions, ideas, and visions that shape future actions and outcomes. Whether the consequences of these forces are beneficial or not is determined to a large extent by the strategic notions held by the individuals who make or shape government policies.

In describing the KMT's defeat on the mainland as a "catastrophic learning experience," Brewster has focused attention on a traumatic episode that had a powerful impact on the KMT leaders' thinking and on the belief of many that their actions on Taiwan provided a "last chance" opportunity to achieve their objectives.[5] The shift to new and remarkably successful policies in Taiwan provides an exceptional opportunity to identify the strategic notions that were key to Taiwan's economic development policies that stimulated impressive increases in agricultural productivity and incomes and that brought about rapid growth of output and employment in the rural nonfarm economy.

## The New Political Economy and the Influence Perspective

For many years, the interpretation of issues of political economy was dominated by Marxists and more recently by new political economy theorists, including both the public choice and collective choice schools.[6] The emphasis in the new political economy theory on the role of interest groups in influencing government decisions is a healthy reaction to the common tendency for economists to ignore the effect of politics on development strategies or to assume implicitly that government will play the role of a neutral and benign protector of broad social interests.[7] There are limitations to the influence perspective, however, and viewing those who wield authority as a completely self-serving group is likely to be as misleading as viewing political leaders simply as disinterested public servants. Taiwan's agricultural and rural development is a particularly clear instance in which the government's activist role made important positive contributions. The same can be said of the successful agricultural development strategies of Japan and the United States during the historical periods when agriculture helped transform the structure of their economies. But Maoist China, Mexico, and Tanzania come to mind as countries where high levels of idealism and activism had unintended counterproductive effects.

More generally, it should be recalled that between 1945 and the early 1960s when many developing countries obtained their independence, highly protectionist import substitution strategies were widely prescribed by development experts. Bhagwati, for example, recalls that "at the outset, few of us realized that controls could proliferate in the way they did. In the early 1950s, industrial controls appeared to be sensible instruments to allocate resources in directions worked out in the planning commission."[8] Although it is now widely recognized that import substitution strategies create "policy rents," Bhagwati's recollections make it clear that was an ex post facto result. Initially, it was the driving force of the prevailing strategic notions that led to the adoption of those policies.

Thus, the influence perspective must be supplemented with a broader view that can explain the many cases where visible self-interest was not the driving force of government decisions. Governments do, on occasion, give priority to broad social and economic goals. While much can be explained in terms of the self-interest of individuals or groups, neoclassical political economy cannot explain the numerous exceptions of "behavior in which calculated self-interest is not the motivating factor."[9]

The ambiguity surrounding the issue of self-interest is hardly surprising because individuals' private interests coexist with collective interests.[10] While influential individuals have incentives to pursue their private interests through financial gain and accumulation of power, concern with their common stake in broader social and economic goals also can motivate actions that transcend narrow group interests.

## The Concept of Strategic Notions

Historical case studies of Japan and the United States, the Soviet Union and China, Taiwan and Mexico, and Kenya and Tanzania indicate that policy priorities and decisions have been shaped by strategic notions held by influential individuals. These strategic notions help explain why government decisions at times appear to be farsighted and consistent with societal objectives, while at other times they have detrimental effects. Because of the complexity and uncertainty of the development process, policy makers usually have only a dim vision of the policies and programs that will catalyze development. Their beliefs are derived from personal experience, the interpretation of others' experiences, and cognitive processes influenced by education, policy research, and analysis. Because policy makers often have similar backgrounds and experience, their strategic notions are likely to be shared, thereby helping them to reach a sufficient degree of consensus to take action.

Strategic notions may also be influenced by the experience of other countries, and their results may be beneficial or disastrous depending on their appropriateness to immediate circumstances. The extent to which a traditional agrarian economy has been transformed into a modern, diversified, and productive industrial economy is a particularly significant determinant of the appropriateness of strategic notions. It will determine, for instance, whether to emphasize the development of existing small-scale farm units or to give priority to achieving economies of farm size. As long as a country's farm labor force is still increasing in absolute size, it is likely to be advantageous to try to foster widespread increases in productivity based on labor-using, capital-saving technologies appropriate for small-scale units. And whether or not a country's farm work force is still increasing in absolute size depends in large measure on the extent to which agriculture is still the dominant source of employment as well as on the growth rate of the total labor force. There are huge differences among countries and over time in agriculture's share of the total labor force (see Table 4.1).

All countries have experienced a first phase of demographic transition characterized by reduced death rates and the persistence of high birth rates. An increasing number have also entered a second phase in which birth rates decline so as to substantially or completely close the gap between death rates and birth rates. The fall in crude death rates in Taiwan was much more rapid than in the United States or Japan.[11] Taiwan appears to have been the first country to experience a very rapid decline in death rates and an upsurge in population growth rates, a trend that became almost universal in the decades following World War II. But it further illustrates that the fall in crude birth rates during

Table 4.1
Percentage of Total Labor Force in Agriculture in the United States, Japan, Taiwan, Mexico, Kenya, and Tanzania

| Country | 1900 | 1930 | 1960 | 1970 | 1985 |
|---|---|---|---|---|---|
| United States | 40 | 22 | 8 | 4 | 3 |
| Japan | 66 | 48 | 31 | 20 | 8 |
| Taiwan | 71 | 68 | 56 | 37 | 18 |
| Mexico | 67 | 69 | 54 | 44 | 33 |
| Kenya | — | — | — | 85 | 79 |
| Tanzania | — | — | — | 90 | 83 |

*Note:* In Japan, 75 percent of the labor force worked in agriculture in 1880. For the United States, agriculture's share of the labor force was 80 percent in 1820 and 55 percent in 1850.

*Sources:* Reproduced from B. F. Johnston and P. Kilby, *Agriculture and Structural Transformation* (N.Y.: Oxford University Press, 1975), p. 454ff., except 1970 and 1985 figures from the Food and Agriculture Organization (FAO), 1988, and Taiwan figures for 1970 and 1985 from Republic of Taiwan, 1988. In recent years, the figures for Taiwan refer to the employed labor force age 15 and over instead of 12 and over; on that basis, the 1960 share is reported as 50 rather than 56 percent.

the declining fertility phase of the demographic transition can also be exceptionally rapid. By the 1930s, Taiwan's labor force was already increasing at 2.3 percent a year, and the growth of the total labor force became even higher following World War II. As a result of the combination of a large share of the labor force in agriculture (still over 50 percent in 1960) and rapid growth in the total labor force, the absolute size of Taiwan's farm labor force continued to increase until the mid-1960s in spite of very rapid growth of nonfarm employment. It was, therefore, of great importance that the strategic notions that shaped Taiwan's agricultural policies and programs included a concern with enlarging opportunities for productive employment in both the farm and nonfarm sectors of the economy by seizing opportunities to apply labor-using, capital-saving technologies.

## The Concept of Strategic Moments

Political economists recognize the critical significance of political constraints and opportunities as well as economic ones. But it is also essential to recognize the importance of strategic moments in a country's history when it becomes possible to seize opportunities that were previously out of reach. The Civil War in the United States and the Meiji Restoration in Japan are examples of strategic moments that made it possible for important strategic notions to be implemented. The Civil War period in the United States is an especially clear example:

the absence of Southern representatives in Congress in 1862 made it possible to enact both the Homestead Act and the Morrill Act. The former contributed greatly to the uniform size distribution of farm units in the American Midwest and West while the latter created the land-grant colleges and universities that have contributed so much to the development of American agriculture.

Clearly, the catastrophic learning experience of the KMT's defeat on the mainland gave rise to a strategic moment in Taiwan. It is difficult to explain why the opportunities opened up by the KMT's last chance opportunity on Taiwan were seized and not missed, but a strong argument can be made that those opportunities were perceived because Taiwan's policy makers came to hold a set of strategic notions that were appropriate to the severe challenges confronting the KMT regime in the 1950s and 1960s. Moreover, as their implementation met with success, those strategic notions were reinforced, gained increased support, and soon evolved into great policies.

## CRUCIAL ELEMENTS OF TAIWAN'S EXPERIENCE

What were the strategic opportunities that led to Taiwan's remarkable economic progress during the 1950s and 1960s? Three features of Taiwan's experience stand out: (1) an integrated perspective was adopted and the organizational requirements for agricultural and rural development were met; (2) policies and programs were adopted that reinforced the broad-based unimodal pattern of agricultural development promoted by the Japanese colonial administration; and (3) strong positive interactions between agricultural and industrial development were facilitated by large intersectoral resource flows and rising agricultural incomes that boosted rural demand for nonagricultural products. Underlying these factors is a set of strategic notions that appears to have facilitated the process of reaching consensus and of supporting the adoption and implementation of effective policies and programs.

### An Integrated Perspective and Meeting the Organizational Requirements

It is important to distinguish between the integrated perspective that shaped the pattern of rural development in Taiwan and the concept of "integrated rural development" that was fashionable in the 1970s, but which proved to be administratively infeasible. It is now widely accepted that development is a generalized process of capital accumulation in which capital is defined broadly to include not only physical capital in the form of plant, equipment, and natural resources but also human capital in the form of skills and professional competence as well as social capital in the form of economically useful knowledge, organizations, and organizational competence.[12] Important complementarities emerge among the various forms of capital, and that is why achieving a well-balanced accumulation of stocks of capital in the various forms is a particularly crucial task for developing countries.

In a 1966 monograph, S. C. Hsieh and T. H. Lee asserted that the key to Taiwan's development was "her ability to meet the organizational requirements."[13] Hsieh and Lee had both played key roles in the Sino-American Joint Commission on Rural Reconstruction (JCRR), and they were well aware of the JCRR's success as a coordinating and catalytic body that was well funded, flexible, and able to seize opportunities to support promising pilot projects implemented by the government or by nongovernment organizations at any level. Hsieh and Lee also stress the contributions of Taiwan's agricultural research institutions, the Farmers' Associations, and the Irrigation Associations, all of which built on experience gained during the period of Japanese rule. In stressing the importance of human factors, Hsieh and Lee stress the role of educational institutions in achieving widespread literacy among the farm population and in providing training in colleges of agriculture and vocational schools for staff members of research institutions and public agencies as well as agricultural technicians working at township and county levels.

The JCRR, being concerned with rural development, included a Rural Health Division. In the early 1960s, the chief of that division was one of the first to perceive that the sharp decline in infant and child mortality had created a potential demand for family planning. A series of demographic surveys in rural as well as urban areas provided guidance for step-by-step implementation of a family-planning program that achieved a rapid reduction in fertility.

An Economic Stabilization Board (which evolved into an Economic Planning Council) and other agencies, including the Central Bank, were responsible for macroeconomic policies. The JCRR monitored the effects of economic policies on farmers' incentives but, more important, shared a commitment to avoid those macroeconomic distortions that have adverse effects on development—an overvalued exchange rate, undervalued capital, and government deficits that fuel inflation.

## Taiwan's Unimodal Pattern of Agricultural Development

Many factors contributed to Taiwan's success in achieving a broad-based unimodal pattern of agricultural development. A great deal of attention has been given to the land reforms carried out between 1949 and 1953. Effective implementation of those reforms was possible because of special circumstances, especially the fact that the Taiwanese landlords who were affected by the reforms had very little power to influence the KMT officials and legislators from the mainland who enacted and implemented land reform. Clearly, those postwar reforms had important positive effects on rural income distribution and producer incentives. But it is important to recall that the pattern of agricultural development was based on a unimodal size distribution of operational farm units during the colonial period even though the distribution of land ownership was skewed.

A striking feature of Taiwan's experience is that underemployment in agriculture was actually reduced despite a 15 percent increase in the size of the farm labor force between 1930 and 1940 and a further 44 percent increase between 1940 and 1964. These changes led to a considerable decline in the average farm size. This was possible because of the application of labor-using and capital- and land-saving technologies. Technology borrowing and local research, together with expansion of irrigation and drainage facilities, made possible dramatic increases in crop yields. Improved water control and a 13-fold increase in fertilizer consumption during the 1911–1915 and 1955–1960 periods were key to the large increases that occurred in multiple cropping and in crop yields. The improvement in total factor productivity made an even larger contribution to agricultural development in Taiwan than in the United States or Japan. Thus, technological change, judicious expansion of purchased inputs, and fuller and more efficient utilization of the still large farm work force represented an economically efficient as well as socially desirable path to agricultural expansion.

### Rising Farm Incomes, the Pattern of Rural Demand, and Rapid Growth of Small- and Medium-Scale Enterprises

Rapid and widespread increases in farm cash income and macroeconomic policies that maintained a level playing field for small and large firms were key factors responsible for the strong positive interactions between agricultural and industrial development. Because of the pattern of technological change and the large increases in total factor productivity, it was possible to achieve a large net capital outflow from agriculture while simultaneously achieving rapid growth of farm output. Much of that capital outflow accrued to Japan during the colonial period, but Taiwan's economy also benefited. This effect is most obvious in the case of investments in infrastructure, notably in irrigation and drainage facilities and in the transport network. Outlays for education were also very significant. By the end of Japanese rule, some 70 percent of children of primary school age were enrolled; and expansion at the secondary and tertiary levels included a number of agricultural vocational schools and two colleges of agriculture.

The importance of productivity growth is underscored by the fact that until the 1950s, outlays for purchased inputs were only about 15 percent of the value of farm production. Those input purchases, which represented about 35 percent of total purchases by farm households, were concentrated almost entirely on fertilizers and other divisible, yield-increasing inputs. As late as the 1961–1965 period, spending on farm equipment and other fixed capital was only about 10 percent of off-farm inputs.[14]

The pattern of rural demand for agricultural inputs, consumer goods, and services encouraged the geographically dispersed growth of small- and medium-scale manufacturing firms and service enterprises using technologies that were labor-intensive and had a low import content. Hence, the expansion of output by the SMEs was less constrained by the scarcity of capital and foreign exchange than was the more capital- and import-intensive growth of large urban firms catering to the demand of large farm enterprises for sophisticated farm equipment and consumer goods.

Reflecting the still predominantly agrarian structure of the economy, it was not until the late 1950s that domestic sales accounted for half of farm cash receipts. The large expansion of marketed farm output in earlier decades, which made possible a huge outflow of funds, was possible only because of rapid expansion of agricultural exports, which increased fourfold during the 1911–1915 and 1936–1940 periods. In 1955, farm products still accounted for 92 percent of Taiwan's exports. By 1970, industrial products accounted for 78 percent of total exports, which had increased more than eleven-fold since 1955.

A distinctive feature of the phenomenal growth of Taiwan's manufacturing sector is the extent to which the growth was due to rapid expansion of the number of firms rather than increases in the size of existing firms. Between 1966 and 1976, the number of firms increased 2.5 times, while employees per firm rose by less than 30 percent.[15]

### The Macroeconomic Environment

Among the macroeconomic policies that were crucial in fostering Taiwan's decentralized pattern of industrial expansion, credit policy is especially noteworthy. Policy makers set interest rates sufficiently high in real terms to stimulate saving and to encourage labor-using, capital-saving technologies. By avoiding the credit rationing that is unavoidable with repressed interest rates, investment was a more effective engine of growth. The rapid and geographically dispersed growth of SMEs, which has been such a significant feature of Taiwan's development, was fostered because those firms had access to credit. They faced interest rates that were appreciably higher than those available to large firms, which benefited from economies of scale in lending, but that disadvantage was usually more than offset by the SMEs' flexibility and ability to hold down total costs. An informal curb market was especially important in facilitating access to credit by start-up firms.[16]

## STRATEGIC NOTIONS THAT SHAPED TAIWAN'S DEVELOPMENT STRATEGIES

Another question arises in reviewing lessons from Taiwan's experience: Why were so many of the strategic opportunities seized and not missed? It is, of course, extremely difficult to answer that question. But it seems clear that certain strategic notions fostered by the KMT leaders' catastrophic learning experience contributed much to the consensus that emerged with respect to the policies and programs adopted to promote Taiwan's economic development.

The need to maintain support of the farm population is perhaps the most obvious of those strategic notions. Closely related, and also of great importance, were the hard-earned lessons related to the supreme importance of food supply for the army and urban population and of avoiding the runaway inflation that had wrought havoc on the mainland. Recognition of the importance of avoiding inflation and the economic chaos that contributed so much to the KMT's failure on the mainland was reinforced by growing awareness of the economic ineffi-ciency associated with import substituting industrialization and concern about an increasingly acute problem of surplus labor. The strategic notions of com-petent professional economists played a major role in determining macroe-conomic policies and helped to ensure support for the most appropriate ones.

The KMT's failure on the mainland had naturally led to considerable soul-searching on the part of key leaders, who explicitly recognized that a major reason for their earlier defeat was the failure to establish a "solid organizational system." Realizing that it was important to have a shared vision of the party's future, they developed a plan for creating a new organizational structure capable of charting a "clear and defined policy."[17] To a surprising extent, the regime in Taiwan managed to avoid the factionalism that had been such a serious problem on the mainland. That awareness of the need for a solid organizational system no doubt contributed to a general determination to achieve a higher level of performance on the part of government agencies, especially in an organization such as the JCRR, to which highly competent persons were appointed and which was given unusual autonomy and substantial resources for carrying out its mandate.

Several other decisions reflected the pragmatism that K. T. Li, one of the ablest and most influential of Taiwan's economic policy makers, attributed to the period by citing the search for a balance of responsibilities between the public and private sectors and by continuing to stress policies aimed at increasing productivity and output on small farms. The latter ensured continuity with Japanese colonial policies and their emphasis on agricultural research and divisible technical innovations with a labor-using, capital-saving bias.

Li also singles out the influence of Sun Yat-sen's Principle of the People's Livelihood as an important guideline for Taiwan's economic policies. He gives credit to that guideline for the early emphasis on "land reform and the promo-tion of industries that provide for the basic needs of life—food, clothing, housing, and transportation." He goes on to argue that the livelihood principle translated into the operational goal of "striving for growth with equity" which embraced "concentrating on the agricultural sector in which most people lived" and concurrently "promoting industries that were open to large numbers of people (that is, required little skill), all the while increasing educational opportunities for everybody."[18] Although Li emphasizes the influence of Dr. Sun's teachings, he also suggests that "in other countries a similar outlook under another name would serve the same purpose: a consensus ideology if you will, favoring growth and a generally agreed framework to achieve it."[19]

## THE TRANSFERABILITY OF TAIWAN'S EXPERIENCE

Li's conclusion poses another question: Is it possible for leaders in other developing countries to use the strategic notions that shaped Taiwan's policies for agricultural development, structural transformation, and the elimination of severe poverty in their own development strategies? Clearly, each country has unique historical circumstances and distinctive economic, social, political, demographic, and agroclimatic characteristics. Those distinctive features obviously limit the extent to which it is appropriate or even possible to borrow policies and technological and institutional innovations that were successful in another country. But there is at least a possibility that an understanding of Taiwan's experience will foster a readiness in leaders in developing countries to rethink past policies and previously held strategic notions. To be sure, a beleaguered elite may (like the ruling class in France prior to the French Revolution) simply procrastinate in the defeatist spirit of "après moi le déluge." But Taiwan's experience shows that there are more hopeful possibilities.

By their nature, strategic notions cannot be analyzed or explained with precision. After all, their influence on policy makers is akin to the half-remembered ideas of some defunct economist to which Keynes referred in *The General Theory*. There seems to be strong evidence from Taiwan, however, that they play an important role in economizing on policy makers' time and attention as they seek answers that are "good enough." Taiwan's catastrophic learning experience led to notable changes in strategic notions: for example, the importance of maintaining the support of the farm population, of controlling inflation, of strengthening the organizational system, and of achieving a proper balance between the roles of the public and private sectors. The response to the challenge and opportunity represented by that situation gave rise to what Montgomery has termed "great policies." It seems all too clear that the enormous challenges—and opportunities—that other developing countries now face are in many ways similar to those Taiwan faced in absorbing a large and growing work force into productive employment and in achieving fuller and more efficient utilization of the country's resources.

## NOTES

1. This chapter draws heavily on Thomas P. Tomich, Peter Kilby, and Bruce F. Johnston, *Transforming Agrarian Economies: Opportunities Seized, Opportunities Missed* (Ithaca, N.Y.: Cornell University Press, 1995).

2. See unsigned article, "Survey," *The Economist* 325, no. 7789 (October 10, 1992): 5.

3. Alain de Janvry, *The Agrarian Question and Reformism in Latin America* (Baltimore: The Johns Hopkins University Press, 1981); I. J. Singh, *The Great Ascent: The Rural Poor in South Asia* (Baltimore: The Johns Hopkins University Press, 1990).

4. Ian Little, "An Economic Reconnaissance," in *Economic Growth and Structural Change in Taiwan: The Postwar Experience of the Republic of China,* ed. W. Galenson (Ithaca, N.Y.: Cornell University Press, 1979); Robert Wade, *Governing the Market: Economic Theory and the Role of Government in East Asian Industrialization* (Princeton, N.J.: Princeton University Press, 1990).

5. J. M. Brewster, "Traditional Social Structures as Barriers to Change," in *Agricultural Development and Economic Growth,* ed. H. M. Southworth and B. F. Johnston (Ithaca, N.Y.: Cornell University Press, 1967).

6. See, for example, Robert H. Bates, *Essays on the Political Economy of Rural Africa* (Cambridge, England: Cambridge University Press, 1983).

7. T. N. Srinivasan, "Neoclassical Political Economy, the State and Economic Development," *Asian Development Review* 3, no. 2 (1985): 38–58.

8. J. N. Bhagwati, "Poverty and Public Policy," *World Development* 16, no. 5 (1988): 539–55, quote at 547.

9. D. C. North, *Structure and Change in Economic History* (New York: Norton, 1981), quote at 11.

10. J. G. March and J. P. Olsen, *Ambiguity and Choice in Organizations* (Bergen, Norway: Universitetsforlaget, 1976).

11. The sharp rise and then fall in crude death rates in Mexico reflect a sharp upsurge in civil strife following the 1910 Revolution followed by a return of peaceful conditions along with the introduction of public health measures and improved access to advances in medicine.

12. See H. G. Johnson, "Comparative Cost and Commercial Policy Theory in a Developing World Economy," *The Pakistan Development Review,* supplement (Spring 1969): 1–33; and Bruce F. Johnston, Allan Hoben, and W. K. Jaeger, "United States Activities to Promote Agricultural and Rural Development in Sub-Saharan Africa," in *Aid to African Agriculture,* ed. Uma Lele (Baltimore: The Johns Hopkins University Press, 1991).

13. S. C. Hsieh and T. H. Lee, "Agricultural Development and Its Contributions to Economic Growth in Taiwan," *Economic Digest Series,* no. 17 (Taipei: Joint Commission on Rural Reconstruction, 1966).

14. T. H. Lee, *Intersectoral Capital Flows in the Economic Development of Taiwan, 1895–1969* (Ithaca, N.Y.: Cornell University Press, 1971).

15. Tibor Scitovsky, "Economic Development in Taiwan and South Korea: 1965–1981," *Food Research Institute Studies* 19, no. 3 (1985): 214–64.

16. T. S. Biggs, "Heterogeneous Firms and Efficient Financial Intermediation in Taiwan," in *Markets in Developing Countries: Parallel, Fragmented and Black,* ed. Michael Roemer and Christine Jones (a copublication of the International Center for Economic Growth and the Harvard Institute for International Development) (San Francisco: ICS Press, 1991).

17. Quoted from Ramon H. Myers and Ts'ai Ling, "Out of the Ashes of Defeat: Revitalizing the Kuomintang in Taiwan, 1950–1952," in *Proceedings of Conference on Eighty Years of the Republic of China 1912–1991* (Taipei: Modern China Publishing Company, 1991), 98, 102.

18. K. T. Li, *The Evolution of Policy Behind Taiwan's Development Success* (New Haven, Conn.: Yale University Press, 1988), quote at 151.

19. Ibid.

# 5

# JAPAN JETS INTERNATIONAL: IMPLEMENTING INNOVATIONS IN EDUCATIONAL POLICY

*David L. McConnell*

The reforms undertaken by the post–World War II occupation government to decentralize Japanese educational policy and administration have been steadily undermined by the Ministry of Education's (MOE) increasing control of personnel movements and educational standards. The political significance of this reversal of course is hotly contested. For those on the political right, the centralization of control is seen as contributing to the success of postwar Japanese education and society. For those on the political left, it symbolizes a return to prewar nationalistic tendencies. Yet the reality of recentralization is rarely questioned.

At the same time, many educational scholars have been reconsidering not only the "myth of centralization" but also the ways in which educational policy making in Japan is shaped by local forces. Some scholars question the degree to which localities really depend on the central government, particularly in the ideologically charged field of public education where a permanent opposition exists.[1] They have found, for example, a relatively high degree of local discretion and autonomy in Japan's high school education policy.[2] Observers paint a complex picture of interaction among MOE bureaucrats and external actors—including the ruling and opposition party leaders, businesses, universities, local

This research was supported by grants from the Fulbright Program of the Japan-U.S. Educational Commission, the Spencer Program of the Woodrow Wilson National Fellowship Foundation, and the Program on U.S.-Japan Relations at Harvard University. Support from the College of Wooster's Henry Luce III Fund for Distinguished Scholarship and from the Pacific Basin Research Center, the Center for Science and International Affairs, John F. Kennedy School of Government, Harvard University, enabled me to return to Japan in May of 1993 for additional interviews. I gratefully acknowledge this assistance. All quotations except those otherwise noted were obtained during these interviews.

educational administrators, and the teachers' union—in the formulation of educational policy.[3]

These competing perceptions suggest that there exists an incomplete portrayal of the interplay among administrative levels and partisan groups in formulating and implementing educational policy in Japan. Relatively little is known about the linkages between administrative levels or about the ways in which actors located in different parts of the policy system reconcile competing objectives. What is the process by which educational policy innovations are formulated, disseminated, and diffused in Japan? How do the distinctive political, social, and bureaucratic environments at each level of administration shape policies and their implementation? How do actors at each level of administration attempt to manipulate the system to their own advantage? These are important questions that can be addressed only by detailed case studies of educational policy making at all levels of the educational system. Although there have been such studies in other sectors—and of policy making in higher education—the process by which a complex, top-down educational innovation is generated and disseminated through the public secondary school system in Japan is still largely a "black box."[4]

This study attempts to fill the gap by examining the linkages and the interplay among national, prefectural, and local school levels in a major educational policy innovation in international education. It focuses on the Japan Exchange and Teaching (JET) program, a government initiative begun in 1987 under the Nakasone administration. The dramatic expansion and reorganization of JET since the early 1970s by MOE allows it to bring over 3,000 college graduates from six English-speaking countries to Japan each year to "foster international perspectives in Japan by promoting international exchange at local levels as well as intensifying foreign language education."[5] After a week-long orientation in Tokyo, the foreign participants are assigned to prefectural, city, and district education offices throughout Japan. These offices of education in turn dispatch them to junior and senior high schools where they participate in the team teaching of English conversation classes with a Japanese English-language teacher.

With an annual budget approaching $220 million, the JET program is clearly an enterprise in which Japan is investing considerable money and resources. It is, perhaps, with some justification then that Japanese government officials have begun to call JET the largest initiative since World War II in the field of human and cultural exchange.

As a policy, JET is both top-down and complex. It is top-down in that it is a national-level policy innovation that is being disseminated throughout the public education system. It is complex because it does not build on existing educational practice in local schools but rather requires some reorganization of practice on the part of Japanese English-language teachers. Moreover, unlike textbook revision or other MOE guidelines that leave classroom implementation to the teacher's discretion, JET confronts Japanese English-language teachers with a foreign innovation in a very immediate and often threatening way. Although individual schools or teachers may choose to take or leave the foreigners, the system as a whole cannot ignore them.

This chapter, based on two years of intensive fieldwork in Japan, views JET as the consequence of competing interests. Its objective is to trace the JET program from the germ of an idea to its implementation. Special attention is paid to MOE politics as well as prefectural patterns of interaction and institutional arrangements that have shaped its outcome in secondary schools throughout the country.

## INTERNATIONALIZATION AS A PROBLEM: THE SOCIAL AND HISTORICAL CONTEXT

Where else in the world but Japan would a government go to such lengths to invite foreigners to internationalize its education system? Since the rise of mass schooling, many countries have grappled with the dilemmas of using public education and public policy to promote the integration of culturally and linguistically diverse populations.[6] Canada is still struggling to fashion a cohesive state in the face of diverse ethnic allegiances. Throughout Africa and much of Asia too, nations are struggling to use public education as a vehicle for social and cultural integration, often in the wake of colonial legacies that have created nation-states with little regard for preexisting ethnic boundaries. The United States is still far from coming to grips with its increasingly diverse population, as is evidenced by the continuing controversy surrounding affirmative action and multicultural education. In all of these cases, the process of integration tends to be driven by politics and to be marked by divisive public debate as social attachments based on race, language, religion, and custom come into direct conflict with government policies aimed at creating a modern, efficient state and a national identity.[7]

In a few places, however, the boundaries of the state more or less coincide with boundaries defined by language, race, or ethnicity. In such folk nations where the degree of population homogeneity is high, national integration has been achieved relatively easily. Instead, the more problematic issue in these cases is global integration, a process fueled primarily by economics. The teaching of English in Scandinavian countries, for example, has been very effective—perhaps crucial—in integrating them into the world economic community. The case of Japan lies in this latter category. Japan is far more culturally distant from the West, however, than Scandinavian countries. For the past 200 years, Japan has been content to pursue global integration by training a cosmopolitan elite to act as go-betweens and buffers with the West and by educating a general population that is quite good at digesting foreign languages and foreign ideas from a distance.

Clearly, this approach has served Japan well. Contrary to the predictions of convergence and modernization theorists, Japan has achieved economic prominence without transforming its social relations into the individualistic model.[8] Similarly, Japan's educational system has contributed to national economic success, not so much by stimulating innovation and individual creativity as by cultivating a high degree of literacy, social order, and national efficiency through the systematic enforcement of uniform guidelines and high academic standards.[9]

Japan's emergence as a world economic power, however, is now beginning to clash with its historical isolation and population homogeneity and requires its leaders to confront the problem of global integration. As Japan has penetrated deeper into the world economic system, Western countries have protested more and more vigorously over what they perceive as the closed nature of Japanese society and Japan's inability to play by the rules of the international liberal trading order. Foreign pressure for reforms in Japan's "feudalistic" value system has become more intense during the past two decades.

Two issues in particular have come to symbolize the conflict between foreign policy and educational and cultural policy. One is foreign language education, and the other is the difficulty in integrating foreigners into Japanese society through face-to-face interaction. Foreign language education in the public schools bears the imprint of the standardized and exam-oriented nature of the secondary school curriculum that has long been criticized for its meager returns on investment. The idea that every Japanese student goes through six to ten years of English instruction but remains unable to converse with a native speaker in even rudimentary terms is now an integral part of Japanese perceptions of their own national character. This situation is increasingly perceived as damaging Japan's international image.[10]

Similarly, Japan's success at integrating foreigners into domestic institutions and social routines has come to be seen increasingly as a litmus test of internationalization by the foreign community. Foreign countries have opened their markets, their schools, and their social institutions to the Japanese, and they expect reciprocal treatment. Japan, for instance, only receives a fraction of the number of foreign students that Western countries accept.[11] In addition, Japanese children who return from living abroad often face subtle pressure from teachers and peers to hide or to give up the cognitive and interactional styles they acquired overseas.[12] Many of the symbolic and legal barriers to integration, such as barring foreigners from teaching in public universities or the law requiring foreign nationals to be fingerprinted, have been dropped or amended in recent years; yet foreigners still complain about strong social and cultural resistance to integration at the local levels.

If nothing else, foreign pressure has created an image problem of acute proportions for the Japanese government. Dependent on the goodwill of the foreign community both for national security and for continued economic prosperity, it has become increasingly important that Japan be able to show that it is, in fact, international, that foreigners really can be part of the group in Japan, and that Japan is an ordinary, not an exceptional, country. Increasingly, certain aspects of Japanese education and culture have come to be perceived as hindering the forward momentum of Japan's foreign policy. The very strengths on which Japan's economic success was built are now seen by some important policy makers as liabilities in the global environment.[13] Influential Japanese policy makers have convinced themselves that mass internationalization is crucial to continued economic progress and that arms-length strategies of global integration are no longer tenable.

Although more and more Japanese are traveling and living abroad, they are still only a small part of the population. The brunt of public "internationalization" has thus fallen on the educational system. The JET program orientation manual sent to local governments in 1989 explained the origins of the program as follows:

> As a result of the increasingly high status of our country in the international community, the manner in which we relate to other countries is in the process of changing drastically. While internationalization until now has primarily involved diplomacy and trade at the national level, the manner in which citizens at each stratum of society are engaging in internationalization has now come to be questioned. In light of this fact and from this point on, the responses of local governments to internationalization will become an important issue that, like our aging population or the emerging "information age," cannot be avoided.[14]

At a time, then, when nations around the world are struggling with ethnic unrest, Japan's problem is precisely the opposite—they need to create diversity and facilitate face-to-face interaction with foreigners. JET thus represents an attempt to integrate a relatively insular and homogeneous population with a global society made profitable and important to Japan by its own economic progress.[15]

### Internationalization as Public Policy: The Emergence of JET

Within this broad context of Japan's role in a changing world, what were the specific factors that gave rise to JET in the mid-1980s? And how did behind-the-scenes negotiations shape JET's specific form? Two events in early 1986 provided impetus for the program. One was the second report issued by Nakasone's own ad hoc council for educational reform. This report called explicitly for "education compatible with a new era of internationalization."[16] Having caught up with other advanced industrialized nations technologically, the report argues, Japan cannot survive in isolation but must interact in cultural and educational spheres as well. From a council that was noted for its power struggles, it is not insignificant that internationalization was one of the few recommendations of the council that garnered unanimous support.[17]

Second, much of the tension surrounding the closed nature of Japanese society reached its height during the 1986 trade conflict between Japan and the United States. It is not coincidental that the announcement of the JET program followed closely on the heels of the Maekawa Report that outlined steps Japan would take to decrease its $50 billion trade surplus with the United States. The JET program would allow the government to use surplus yen to deflect foreign criticism of Japan as a closed society and an "economic animal" interested only in reaping larger and larger annual trade surpluses. In this sense, the JET program can be categorized as a reactive policy. It was generated by pressure from the outside and was aimed at demonstrating Japan's commonality with other countries in order to protect what Nakasone himself described as Japan's "vulnerable security system and international economic encirclement."[18]

The process of moving from the germ of an idea to a nationally administered program, however, meant changing from a relatively straightforward and appealing concept to a politically complex coalition of diverse interests. Under the agreed-upon division of labor for the administration of the JET program, the Ministry of Foreign Affairs (MOFA) would be responsible for the recruitment of participants abroad, MOE would guide the educational portion of the program involving the teaching of English in the local schools, and, most curiously, the Ministry of Home Affairs (MOHA) would be responsible for the overall administration and coordination of the program.

First, MOHA set up an administrative office called the Council of Local Authorities for International Relations (CLAIR) to oversee program implementation. Why would MOHA, which by almost any measure is probably one of the least international ministries in Japan, take control of a program that primarily concerns foreign language teaching in the public education system? As it turns out, the initial idea for JET came from a middle-level bureaucrat in the MOHA secretariat, Kuniyuki Nose, as part of a larger ministry effort to get on the bandwagon of internationalization and to reassert its leadership with local governments that had begun forging international linkages on their own. When Nose first proposed the plan in 1985, it was initially rejected by Vice Minister Yoshiteru Tsuchiya, who thought the proposal would be seen as encroaching on MOE's turf. By the following year, however, U.S. criticism of Japan's trade surplus had escalated, and when Tsuchiya brought the idea to Yoshio Okawara, a senior advisor in MOFA and a former ambassador to the United States, Okawara jumped at the prospect of presenting the idea at the Reagan-Nakasone summit as one solution to the ongoing trade wars.[19]

MOE—upset at the prospects of losing control of its own smaller Mombusho English Fellow (MEF) and British English Teaching (BET) programs and also realizing that there would be considerable resistance among local teachers if the numbers of foreign teachers were increased tenfold—initially opposed the program. It was only after a series of meetings and compromises among the vice ministers in MOE and MOHA that any progress was made. Why did neither MOE nor the Japan Teachers Union decide to press the issue and block the program? It appears that, at one level, both understood and sympathized with the logic behind the program—Japan had to do something to survive in an increasingly interconnected world.

Moreover, they realized that public resistance to the concept of internationalization was simply not the politically correct thing to do. MOE was already committed to the idea of using native foreign-language speakers in the classroom, and the teachers' union had long criticized MOE for promoting "examination English" at the expense of conversational skills. A top MOE official in charge of JET emphasized the high ideals of internationalization, but implied that many bureaucrats were merely going through the motions of accommodating those ideals.

Subsequently, the ministries and other actors who were involved adopted very different goals and priorities for the JET program. From the very start, it was subject to competing goals and rivalries among the inward- and outward-looking ministries that were directly charged with its implementation (and with a whole host of other agencies and organizations as well). Several examples illustrate the point. One of the most curious structural features of the JET program is the classroom arrangement known as team teaching, in which the foreigner serves as assistant to the regular Japanese English-language teacher. Ironically, the very existence of team teaching was the result of a compromise among the ministries. MOE would go along with the program only if team teaching was adopted and Japanese teachers would not feel that their own jobs were either legally or symbolically threatened by the influx of native speakers. In fact, the designation assistant English teacher (AET), used in the early years of JET, represented an important symbolic lowering of status from the name English Fellows that had been used under the previous program.

In addition, MOE tended to view the goals of the program primarily in terms of English-language education, whereas MOHA saw its objectives more in terms of social education and exposing prefectural and local officials, as well as citizens, to foreigners. One result of this turf war is a large degree of compartmentalization in the implementation of the program, and all sides have been extremely sensitive and protective of their roles. At the Tokyo orientation or midyear conferences for the foreign teachers, for instance, the entire conference is divided into two parts: one sponsored by the Council of Local Authorities for International Relations (CLAIR), the administrative arm of the MOHA; one by MOE. The two ministries have also disagreed over the extent to which demands made by the foreign teachers should be accommodated, with MOE arguing that CLAIR has bent over backwards to do whatever the foreign teachers demanded. This tension became clear when the foreign teachers, soon after their arrival in August 1987, formed a quasi union to counter the perceived inability of the Japanese side to respond effectively to a variety of problems. MOHA was much more willing to work with this association than was MOE, whose leaders viewed the support group as an illegitimate organization that threatened their policy-making authority.

But MOE and MOHA were not always on opposite sides. MOFA, for its part, has tended to emphasize the contribution of the program to Japan's diplomatic relations at the expense of considering domestic realities. The way in which the number of countries eligible to send foreign teachers was expanded provides a good example. During the first year of the JET program, participants were recruited from the United States, Britain, Australia, and New Zealand. The following year, Canada and Ireland were added, and French and German participants became eligible in subsequent years. As it turned out, this diversification of participating countries was part of the Japanese government's larger foreign relations strategy to move beyond the elliptical affair with the United States and to reposition itself in relation to the European market by expanding networks and liaisons with a variety of other Western countries. This strategy became obvious when former Prime Minister Takeshita, on a visit to Europe in 1988, suddenly promised to include French and German participants the following year. The script of his speech was written by MOFA, and the announcement came as a shock and a complete surprise to MOE and MOHA. In any event, these officials were forced to scramble to find schools where foreigners could teach French and German, not an easy task in the English-dominated foreign language environment in Japan. In the end, only a token number (fewer than a dozen) of French and German participants were invited the next year, and most ended up teaching English in addition to a few classes in their native language. The policy had another ironic twist as well in its effects on the Canadian Embassy's request to allow French Canadian participants on the program. With France admitted, however, the government felt that the few slots available for French teachers had to be reserved for participants from France.

The sheer size of the program also meant that many other actors at the national level had to be involved in the program. The Ministry of Justice had to approve the special visas granted to the foreign teachers, but, as a ministry concerned with regulating the flow of foreigners into and out of Japan, it has taken a fairly conservative stance on allowing the foreign teachers to stay in Japan after their contracts with JET expire. The National Audit Board got involved when it learned that local governments were not covering the foreign teachers under the required insurance policy. Much to the dismay of many of the foreign participants, a portion of their monthly salaries are now deducted for health insurance and for pension benefits which they never receive.

What is clear from these examples is that there were a variety of interests and objectives that had to be managed and reconciled even at the ministerial level. Although the daily lives of the foreign teachers at the local level centered around schools and offices of education, MOE was only one player among many at the national level. In fact, JET in many ways represented an attempt by MOHA and MOFA bureaucrats, with support from the prime minister's office, to bypass MOE. The result was a great deal of confusion during the early years of the program among the foreign teachers when they realized that the realities of Japanese schools were very different from their expectations and began to cast around for someone to blame.

Nevertheless, in spite of the differences in the outlooks of the various ministries, what is most striking is that no one deterred the adoption of the policy itself. In fact, for the politicians and bureaucrats concerned, the proclamation of the JET program was at least as important as the details of the policy's execution. This is not because politicians and bureaucrats are hypocritical but because they have practical concerns about maintaining electoral support and realize the substantial symbolic significance of political actions.[20] Indeed, as noted earlier, the national level differs from prefectural and school levels in that the environment is one of intense outside pressure on Japan to open up its system to foreigners. It is an environment in which matters of foreign relations often have a great impact on policy making and where diplomatic relations and a consideration of Japan's role and image in the world often receive high priority in policy formation. In such an environment, the JET program makes perfect sense and meets a real need. Moreover, the stakes are highest at the national level to ensure that the appearances of Western-style internationalization are in place. Ministry officials charged with the program's management thus have a very strong interest in ensuring that implementation goes smoothly and that signs of discord and discontent on the part of the foreign teachers are minimal. The last thing they want is negative publicity or the program to be pronounced a failure.

## A CONTINGENCY THEORY APPROACH TO POLICY IMPLEMENTATION

During the past fifteen years, research on policy implementation has increasingly recognized the importance of taking into account the perspectives of those who are actually charged with implementing policy innovations. Systems management and bureaucratic process models have increasingly fallen into disfavor as more attention is focused on the issue of whether or not the goals and resources of policy makers fit the needs and perspectives of those actually affected by top-down policies.[21] This view of policy thus attends not only to the resources, plans, and choices available to policy makers at the national level but also to values and expectations, multiple and competing objectives, and processes and actors located in all parts of the policy system.

For lack of a better term, this approach becomes a "contingency theory" of policy implementation: policy forms and outcomes are assumed to be contingent on the particular nature of the social and political environment operating at each bureaucratic level. Indeed, MOE, prefectural offices of education, and local schools constitute distinct levels of the institution of public education, and each has its own priorities and world view.[22] Each bureaucratic level is, in other words, a distinct sociopolitical subsystem that has its own manner of participating in and shaping the implementation of a top-down policy such as the JET program. This section assesses the ways in which JET is the administrative product of competing goals and priorities that operate at the prefectural and local school levels.

### The Prefectural Level: The Eclair Model

Government ministries, in spite of being highly compartmentalized, share a common view of the implementation process that comes from their position at the top of a relatively centralized system. The prevailing assumption at the ministerial level is that the barriers to successful implementation lie primarily at the prefectural and local levels. They subscribe to a theory of top-down change that sees the national government providing training, encouragement, guidelines, and subtle pressure on prefectural governments, which in turn leverage the next level of the system, and so on, until satisfactory outcomes are achieved.

How responsive have prefectural offices been to hiring foreign teachers and to accepting the directives of MOE and CLAIR regarding program content? First, consider the issue of receptivity to employing the foreign teachers. In general, the receptivity of prefectures has been astounding. Even in the first year of the program, every one of Japan's forty-seven prefectures and eleven designated cities requested foreign teachers, and some now employ more than 100. Significantly, not a single prefecture or city has reduced its number in subsequent years. Because MOHA is running the program, however, it has been primarily the governors and mayors who have set the tone for requests. Eager to get on the bandwagon of internationalization and anxious not to be left out of a major government initiative, these politicians have, in many cases, instructed superintendents of education (who are political appointees) and their subordinates on how to respond. As a result, the demand for foreign teachers from the prefectures has outstripped the supply of qualified applicants in every year of the program.

The response of educational administrators working within offices of education, however, has been quite different. Bureaucratic capacities and priorities shape the program in distinctive ways, and educational administrators are only partially receptive to top-down guidance. At the prefectural level, the people directly responsible for the foreign teachers are the English teachers' consultants. These are experienced teachers temporarily assigned to administrative duties, after which they return to schools in leadership positions. They have been described as "respected, hardworking and aligned with the administrative goal of maintaining efficient schooling."[23] These people are chosen for their loyalty, pragmatism, and political savvy rather than on the basis of their English skills or international experience. If anything, they represent the more conservative teacher with a tendency to toe the administrative line.

Eager to make internationalization a success and anxious to remain true to the spirit of the program and feeling very acutely the pressure from the superintendent, the governor, and even Tokyo, prefectural administrators strive to create support and momentum for English conversation and international activities. Every prefecture in Japan now sponsors numerous team-teaching workshops and seminars as part of its instructional guidance and has published guidebooks on team teaching and how to work with a foreign teacher. And, in virtually every prefecture there is an international high school with a special course in English conversation where a number of foreign teachers are concentrated. Interestingly, however, these efforts often occur while the same administrators are engaged in other projects that seek to raise the exam scores of prefectural students. Prefectural offices of education also go to great lengths to try to prevent foreign teachers from returning home early since this is perceived as a great embarrassment to the prefecture and an inconvenience to the host schools.

Not surprisingly, the English teachers' consultants have employed a variety of methods to create a "soft landing" and minimize interruption to established routines and to existing institutional priorities. For instance, they have put great pressure on MOE to recruit foreign participants overseas and have emphasized the idea of locating people who are sensitive, flexible, stable, and friendly more than people who have teaching experience, an English as a Second Language (ESL) degree, or special knowledge of Japanese culture. Personality and even physical characteristics seem to have taken precedence over formal qualifications. Social fit and social type are seen as very important. Consequently, the lack of high-quality applicants has been perceived as one of the most pressing problems from the prefectural level on the Japanese side. Pressure on MOFA to tighten the screening process in this direction has increased dramatically in recent years with the suicides of two foreign teachers and several serious incidents of drunken driving. In 1991, at the top of the rating sheet given to members of the screening committees (mostly comprised of foreigners) at the various consulates abroad, was written, "If the applicant appears to be overly sensitive/emotionally fragile, not sociable, cheerful or polite, or does not appear to like children, DO NOT RECOMMEND their acceptance to the program."

Since prefectures until recently could request certain kinds of foreign teachers (with the exception of race), they have also tried to influence the system to maximize their chances for getting high-quality teachers. In one prefecture, officials decided that since they had considerable trouble with Americans and Australians, they would request only British and Canadian participants the following year. When that failed to solve their problems, they requested only males the next year after having noticed that women had a harder time adjusting to Japanese society than men.

Another persistent problem from the point of view of prefectural administrators is the difficulty of telling troublesome and recalcitrant foreign teachers that they may not renew their contracts, even though the prefectural office has the legal power to do so. The thought of face-to-face confrontation with foreigners demanding to be shown evidence for why they cannot renew their contracts is enough to ensure that any foreign teacher who so desires may renew his or her contract. Faced with a situation in which some foreigners who had learned how to milk the system continued to renew their contracts for extended periods of time, the prefectural administrators quietly asked ministry officials to establish a three-year limit on participation as a program policy at the national level. This was done in 1990 and provided the "Japanese who can't say No" (as they jokingly referred to themselves) with a ready-made rationale for not allowing these bad apples to renew their contracts. What is striking in this case is the similarity in the views of the foreign teachers held by both local administrators and ministry officials—a shared conception that readily led to the proposed solution.

Two features of prefectural responses are worth highlighting. One is the degree to which educational policy in the JET program is influenced even at this level by other offices within the prefectural government. Even the office of education is staffed with people who are not professional educators but rather local civil servants; it is they who often have ties with other sections in the prefectural office, and their cooperation can be instrumental in securing funds or otherwise making or breaking an initiative. Second, prefectural offices of education are crucial links in a very complex policy. Anxious to stay within the framework set by national policy and thus to remain faithful to their relationships with ministry officials, they are partially receptive to top-down guidance. On the other hand, they also work in a system dominated by bureaucratic priorities, and they must respond to the particular concerns of those in local schools without sacrificing their own authority. These administrators view themselves much like the creamy filling of an eclair. Although there is chocolate on both sides of them, it is they who link the top and the bottom and provide the sweetness and substance of the entire pastry. Prefectural offices of education thus strive to maintain the formal goals of the program while at the same time shaping its structure and content in ways that conform to the bureaucratic priorities of their offices.

### The Local School Level: Propriety and Organizational Maintenance

Prefectural officials, of course, must turn the foreign teachers over to school-based personnel, and it is at the school level where the symbolic agreement, so easy to maintain when the concept of internationalization is kept at a certain level of abstractness, really begins to break down. Undoubtedly, one of the reasons JET has been so popular with governors and mayors is precisely because it allows them to be international without having to interact with the foreigners on a daily basis.

The translation of the buzzword internationalization into the reality of three thousand foreigners arriving at public schools throughout the country thus produces a kind of conflict that is unusual in the institution of public education in Japan. Observers have noted that in public education in Japan, the higher the administrative level, the greater the degree of overt conflict, so that conflict is highest at the national level where the sides are clearly drawn and most institutionalized. At the small group level in local schools, by contrast, there is much greater pressure to work together cohesively; thus, ideological considerations take second seat to the more practical concerns of cooperating together to run the school.

The JET program is a case, however, in which the level of agreement is highest at the symbolic level: everyone expresses agreement on the importance of internationalization. Instead, the JET program produces conflict at the very lowest levels of the system. The foreign teachers are problematic precisely because they assert ethical principles of the universal kind that can be very contradictory and damaging to the norms of group process. In this sense, the JET program shares similarities with the women's movement and other social movements that disrupt (often, purposefully) social order at the lowest levels of the system.[24] The Japanese preference for situational ethics and the maintenance of harmony in face-to-face interaction contrasts with the tendencies of the foreign teachers to confront and debate differences and to attempt to bring behaviors in line with general principles. What many of the foreign criticisms amount to is a demand that the Japanese reconstitute themselves and their society so as to make them more compatible with Western norms and expectations.

As a result, it is very unclear how the foreign teachers fit into the day-to-day priorities and social routines that characterize Japanese schools. In fact, by the relevant criteria of this environment, the foreign teachers unintentionally often behave very poorly because their cultural assumptions lead them to view the goals of education very differently. From the Japanese point of view, the confrontational base of their actions is countereducational.

The mere arrival of reform-minded native speakers into an exam-oriented school environment creates a dilemma of considerable proportions for many Japanese English-language teachers. During the Tokyo orientation, foreign teachers are given a crash course in the assumptions underlying ESL methodologies: student as active learner; teacher as facilitator; focus on the content of language as opposed to its form; curriculum that is inherently interesting and relevant to students' lives; and classes marked by liveliness and spontaneity.

These assumptions run directly counter to cultural theories of learning in Japan as well as to teaching practices that are honed to entrance-exam preparation and wedded to ministry-approved textbooks.[25] Indeed, the most striking response of the foreign teachers is the degree to which they try to use games and other fun activities in the team teaching of English. From playing the guitar to turning the class into a drama or playing such games as Hangman and Twenty Questions, foreign teachers seem to be trying to do anything that will liven up the class by using "living English" and thus produce evidence in the form of critical thinking and self-expression that "real" learning is taking place. Yet, the conversational English lessons so enthusiastically supported by the foreign teachers and publicly endorsed both by MOE as well as prefectural teachers' consultants are viewed by Japanese teachers as largely irrelevant to the reality of entrance exams that require the memorization and manipulation of discrete lexical items and direct translation.

School-level receptivity to a foreign teacher varies widely depending on the composition of the faculty as well as the personality of the foreign teacher. In general, however, the cultural and organizational realities of Japanese schools mean that staff must work to manage and control the foreign teacher's visit. One way this can be accomplished is by ensuring that the school does not receive a foreign teacher. Exam-oriented schools are much less likely to receive foreign teachers than other schools, and third-year students at any school are usually less likely to receive regular team-teaching classes than are students in other grades who are not immediately confronting entrance exams. Although some prefectures still allow schools to request a foreign teacher, the rapid increase in numbers since 1987 has meant that, in many cases, foreign teachers are placed in schools where the large majority of the Japanese English-language teachers are ambivalent if not opposed to the idea. In one school, for example, when the head English teacher brought up the board of education's request that they serve as a base school for a foreign teacher the following year, the proposal was greeted with complete silence. No one wanted the extra work and tension that it would produce, yet no one dared voice opposition. As a result, the head English teacher, declaring that internationalization was a must, effectively made the decision.

The foreign teachers are often, but not always, given so few classes that they have an inordinate amount of free time on their hands, and in extreme cases they serve as little more than decorations in the workplace. Much to their frustration, they find it extremely difficult to get the Japanese teachers to sit down with them during the day to make out their lesson plans. In the case of foreign teachers who conduct one-shot visits, district offices of education often require the Japanese teacher to fill out a lesson plan and mail it to the office of education before the foreign teacher's visit, but this time-consuming practice is widely viewed by the Japanese teachers as a considerable burden. The resolution of where the foreign teacher's desk will be placed and who will end up team teaching with him or her is quite sticky and more often than not goes against the wishes of one or more of the Japanese English-language teachers. Younger teachers, because of their lack of seniority, often end up with the task of team teaching.

Although individual Japanese teachers use the foreign teachers in a variety of ways, their strategies tend to cluster around two extremes. Either all or part of a class is turned over to the foreign teacher, or the foreign teacher is integrated into the regular classes as a kind of "human tape recorder." Significantly, both cases serve to minimize the possibilities of spontaneous interaction in the classroom, for students are watching carefully to see how well their teacher handles himself or herself when put on the spot. Even though Japanese teachers may give the foreign teacher considerable leeway in class, in private they usually described the classes led by the foreign teachers as classes that were not challenging or were just plain playtime. Some complain that they must work extra hard in solo classes to compensate for the lost time in the team-teaching class. They will routinely mark the shift from conversation practice or a game led by the foreign teacher to textbook work with the phrase, "Now it's time to get down to studying."

The problem for the Japanese teachers is compounded by the fact that the foreign teachers are extremely popular with the students. This makes it very difficult for the Japanese teacher, concerned only with exam preparation, who may be viewed as putting a damper on things. One cartoon in a national newspaper depicted a team-teaching situation in which a foreign teacher is being besieged with attention from the students while the Japanese teacher, suddenly ignored, is shown tapping his foot angrily behind the podium.

If the goals of conversational English suffer under the organizational rigidities of local schools, it is also difficult for the foreign teachers to find evidence (other than their own presence) of the Japanese school system's commitment to cultivating in students an appreciation for diversity. One of the greatest surprises that awaits the foreign teachers upon their arrival in Japan is the extension of preferential treatment. At the national level, in addition to the red carpet treatment at the week long Tokyo orientation, the salaries for the foreign teachers were set at 300,000 yen per month, much more than a starting teacher in Japan would make. This, not surprisingly, has been a very sore point with Japanese teachers. Furthermore, the foreign teachers are required to work only a five-day week, in contrast to their Japanese counterparts who regularly work on Saturday mornings.

This special treatment is also pronounced in the school visits. In a typical instance, an American female teacher visited an academic high school in the suburbs of a large city in southwestern Japan. Before she came to their school, three of the teachers visited another school currently hosting a foreign teacher to get advice. The teachers circulated around the teachers' room a copy of her picture and vital statistics, and there was much speculation about what kind of person she would be. The Japanese English-language teachers met five times to decide how to handle her school visit and to divide up the labor. Different teachers were chosen to be responsible for her orientation and counseling, for paperwork and administrative matters, for planning seminars related to team teaching, and for parties to be held for her. When the foreign teacher visited the school, she was greeted by students staring, waving, and even venturing a bold, "Hello! Hello!" Her shoes were placed in the shoe box reserved for guests. There was a schoolwide assembly to introduce her to the student body. The Japanese English-language teachers held a welcome party for her and later gave her a present on her birthday, something that was not a common practice in Japan. She was called on to give a speech to the Parent Teacher Association (PTA) and to write an article for the local newspaper. One night she was on the local eyewitness news. She had a fan club among the boy students, and towards the end of her visit, students approached her for an autograph or a handshake. Finally, there was a farewell party that the Japanese teacher of English describes as follows:

> For the students she was nothing less than a celebrity. All she had to do was say something and everyone would marvel at her beautiful pronunciation. For her farewell party the student council planned for weeks. They conducted a survey of all the students and then we made up a song to the tune of "You Are My Sunshine." Except we sang "You are my teacher, my wonderful teacher, please don't take my wonderful teacher away." They gave her paper cranes they had made and there were speeches from student representatives and from [the AET]. Then they gave her roses and she paraded out of the gym to the music of "Let It Be." It was an incredibly touching occasion.

The other side of preferential treatment, of course, is that the foreign teachers are rarely integrated into social routines and social groupings at their schools beyond a very superficial level. Schools differ somewhat in the degree to which they integrate the foreign teachers, but, in some cases, the arrival of a foreign teacher seems actually to heighten the sense of "Japanese-ness" among teachers and to foster increased boundary maintenance activities. Japanese teachers of English report that it is often very difficult to talk freely with the foreign teacher in school because other teachers may feel they are showing off. As one veteran Japanese English-language teacher commented, "Whenever the AET calls me over in the teachers' room, I have to walk gingerly and interact in a very hesitant manner." Some Japanese teachers also told of being ostracized or teased as a result of spending too much time with the foreign teacher. Japanese teachers also seem to feel they had much more in common with their students than with a foreigner who happened to share the same occupation. It is not uncommon for teachers to prep their students on how to behave and to coach them on English phrases prior to the foreign teacher's visit. And, in cases where Japanese teachers, at the urging of their foreign guests, have tried to speak only English in the classroom, students' reactions (such as, "You act just like a foreigner") often led them to abandon the attempt because it felt strange.

This is not to deny that there was variability in Japanese reactions to the foreign teachers. There were Japanese teachers and administrators who viewed foreign teachers as a virus that had to be controlled, just as there were those who viewed them as medicine for an outdated and rigid system. In neither case, however, were the foreign teachers expected to join the group. The foreign teachers themselves were extremely critical of all the special treatment and the exclusion from social routines that went with it. The terms "panda mentality" or "star complex" are widely used and understood by all foreign teachers in the JET program. It was not uncommon for the foreigners to take a conspiracy theory view of the preferential treatment as part of an elaborate plan on the part of Japanese to keep foreigners at arms' length.

Two points must be made here. First, preferential treatment, from the Japanese point of view, is quite natural, and, in fact, it constitutes expected social etiquette. It is the polite and hospitable thing to do and speaks to the high esteem in which Japanese hold foreigners. To the accusations of the foreign teachers, Japanese have countered that if it is discrimination, it is inadvertent since the intent is benign. Indeed, the roots of Japanese responses to the foreign teachers lie in the sense of separateness and the very different formulations of ethnicity that Japanese at all levels bring to the policy process. The Japanese tendency to assume that linguistic and cultural competence, much less identity, is, a priori, inaccessible to foreigners lies in sharp contrast to the tendency of Americans to assume that those of foreign backgrounds not only can, but should, learn English and become Americanized. In Japan there is no expectation that foreigners will become part of the group. The Japanese quite naturally see internationalization as implying the development of techniques for the improvement of understanding and communication between cultures and groups that, it is assumed, will always be fundamentally different. By contrast, many (though not all) of the foreign teachers, having grown up in societies where ethnicity is viewed as a personal religion, see internationalization less in terms of building bridges between people than in breaking down the walls between them.

There is also a pragmatic element involved. So finely tuned are Japanese sensitivities to interpersonal relations that the foreign teachers inevitably are viewed as bumblers. It is simply a lot more work to include foreigners because they do not understand many of the subtle messages that are so vital to the smooth workings of small groups in Japan.

The second point is that this preferential treatment and exclusion of foreigners, which is commonsense behavior to the Japanese, actually runs directly counter to the stated goals of the program, at least as interpreted by the foreign teachers. In response to vigorous complaints by the foreign teachers, MOE and CLAIR have increasingly exhorted local governments, which have in turn counseled local schools, to try not to extend preferential treatment to the foreign teachers. Yet this view of foreigners runs so deep in Japanese society that it continues to shape policy decisions and interactions. At numerous schools, for instance, Japanese teachers complained that the students had come to take the foreign teachers too much for granted. This seemed like a curious comment, and when asked for clarification, the Japanese teachers explained that if the students become too accustomed to the foreign teacher, then the power of the foreigner to motivate the students is lost. Here, then, Japanese cultural sensibilities led them to negatively evaluate a process with which the foreign teachers are obsessed: breaking down the barriers and cultural distance between themselves and the students.

In sum, because of the organizational and cultural priorities of Japanese schools, local school teachers engaged in behaviors that were perfectly common-sense to them but ran directly counter to the national-level goals of improving English conversation and accepting foreigners. All of this led to a great deal of frustration and disillusionment on the part of the foreign teachers. Having been exhorted at the Tokyo orientation by distinguished Japanese politicians and bureaucrats to take on the role of cultural ambassadors and reformers of English-language education, the realities of local schools left them feeling underused and confronting an impossible mission. Most disturbingly, from Tokyo's point of view, negative articles in the press began appearing regularly as the foreign teachers vented their frustrations in the way that they knew best—by confronting and challenging the system. Such demands and ultimatums, in turn, produced considerable resentment among Japanese teachers. It was not uncommon to hear Japanese teachers talk of the "AET problem," and they privately describe their interactions with the foreign teachers as burdensome. In fact, at the school level, teachers have jokingly taken to referring to the JET program as "the second coming of the black ships" and to drawing a parallel between Commodore William Perry's uninvited "opening" of Japan to Western trade in 1854.

### The Learning Curve

Yet, in spite of the fact that most Japanese teachers of English are not thrilled by the JET program, what is perhaps the most fascinating aspect of their response is that they see team teaching and internationalization as a cause. Again and again one is struck by the seriousness with which Japanese teachers of English have taken on the task of learning how to team teach. Workshops and books on the how-to's of team teaching now comprise a cottage industry in Japan, and English societies all across the country have taken up this theme in workshops and seminars. Japanese teachers of English, in other words, are not giving up; in fact, many talk frankly about the need to master team-teaching techniques. Most feel that they should be able to speak and teach conversational

English. In any event, workshops on team teaching are often very well attended. In one district where teachers could choose between a traditional class and a team-teaching class, the team-teaching seminar attracted five times as many teachers as the other. Japanese teachers, in other words, are surprisingly willing to put themselves in the position of learner even though they complain about the youthfulness of the foreign teachers. The cultural predisposition that allows teachers to put themselves in the place of learner without feeling that it is degrading (to which American notions of maturity lend themselves) is of critical importance in explaining teachers' reactions. Given the centrality of teachers in creating educational change, any top-down reform at least has a fighting chance. Indeed, the sharp learning curve of Japanese teachers is in large part responsible for the relative success of the program after a very shaky first couple of years.

### State as Change Agent

This case yields competing portrayals of the power and limitations of the state to facilitate top-down change. On the one hand, viewed from an organizational perspective, the JET program appears much more fragmented, loosely coupled, and marked by competing goals and communication breakdowns than one would expect. JET makes perfect sense in terms of foreign policy objectives at the national level, but the relevance of the foreign teachers to the daily priorities of offices of education and local schools is ambiguous at best. The fit between national-level objectives and local realities becomes more problematic as the program moves down through the various layers of the educational system. The picture is one in which the "fudge" factor, as it were, on the part of those administering the program becomes greater and greater, and there are numerous cracks in the policy implementation process.

The actions of local school personnel, in many cases, run directly counter to the public objectives of the program. It would appear that one of the JET program's many ironies is that this solution to one set of political problems—trade relations and Japan's image in the world—gave rise to a whole host of other problems, whose solutions in turn created new dilemmas in a snowballing fashion. Judged by the formally stated goals—promotion of the acceptance of diversity and promotion of conversational English—the rock is simply too heavy for the policy lever being applied.

On the other hand, with a few exceptions, the policy has been marked by very little public controversy on the Japanese side, and the government has achieved an extraordinary degree of compliance in getting the forms of implementation in place. Through its bureaucratic arm, the Japanese government has ensured placement in schools all over the country of over 3,000 foreign teachers invited through a program whose origins were entirely top-down. Thus, since the program began, foreign teachers have probably visited and conducted team teaching on at least one occasion in virtually every one of Japan's more than 16,000 public secondary schools. This has been done with no public resistance from the Japan Teachers Union, which has systematically opposed virtually every government initiative in the postwar period. Nor was there public resistance from Japanese English-language teachers who were placed in the difficult position of having to team teach with the threatening foreigners without ever having been consulted about the program.

Given the current wisdom in the United States that top-down interventions rarely get through the classroom door, the receptivity of the Japanese system appears to be nothing short of phenomenal. In spite of great private ambivalence and even dissatisfaction with the program, particularly among those charged with handling face-to-face interactions with foreigners, Japanese at all levels continue to go along with it and even put forth great effort to make it work. Actors in all parts of the policy system mouth the same words that were used by the prime minister's office to justify the program in the first place: "This is something Japan must do to survive in the new international world order."

The parallels between the dynamics of current policy for internationalization and policies for democratization and modernization in past eras is certainly more than coincidental. It is almost as if every decade or two the government concocts a label and defines it, and then throughout the country, everyone bends over backwards to accommodate it, even though it creates private discomfort. It is well to note, however, that the orchestration of compliance at the public level throughout the system is not achieved through coercion but rather through persuasion and gentle pressure and a prior degree of cultural consensus. That the national government is so effective in attaining compliance in simply getting the foreign teachers into schools is testimony not so much to their sweeping powers as to the similarity in assumptions in the general population to begin with. To put it another way, in spite of the differences in opinion among various Japanese, there is a much higher degree of shared consensus that "We're all in the same boat": This is something Japan has to do to survive in an increasingly interconnected world.

The result is that, in effect, there are two social orders operating in the implementation of the JET program. What is striking in this case is that everyone continues to go along with the public objectives of the program while at the same time devising ways to subvert it in instances where local priorities and institutions are at stake. By defining internationalization as situational accommodation to Western demands, Japan's policy response in one sense demonstrates a very pragmatic instrumentalism. As in the government's handling of the "returnee children," the JET program seems to provide a means by which Japan can "do" Western-style internationalization while protecting local meanings and institutions.

In spite of the cross-cultural misperceptions that are an integral part of JET, however, there are signs that the program is having an impact. With respect to language education, for instance, Tokyo University's move to include a hearing component on its entrance exam was widely perceived as a result of the JET program. So too was the recent revision in the course of study that emphasized more communication-oriented language teaching. Although individual AETs do not see much progress, the cumulative effect may be much greater.

Perhaps an even larger, and somewhat unintended, effect of the program lies in the changes in foreign participants themselves. Some are returning home to study Japan-related topics in graduate school and may become Japanophiles for life. Others have managed to stay in Japan, and there have even been a number of intercultural marriages. There is an increasingly active JET Alumni Association in most participating countries, and the Monterey Institute of International Studies has recently instituted a JET Alumni Scholarship for its Teachers of English as a Second Language program. Moreover, despite the shaky start, JET now seems to have generated a tremendous amount of goodwill among college faculty in Japan-related fields in the participating countries. At a time when job prospects for graduating seniors are less than certain, JET offers an attractive option both for students interested in pursuing Japan-related careers and for students interested in a cross-cultural learning experience before entering graduate school or tackling the job market at home. During a recent visit, Japanese leaders privately assured me of the continuation of the JET program no matter what the state of the Japanese economy. As with the U.S. Peace Corps, the benefits of the program in terms of cultivating international goodwill and cross-cultural ties among individuals may far exceed the narrow goals of the program in English-language education.

## NOTES

1. Richard Samuels, *The Politics of Regional Policy in Japan: Localities Incorporated?* (Princeton, N.J.: Princeton University Press, 1983).

2. Steven Reed, *Japanese Prefectures and Policymaking* (Pittsburgh: University of Pittsburgh Press, 1986).

3. Leonard J. Schoppa, *Education Reform in Japan: A Case of Immobilist Politics* (London: Routledge, 1991).

4. Haruhiro Fukui, "Studies in Policymaking: A Review of the Literature," in *Policymaking in Contemporary Japan*, ed. T. J. Pempel (Ithaca, N.Y.: Cornell University Press, 1977), 22–59.

5. The great majority of participants come from the United States (53 percent), the United Kingdom (17 percent), and Canada (17 percent), while Australia (5 percent), New Zealand (5 percent), and Ireland (2 percent) contribute smaller numbers. Less than 1 percent of participants come from non-English-speaking countries (France, Germany, South Korea, and China), and most of these persons are placed in prefectural offices rather than schools.

6. See Christine E. Sleeter and Carl A. Grant, "An Analysis of Multicultural Education in the United States," *Harvard Educational Review* 57 (1987): 421–44; Michael R. Olneck, "The Recurring Dream: Symbolism and Ideology in Intercultural and Multicultural Education," *American Journal of Education* 98, no. 2 (1990): 147–74.

7. Clifford Geertz, "The Integrative Revolution: Primordial Sentiments and Civil Politics in the New States," in *The Interpretation of Cultures*, ed. Clifford Geertz (New York: Basic Books, 1973), 255–310.

8. See Yasusuke Murakami and Thomas Rohlen, "Social-Exchange Aspects of the Japanese Political Economy: Culture, Efficiency and Change" in *The Political Economy of Japan*, vol. 3 of *Cultural and Social Dynamics*, ed. Shumpei Kumon and Henry Rosovsky (Stanford, Calif.: Stanford University Press, 1992), 63–105; and Ronald Dore, "Goodwill and the Spirit of Market Capitalism," *The British Journal of Sociology* 34, no. 4 (1983): 459–81.

9. Thomas P. Rohlen, *Japan's High Schools* (Berkeley: University of California Press, 1983); and Merry I. White, *The Japanese Educational Challenge: A Commitment to Children* (New York: Free Press, 1987).

10. Viewed in terms of foreign language requirements at the secondary level, Japan is far more "progressive" than the United States where less than 30 percent of graduating high school seniors have studied a foreign language. What is viewed as increasingly problematic by some Japanese policy makers and by many in the general population is the fact that the return on investments seems so small in the Japanese case. This is reflected in such media events as a prime time television special that aired in 1989 called *We Don't Need This!*, in which a panel of distinguished guests explored the reasons for Japan's poor performance in English education.

11. See, for example, Kazuhiro Ebuchi, ed., *Foreign Students and the Internationalization of Higher Education* (Hiroshima, Japan: Hiroshima University Research Institute for Higher Education, 1989).

12. White, *The Japanese Educational Challenge*; and Roger Goodman, *Japan's "International Youth": The Emergence of a New Class of Schoolchildren* (Oxford: Clarendon Press, 1990).

13. As long as Japanese development was primarily an internal affair, Japanese culture and education were largely irrelevant to the conduct of Japan's foreign policy. The increasing importance of the world to Japan's economic success, however, has had a kind of boomerang effect in which Japan's leaders have begun to rethink what's happening at home. For a similar account of how this process has created conflict between Japan's security policy and her foreign assistance policy, see Susan J. Pharr, "Policy Interactions in Japanese Foreign Affairs," in *Values in Conflict*, ed. John D. Montgomery (Cambridge, Mass.: Soka University of America and John F. Kennedy School of Government, Pacific Basin Research Center, Harvard University, 1990), 14–17.

14. *Japan Exchange and Teaching Program*, advertising brochure (Washington, D.C.: Embassy of Japan, 1988): 1.

15. Contextualized in this way, the Japan Exchange and Teaching (JET) program differs from the use of education in the West as a vehicle for global integration. The United States and many other Western countries have tended to pursue global integration through "exporting" personnel and educational services (such as the Peace Corps and the British Council), whereas Japan has preferred to pursue selective integration through "importing" people and ideas. Though Japan's conduct during World War II should remind us of the danger of postulating any inherent tendency towards contraction, this is the form most efforts have taken for the past century. In fact, during the late 1800s under the slogan Japanese Spirit, Western Knowledge, roughly 3000 foreign technicians, teachers, and consultants were imported in exactly the same manner. See Hazel J. Jones, *Live Machines: Hired Foreigners in Meiji Japan* (Vancouver, B.C.: University of British Columbia Press, 1980).

16. National Council on Educational Reform, *Second Report on Reform* (Tokyo: Government of Japan, 1986).

17. The council was sharply divided between members chosen by Nakasone, who favored liberalization but were fiscal conservatives, and representatives from the Ministry of Education (MOE), including Liberal Democratic Party diet men with a special interest in education. For

a detailed account of the politics of postwar educational reform, see Schoppa, *Education Reform in Japan.*

18. Quoted in Takashi Inoguchi, "The Legacy of the Weathercock Prime Minister," *Japan Quarterly* 34, no. 4 (Summer 1987): 363–70, quote at 365.

19. Interestingly, Nose's initial proposal called only for a program that would bring local government personnel to Japan to work in prefectural and municipal offices for the promotion of international activities. Given the small number of local governments in Japan, however, it soon became clear that public secondary schools were the only vehicle that would allow for a program with a large enough profile to catch the media's attention. Nevertheless, a separate category within the JET program was reserved for participants who wanted to work in local government offices. Unlike the assistant language teacher (ALT) portion of the program, the coordinators of international relations (CIR) portion of the program is administered solely by MOHA.

20. James G. March and Johan P. Olsen, *Rediscovering Institutions: The Organizational Basis of Politics* (New York: The Free Press, 1989).

21. In this vein, Lee Sproull, "Response to Regulation: An Organizational Process Framework," *Administration and Society* 12, no. 4 (1981): 447–69, offers an organizational process framework that focuses not on the properties of programs but rather on the processes by which organizational attention is captured, external stimuli interpreted, response repertoires invoked, and behavioral directives communicated. Karl Weick, "Educational Organizations as Loosely Coupled Systems," *Administrative Science Quarterly* 21 (1976): 1–19, describes educational organizations as "loosely coupled systems" characterized by a lack of structure and determinacy and the dispersion of resources and responsibilities and emphasizes that commonality of purpose cannot be assumed.

22. See Thomas P. Rohlen, "Conflict in Institutional Environments: Politics in Education," in *Conflict in Japan*, ed. Ellis Krauss, Patricia Steinhoff, and Thomas Rohlen (Berkeley: University of California Press, 1983), 136–73.

23. Rohlen, *Japan's High Schools*, quote at 159.

24. Frank K. Upham, *Law and Social Change in Postwar Japan* (Cambridge, Mass.: Harvard University Press, 1987).

25. John Singleton, "Gambaru: A Japanese Cultural Theory of Learning," in *Japanese Schooling: Patterns of Socialization, Equality and Political Control*, ed. James J. Shields, Jr. (University Park: Pennsylvania State University Press, 1989), 8–15.

# 6

# REVERSING CHINA'S BRAIN DRAIN: THE STUDY-ABROAD POLICY, 1978–1993

*Paul Englesberg*

In 1978, Deng Xiaoping led the People's Republic of China on a modernization drive, using science and technology as its main engine. But that engine needed a jump-start, which Deng decided to provide by a vast program of Western training. The result was a policy that sent tens of thousands of Chinese students and scholars (CSS) to the West and that also included a series of improvisations for luring them back home. Only a third of the 200,000 students and scholars who had left China had returned by the end of 1993. Getting them back called for new conceptions and strategies, and China's leaders found themselves producing, almost in spite of themselves, a megapolicy.

The study-abroad program offers an opportunity to view policy making and implementation over a period of time when the Chinese government was not only opening doors to the West but also experimenting with decentralized and voluntary approaches for the first time since the 1950s. The foreign study policy involved a range of cross-sectoral interests: scientific research and higher education were foremost, and industry, foreign relations, and defense were secondary interests. The two primary government sectors involved were the science and education institutions, but the policy called for coordination across sectors, negotiations between policymakers and the various stakeholders, and government interrelationships at the central, regional, and local levels.[1]

In the 1950s, approximately 10,000 engineers, scientists, and other scholars—virtually all of whom returned to China—had been trained in institutions in the Soviet Union and Eastern Europe.[2] The study-abroad program had been managed by a committee within the Ministry of Education (MOE). With the Sino-Soviet rift in the early 1960s, the exchange of Chinese students and Soviet experts was curtailed, and the Chinese government adopted the principle of self-reliance. Although some students were sent abroad in the early 1960s, the Cultural Revolution that erupted in 1966 closed the gates of China's colleges and universities for several years, made educational exchange anathema, and branded many foreign-trained scholars and officials as counterrevolutionaries.[3]

## POLICY INITIATION

China's study-abroad program was initiated in 1978 as part of the much-heralded Four Modernizations of agriculture, industry, defense, and science and technology (S&T). In reversing the leftist policies of Mao and the Gang of Four, Deng Xiaoping and his followers revived many of the programs that Deng had helped to develop under Liu Shaoqi and Zhou Enlai. The Four Modernizations had first been promoted under Zhou's name in 1975, the year before his death, and was widely seen as the brainchild of Deng Xiaoping. In 1976 during the vilification and purge of Deng as a "capitalist-roader," the program was severely attacked and scuttled. Apparently, the struggle over the Four Modernizations policy, and especially over the leading role of S&T development, was inextricably bound up with the political battle for succession.[4] One of the chief accusations against the so-called Gang of Four was that in their struggle for power, they had obstructed progress in education and science and kept China backward. When Deng was "rehabilitated" and consolidated his power as vice premier in 1977, the Four Modernizations was rapidly resurrected as the forward-looking slogan signifying an all-out program to catch up with industrialized countries by the turn of the century.

The strategy for training the scientists, technicians, and managerial personnel required for such rapid modernization was not worked out in detail when the Four Modernizations policy was first announced, and early speeches and presentations of the policy made no mention of foreign training. Deng personally shaped the broad outlines of education and science policies in 1977 and 1978 and specifically advocated reliance on Western training. According to one education official, "It was Comrade Deng Xiaoping's initiative to implement on a larger scale the policy of sending many students and scholars abroad."[5]

Several reasons have been proposed for the rather sudden policy move to train thousands of scholars in the West. Deng Xiaoping himself went to study in France in 1920, and, although he was mostly involved in radical political activities, he may have had a vision of the value of foreign study. Deng Zhiduan suggests that as the "chief architect of China's open-door policy," with foreign study as a key element, Deng Xiaoping was able to strengthen his own political position domestically and signal "a new Chinese outlook on the world."[6] It may not have been clear to Deng and other leaders at first that the training of thousands overseas was necessary or advisable. According to several sources interviewed, it was prominent Chinese scientists, both those at home and those living overseas, who convinced government leaders of the necessity of training students abroad.

The new policy towards science, research, and professional training was announced in March 1978 at the National Science Conference, the first of its kind since 1950. In recognition of the urgent need for trained professionals in scientific areas, government leaders called for the training of 800,000 scientific researchers by 1985. The conference identified several areas for top priority development: agriculture, energy, materials science, computers, laser and space technology, high-energy physics, and genetics. The high-profile participation of top leaders Hua Guofeng and Deng Xiaoping was a clear indication of the priority placed on science.

During the conference, the first official mention was made of expanding overseas study, but no specific plan or policy change was indicated. During his comprehensive report on the national plan for the development of science, Fang Yi, vice premier and vice president of the Chinese Academy of Science (CAS), said that China should "actively and systematically enlarge the scope" of sending S&T personnel and students abroad for advanced training.[7] Deng Xiaoping, in his opening speech, announced, "We must actively develop international academic exchanges and step up our friendly contacts with scientific circles of other countries."[8] Premier Hua Guofeng, the transitional leader between Mao and Deng, also emphasized the importance of learning from other countries while still affirming homage to the Maoist principle of self-reliance which had been the doctrine since 1966. Hua's stance demonstrated the significance of this break with the Maoist doctrine and hinted at the political sensitivity of increased dependence upon foreign countries for training. "While upholding independence and self-reliance, we should learn from other countries analytically and critically," he argued.[9] "In order to raise the scientific and cultural level of our nation, it is necessary to reiterate Chairman Mao's slogan of learning from other countries."[10]

Similarly, at the National Education Work Conference held in April 1978 to chart new directions for the nation's entire system of schools, leaders mentioned expanding international academic exchange but presented no specifics or guidelines. Education Minister Liu Xiyao only said, "Efforts should also be made to increase college-level academic exchanges with foreign countries in order to better understand new achievements in science and technology in foreign lands and related trends and management experiences."[11] At that point, no mention was made of the need for overseas training to upgrade the higher education system itself. Although both the selection of candidates for studying abroad and preparation in foreign languages were reportedly discussed, the content of this discussion was never released.

According to later press reports, the Communist Party Central Committee (CPCC) made the decision to expand study abroad in June 1978, but official ratification of the new policies was not made until late December 1978 at the

Third Plenum of the Eleventh CPCC.[12] No documentation of the policy debate among party leaders has been released, but no opposition to Deng's position has been suggested.[13] Following the CPCC decision, progress toward policy implementation was swift. That month, a U.S. government science delegation meeting with Deng and Fang Yi found the Chinese side expressing a new interest in a larger-scale exchange program even before the normalization of diplomatic relations, which had been the major obstacle.

By August, reports began to circulate that China had plans to send thousands of students and scholars overseas.[14] In an internal directive (still unpublished), MOE called for the selection of at least 3,000 undergraduates, scholars, and graduate students in the sciences and engineering.[15] Early information estimated that for the first year, at least 500 would be sent to each of several countries, including the United States, Australia, Japan, and several countries in Western Europe. They would mostly study fields in science and technology, and some would study management.

Following what Leo Orleans has called "the more the better" principle, the major policy during the first years was simply "to send as many students and scholars abroad as acceptances could be procured and as funding would allow."[16] However, the national priority for training in basic and applied sciences and engineering was broadly implemented, and as the program evolved, candidates were to be selected according to national plans in specific fields.

According to one source, Deng Xiaoping had wanted to send 3,000 students the first academic year (1978–1979) and increase the numbers sent to 10,000 for the second year. MOE officials in charge of crafting and carrying out the policy felt 10,000 was unrealistic and dissuaded Deng. This is one of the most concrete examples of Deng's personal influence and involvement with the details of the study-abroad policy. Government documents confirm that the original goals of 3,000 and 10,000 were officially adjusted following the August 1979 meeting on study-abroad work. A quota of 2,000 was set for 1980 and 1981 during this meeting, for the government had difficulties in filling its quotas. But throughout most of the 1980s, Deng's 3,000 figure became the standard for the government-sponsored program.[17]

From 1978 through 1981, most of those sent abroad were older, usually in their mid-thirties to late forties. They mostly went under the category of visiting scholars (*jinxiu renyuan*) for one to two years and did not enroll in degree programs. The emphasis on sending visiting scholars was due in large part to the large number of older specialists whose professional careers had been interrupted during the Cultural Revolution period.

When the Chinese education delegation to the United States proposed to send the first group of 500 to 700 students and scholars to the United States, they indicated that 80 percent would be visiting scholars and that matriculating undergraduates and graduate students would each comprise about 10 percent of the total.[18] Visiting scholars comprised approximately 70 percent of the state-sponsored program (*guojia gongpai*) and 68 percent of the unit-sent program (*danwei gongpai*) between 1978 and 1989. Only at the height of the emphasis on training graduate students in 1983 did the numbers in the visiting scholar category drop to near 50 percent in the state program.

When concern about delayed return and brain drain mounted in the late 1980s, policies were shifted again to favor sending mostly older professionals for shorter stays as visiting scholars. Renewed emphasis on advanced nondegree studies were partly justified on the grounds that China was capable of training graduate students in most fields in domestic master's and doctoral programs. However, criticisms of this approach pointed out the limited value of the six-to-eighteen months stays and the continued need for the kind of training provided by foreign graduate programs.[19]

During the first years of the exchange program, a relatively small proportion of students was enrolled in graduate degree programs because few young students could meet the qualifications. In 1982, the first group of college students admitted under the revived examination system graduated. This cohort was considered the best and the brightest, as it included those who had not been able to continue their studies during the 1966–1977 period. They also had higher language proficiency, the absence of which had severely limited numbers of candidates during the first few years of the study-abroad program. Starting with this graduating class of 1982, more relatively young students began to be selected for studying abroad as graduate students. Most were initially sent for two- to three-year master's degree programs, and some in the visiting scholar category were able to switch to degree programs. Due to the relative ease with which qualified students could prolong their stays in order to pursue doctoral and postdoctoral work and also due to the younger age of most of these students, they tended to return to China at a much lower rate than visiting scholars.

Although the graduate student category expanded from under 7 percent in 1979 to 44 percent in 1983, it never exceeded the number sent as visiting scholars under government sponsorship. As the domestic graduate programs which were started in 1981 trained larger cohorts, especially at the master's level, the study-abroad plan was adjusted to send more students at the doctoral and postdoctoral levels.[20] The adjustment was also a response to the low rate of return among graduate students, which made graduate study a riskier investment for the government. In 1989, the State Education Commission (SEdC) sharply reduced the graduate student quota by sending only 411 (13.8 percent) of the total. However, with adequate support from foreign universities, graduate study would continue to be the objective for most self-financed students.

A small group of undergraduates was also sent each year. Initially, this was to ensure that they would become highly proficient in foreign languages since most of the older professionals had been trained only in Russian. There was some disagreement over the efficacy of sending undergraduates, and they were sent in limited numbers each year. In 1981, MOE decided to decrease the number of undergraduates abroad by limiting them to those training to be foreign language teachers and interpreters.[21] Nearly 1,000 undergraduates had been sent by 1982; a total of 1,874 by 1989. But by 1993, only a small number had returned to work in China, and officials interviewed did not consider the sending of undergraduates to have been a successful part of the program.[22]

## POLICY IMPLEMENTATION

The comprehensive strategy for S&T development, which included personnel, organization, and equipment, was worked out under the State Science and Technology Commission (SSTC) with a strong role played by CAS. Coordination of the many government organizations with different interests—military, research, education, and economic development—was needed. However, there were indications that SSTC was less than effective in fulfilling this need.[23]

### Organization of the Study-Abroad Program

Once the study-abroad policy was initiated in 1978, detailed implementation was handled by three organizations at the national level: Bureau of S&T Cadres (BSTC) under the State Council, MOE, and CAS. At the provincial and regional levels, both educational and S&T departments were involved. This shared responsibility was due to organizational jurisdiction over separate categories of personnel to be trained abroad. By the end of 1979, a total of 2,700 people— mostly in the sciences but also including 2,100 under education departments and 600 under CAS—had been sent overseas.[24]

The involvement of many sectors of government in the initial stage of the study-abroad policy can be seen from the composition of the Chinese group who met with the first U.S. government science delegation in July 1978. The delegation included high-ranking leaders (mostly vice ministers) of CAS; the Science and Technology Association of the People's Republic of China (STAPRC); SSTC; the Ministries of Foreign Relations (MFR), Agriculture and Forestry, Petroleum Industry, and Foreign Trade; the Chinese Academy of Space Technology; the Chinese Academy of Medical Sciences; the State Bureau of Metrology; and the State Geological Bureau. Noticeably absent was formal representation from MOE even though Jiang Nanxiang, vice minister of the SSTC, fulfilled this role as he was about to be named Minister of Education.[25]

The first meetings held to evaluate the study-abroad program and make plans for its continuation showed that MOE was in charge, but other governmental offices continued to be involved. In December 1979, the first work conference on overseas study was convened jointly by MOE and BSTC. The emphasis placed at this conference on the training of faculty in higher education is an indication of the primary role of MOE. Because CAS conducted a separate program stressing the foreign training of scientific researchers, it became less involved in guiding general study-abroad policy.

The next year, a larger conference was held to discuss the program and, in particular, to consider the question of allowing privately financed study abroad. The joint conveners included MOE, MFR, the Ministry of Finance (MOF), the Ministry of Culture, BSTC, and CAS. In 1981, the authority of MOE, in most aspects of the program, was explicitly sanctioned by the State Council, the government body with authority over all the state ministries, academies, commissions, and bureaus. MOE was authorized to control selecting and sending people in all three categories—visiting scholars, graduate students, and undergraduates—and to oversee international exchange activities, such as lectures, academic visits, and exchanges between institutions.[26] BSTC became less prominent as MOE assumed major responsibility for the program. It is not clear what this change signified, but it may have been a means of tightening control over the selection of personnel. There were signs of dissatisfaction with the role of BSTC and with unqualified personnel being sent abroad because of their familial and other relations to officialdom. According to one education official, MOE had overall responsibility while the role of BSTC, which later merged with the SSTC and the Ministry of Personnel (MOP), was limited to the training of personnel in government bureaus in the noneducation (*feijiaoyu*) sector.

In 1984, CPCC directed a "leading group for attracting foreign talent" to oversee the study-abroad policy and study-abroad work and, thus, set up a structure over MOE, CAS, and other ministries sending students and scholars abroad.[27] This group, which became the Foreign Experts Bureau under the State Council, was largely responsible for the central recruitment and management of foreign teachers and specialists and actually had only limited involvement in study-abroad policy despite the CPCC directive. In fact, MOE remained in charge of the actual day-to-day management of the study-abroad program, with some degree of coordination and shared decision making among government sectors during major meetings.

Various government sectors involved in the program were represented at the opening and closing of the November 1984 study-abroad conference: the State Council; SSTC; MOE; the Commission of Science, Technology, and Industry for National Defense; the State Planning Commission; the State Economic Commission; the China People's Association for Friendship with Foreign Countries; the Ministries of Agriculture, Animal Husbandry and Fisheries, Electronics Industry, and Public Health; and representatives from consulates and embassies (under MFR). It is significant that State Council member Zhang Jingfu opened the conference and stressed the involvement and concern by the top state and party officials.[28] Both CPCC and the State Council recognized that MOE lacked sufficient authority needed to coordinate policy involving many competing ministries and bureaus.

The reorganization and elevation of MOE in 1986 as SEdC, directly under the State Council, allowed, for the first time, coordinated central authority over the various ministries, provinces, and municipal governments which ran nearly 1,000 institutes and universities. The State Council and CPCC gave SEdC clear responsibility both for sending personnel abroad and for placing returnees.[29] SEdC held the conferences and drafted the regulations on the program, but the State Council often issued the final versions of decisions that gave them more authority. But even with this authority, the policy decisions were by no means left to SEdC alone. Press releases on the policy frequently mentioned the concern with and discussion of study abroad by CPCC and the State Council. Top leaders, including Deng Xiaoping, Li Peng, and Jiang Zemin, addressed the study-abroad policy in major speeches at critical points and were undoubtedly involved in behind-the-scenes policy decisions at the CPCC level.

One of the greatest powers wielded by MOE, and later SEdC, was in the distribution of annual quotas for state-sponsored overseas training slots to the various universities under its control and to the ministries, provinces, and CAS, all of which ran institutes and universities. MOE/SEdC also controlled the final evaluation and approval process of candidates for study abroad proposed by the institutions. In 1989, China's 1,075 regular higher education institutions employed nearly 400,000 full-time faculty members plus another 280,000 supporting staff and administrative personnel.[30] CAS administered 123 research institutes and 20 other units employing 57,000 researchers and another 23,000 staff.[31] Thus, the 3,000 annual state-funded positions for foreign training were coveted by the various institutions, and these decisions by SEdC had far-reaching impact on the development of personnel, research, and academic disciplines for individual institutions. Data collected for this study in 1992 and by other researchers show that the state quotas had significant though quite uneven effects on the development of different types of universities. This will be discussed in the following section.

## Coordination of Returning Students

Another shifting area of authority that was shared among organizations was the assignment of jobs to returning students. The resulting lack of overall coordination and responsibility was one of the causes of problems with improper job assignment and poor utilization of foreign-trained personnel. By 1983, more students who had not been assigned to work units before studying abroad were returning, and responsibility over their job assignment was shared by the Ministry of Labor, the Ministry of Personnel (MOP), and MOE.[32] After the establishment of SEdC in 1986, job assignment responsibility was placed under both SEdC for university personnel and CAS for its researchers.[33] MOP managed job placement for those returning from abroad who belonged to noneducation sectors and for postdoctoral researchers.

After 1989, SEdC's stricter policies not only failed to attract students to return but also drew intense criticisms by students overseas. Realizing the need to adopt a more flexible approach to employment and better job recruitment to attract returnees, the government apparently strengthened the role of MOP. The increased activity and visibility of MOP may have been an attempt to signal a new approach of accommodation and flexibility. Furthermore, the development of an array of professional opportunities outside the education sector, including enterprises, open laboratories, postdoctoral centers, and joint ventures, required coordination of an increasingly broad network for personnel placement.[34]

### Financing the Program

When the study-abroad policy was first formulated in 1978, the Chinese government decided to break with past principles and precedent by seeking and accepting funding from foreign governments and institutions, international organizations, and private sources. In fact, the structure of the program was, in part, a response to the availability of funding in certain fields. The CAS program started with significant aid from West Germany's Humboldt Foundation and the Max-Planck Institute for the Sciences. The Ministry of Agriculture was maintained as a separate program in order to take advantage of Food and Agriculture Organization (FAO) funding. Similarly, the Ministry of Public Health obtained funds from the World Health Organization (WHO) for overseas training in the field of medicine.

Funding data was generally deleted from published government documents; however, according to one official government report issued in 1979, the average cost of maintaining one student overseas for one year was U.S.$ 10,000.[35] Other reports from Chinese sources and surveys of students receiving government support have indicated average annual expenditures per CSS ranging from U.S.$ 6,000 to 10,000.[36]

In addition to the central SEdC and CAS funds, most provinces and autonomous regions began study-abroad programs in the mid-1980s using their own funds. Guangxi, one of the first regions to develop its own program, reported an annual budget of $500,000 for 139 students sent abroad between 1982 to 1986 and a 1986 budget of $1,000,000 to enable it to send as many as 56 more. Despite substantial expenditures by the Chinese government for the program and professed commitment to support its government-sent (*gongpai*) personnel studying abroad, the majority of financial support for CSS has come from foreign sources since the mid-1980s. The overall annual budget by the central government for the study-abroad program was in the vicinity of U.S.$ 100 to 200 million for the early 1990s according to an unofficial estimate. China's support for the students and scholars in the United States for the three-year period, 1985–1988, was reported to be U.S.$ 75 million.[37] CAS reported that it had spent $40 million from 1978 through 1991 in sending 7,500 of its staff as graduate students and visiting scholars abroad.[38]

The wide array of bilateral agreements, nongovernmental academic exchange agreements, and various fellowship opportunities supporting CSS make the total amount of foreign financial support for the study-abroad program difficult to estimate. The largest single source of outside support was the $200 million World Bank loan for the Chinese university-development project (1982–1986) of which approximately 25 percent was used for foreign training of university faculty.[39]

U.S. universities provided a very large share of the support for Chinese students. Between 1979 and 1983, an estimated 40 percent of the cost of CSS in the United States was borne by the host institutions.[40]

In order to maximize the number of CSS trained overseas within a limited budget, the Chinese government sought to utilize multiple channels, including bilateral exchanges of scholars, fellowships from foreign governments and private foundations, and institutional scholarships. By 1979, policy makers began considering opening the doors wider to allow those students who could obtain private funding (*zifei*) to study abroad also. The *zifei* option was in part a response to requests by overseas Chinese who wished to support their relatives, and it was also seen as a way for the government to expand the numbers of trainees without increasing its financial burden. Despite some objections from university and institute leaders who feared the loss of staff, the *zifei* policy was approved because at that point nearly all scholars were returning from foreign study on time as expected.

## UNANTICIPATED PROBLEMS AND UNINTENDED CONSEQUENCES

By the end of 1981, the government recognized that several serious problems had developed as a result of an estimated 6,000 people leaving China as self-financed students. Chief among these problems was that party cadres and other government officials were using their power to send their own children and other relatives overseas as *zifei* students. A second problem was that university students were applying to study abroad in larger numbers, thereby decreasing the government's control over higher education and job assignment and creating a study-abroad craze on campuses. A third problem was the bourgeois corruption of students, including the children of government officials. In response, regulations issued in March 1982 placed new restrictions on the *zifei* category, including a ban on undergraduates and graduate students, a two-year work requirement for college graduates prior to eligibility for study abroad, and stricter controls regarding government and party officials and their children. Because this regulation affected high-ranking party officials, it was issued by CPCC rather than MOE.[41]

## Controlling *Zifei* Students

A major difference in the treatment of *zifei* and *gongpai* students in the relation to the work unit was stipulated in further regulations in 1982. While government-sponsored students were entitled to receive their salaries and build up seniority, self-financed students lost their salary and were kept at the same seniority level.[42] The comprehensive 1986 Provisional Regulations granted self-financed students earning doctorates abroad the same seniority treatment as state-supported students, but as of 1994, few self-financed students with Ph.D.s earned abroad had returned to China.[43]

In the early 1980s, despite the *zifei* policy, many candidates were not permitted to leave by either their school or work unit, and complaints to MOE mounted. Since most universities were under provincial governments, MOE's authority was limited; it could only urge them to allow their personnel to leave or use the state quotas as a bargaining chip. To solve the problem, the State Council, with authority over all ministry and provincial institutions, further relaxed the regulations for self-financed study in 1984 and simplified the approval procedures for most applicants so that they needed only to obtain approval from Public Security Bureau offices. The schools and work units to which student or worker applicants belonged could only "give comments and sign" (rubber-stamp) the applications. Such core professionals as college faculty, researchers, doctors, and graduate students, on the other hand, were still required to obtain permission from their units and approval from government offices in charge of cadres.[44]

No accurate data on the numbers of those studying overseas through private channels was available, and from the numerous drastically conflicting figures released, it is clear that neither the Chinese government nor the individual institutions had an effective system to keep track of students and scholars leaving for foreign study. Once it liberalized the granting of passports and decentralized the approval for study abroad so that each local Public Security Bureau and university could grant permission, the government apparently had no system at all.

Although specific data is lacking, two important facts are clear: at least 100,000 people left, and very few of them returned. Tens of thousands of students left during the 1980s and continuing into the 1990s, and the vast majority are now in the United States. According to one SEdC official interviewed in November 1992, an estimated 100,000 self-financed students went abroad.[45] A higher figure of 140,000 self-financed students since 1978 given by the Ministry of Public Security probably includes work-study students in language schools, especially in Japan and Australia, who are not included in other figures.[46] The low return rate of self-financed students is widely acknowledged, but the patterns and numbers of those returning or emigrating remains to be studied.

### Utilization of Returnees

In 1981 and 1982, the first large groups of visiting scholars began to return. Because most scholars already had positions in their institutes and universities, utilization of the first cohorts of returned scientists was expected to be simple. But as they attempted to set up laboratories and to conduct research, difficulties soon became apparent. Equipment shortages, lack of funding, logistics, and improper job assignments were the most frequent complaints. Utilization of returnees was, of course, closely related to problems in the general organization of S&T research and personnel in these institutions, but waste of top talent after the investment of large sums of money on overseas training brought the problems into sharper focus. As thousands returned each year, the problems were compounded. By the mid-1980s, the problem of returnee absorption and utilization became a top priority concern. Frequent criticisms and calls for reform of the personnel system were published in the press in the mid-1980s; the most common phrase was that returned scientists' skills and training were not given "full play" (*fahui tamen de zuoyong*).[47] Those who had studied overseas through private arrangements, whether by means of scholarships or relatives' support, often faced a more difficult struggle as their training and degrees were sometimes not recognized and proper employment opportunities were not offered to them.

In response to the problems of *zifei* students, MOE declared the principle of equal treatment of self-financed students and government-sponsored students studying abroad as official policy, and the State Council issued a regulation liberalizing self-financed study abroad in December 1984.[48] But despite new regulations, self-financed students continued to face difficulties and unequal treatment when returning to work units.

Policy makers tended to see the utilization problem in terms of irrationalities in the selection and distribution of personnel who could be controlled rather than as a matter to be solved by reforming structures, such as the personnel system, research bodies, and funding. While state sponsorship was maintained at a constant level, provinces, cities, and institutions were encouraged to expand their own programs. Through the decentralization policies of 1987, the government yielded substantial control over the selection and fields of study with the expectation that these entities would achieve a closer link between their needs and foreign training.

### Brain Drain and Delayed Return

As opportunities expanded through private sponsorship and institution-level sponsorship and exchanges, Chinese campuses erupted in what was commonly called "study-abroad fever." Many factors from cultural to economic contributed to this phenomenon, but the most important motivation seemed to be the common dissatisfaction among students and young faculty and researchers with their work and with their prospects. Because many who wished to go could not leave, the policy tended to have a negative effect on those who stayed behind. Their work burdens increased and their morale declined as more and more young and capable teachers and researchers either left or concentrated efforts on studying for language exams and applying to foreign universities.[49]

Utilization problems and the study-abroad fever fueled what is commonly referred to as the brain drain but might be better described as the problem of "delayed return" as Paul Pedersen suggests.[50] Although a high proportion of visiting scholars returned, many undergraduates and graduate students, especially those in the United States and Canada, extended their studies. One early measure to encourage privately funded students to return was the offer of one-way airfare back to China for those with advanced degrees. But few self-financed students chose to return. The government's policy of encouraging sponsored students to find scholarships, assistantships, or other financing after the first year made them more independent of the government. The prospect of mismatched positions, low ranks, little funding, and housing problems were strong disincentives to return: the "push." Opportunities to save money while working and studying abroad "pulled" students. The political climate was also a concern for many, especially in 1987 with the purge of Hu Yaobang and several prominent intellectuals and also with the hardline taken against the 1989 democracy movement.[51]

## POLICY RESPONSES: CHANGES IN THE STUDY-ABROAD PROGRAM

In response to the challenge of delayed return, the government turned to a variety of strategies. Some were simply changes in the regulations, that is, attempts to make incremental adjustments to existing policy. Other strategies were more creative and demonstrated both a willingness to follow examples from the experiences of Taiwan and South Korea and a responsiveness to the suggestions of the students and scholars themselves.[52]

### "Carrots and Sticks"

Various bureaucratic measures were implemented both to try to restrict the flow of those most likely to remain abroad and to require those leaving to return within a contracted period of time. Regulations imposed a minimum of five years of work before studying abroad for certain categories and also assessed training fees for those leaving before meeting the work requirements. Although the SEdC opposed penalties, some provinces and institutions levied fines on the families of students who failed to return by the stipulated time. Deviations from national policy occurred because the central government lost much of its control over the study-abroad program through decentralization. Self-financed study was encouraged for those who wished to study for degrees, but government funds would mostly be used to sponsor older professionals for shorter nondegree tours as visiting scholars.

The government tried to offer the "carrot" as well as brandish the "stick," but incentives to return proved difficult to implement. The living and work conditions for returnees were largely controlled by local institutions and the various government offices to which they belonged. Both the government and the institutions were reluctant to give returned students overt preferential treatment for fear of demoralizing those who stayed behind and further feeding the going abroad frenzy. The allocation of five million yuan for housing in 1991 was the first attempt by the central government to address one of the most intractable problems for returnees. In general, preferential treatment in housing has amounted to an additional several square meters of space. Other preferential measures announced in 1991–1992 have included duty-free import of computers and other items and duty-free domestic automobile purchase.[53]

### Maintaining Goodwill

Although return was not identified as a major problem during the first years of the program, the Chinese government relied on several means to ensure that the sponsored students and scholars not only would return but also would retain their loyalty. Patriotism and political ties were promoted through organizations on university campuses led by student cadres who organized activities, supervised students, and acted as liaisons with consular officials.[54] MOE assigned their attachés to consulates in part to monitor and supervise CSS. Copies of the Communist Party newspaper *People's Daily*, official notices, and Chinese films were distributed through these organizations.

As the number of CSS abroad surpassed 10,000 in 1984 and brain drain fears began to grow, government leaders showed more concern for maintaining close relations with them and ensuring their patriotism. Top party leaders, including Hu Yaobang and Zhao Ziyang, sent personal new year messages to students via videotape, and the party and the State Council sent special "support teams" (*weiwentuan*) to visit students in the United States and Canada. In 1985, support teams visited students in North America, Asia, and Europe and stressed the new policies guaranteeing equal treatment and concern for self-financed students.[55]

In 1987, the magazine *Shenzhou xueren* (China's Scholars Abroad) was established by SEdC, in the words of its cover slogan, "to provide services for studying abroad; to introduce the lives of those studying abroad; to report on their achievements; and to provide information about developments in study abroad." Ruth Hayhoe analyzed its apparent mission as "intend[ing] both to reassure and to attract scholars abroad who might be thinking twice about whether they should return."[56] To reach more students, in 1990, the People's

Daily Overseas Edition began to devote a special page each week to study abroad, co-edited by the *Shenzhou xueren* staff.

## Providing Assistance: Service Centers and Job Placement

In 1989, as one component of the new policies aimed at improving the utilization of returned personnel and attracting more students to return, SEdC opened in Beijing a Service Center for Returned Students to help match returning students with work units. The new guiding principle of "mutual selection" by student and work unit was an attempt to solve the problem of improper job assignment, a major deterrent to return.[57] After the 1989 crack-down, both SEdC and MOP opened more service centers in efforts to create a network in major Chinese cities and in foreign countries. Special economic zones and a few municipal governments began to establish their own service centers in 1992.[58]

Expanding needs for trained professionals, especially in high-tech industries and enterprises, also created increased demand for overseas-trained personnel. Capital Iron and Steel, China's largest business with 180,000 employees, established a service center for returning students in 1992 which offered "excellent working and living conditions . . . [and] high salaries."[59] The opening of this first enterprise-based service center demonstrated the increased attraction of the business sector for highly trained professionals.

## Supporting Research: Postdoctoral Stations

Following the 1984 decision to allocate 20 million yuan in special funds for the establishment of ten postdoctoral research stations, plans were developed for enrolling 250 students in over 100 postdoctoral programs and for creating a system of fellowship support. In 1986, a National Coordinating Committee was formed under SSTC and was composed of representatives from SEdC, CAS, the Ministry of Aviation Industry, and the Beijing Municipal S&T Commission.[60] New regulations stipulated the qualifications, application and selection procedure, work conditions, remuneration, housing allowance, and future work assignment. In 1987, the first grants for postdoctoral research were awarded by both the National Coordinating Committee and SSTC.[61]

By 1989, the system was fully developed with MOP in charge of the actual administration of the researchers in these centers. The system included a special postdoctoral research foundation that was administered by MOP as well as modest support (5,000 to 10,000 yuan) and funds for housing for postdoctoral researchers that were provided by the State Planning Commission. But prior to the June 1989 crackdown, the 145 stations had attracted only 140 returned students (40 percent of the total returned Ph.D. recipients).[62] In an attempt to encourage more returnees, SEdC and MOP jointly granted further preferential treatment to postdoctoral researchers and their families in 1992.[63]

In 1993, the Chinese press reported that 354 students had returned to China for postdoctoral research and that China's 283 postdoctoral stations had received over 1,800 researchers, including those trained both domestically and overseas. For the mid-1990s, the government announced its aim to recruit 500 postdoctoral students from overseas each year—a sharp reduction from the 1,000 Ph.D. students it had expected annually before the events of June 4, 1989. The opening of sixteen new postdoctoral research stations in the social sciences was an attempt to broaden the fields of recruitment. Although the Chinese media have lauded the success of these stations at attracting students from overseas, they have primarily served those receiving doctorates in domestic programs.[64]

Increased funding for research in the sciences was another major part of policies to attract students. Some funds, such as the Study Abroad Foundation established in January 1989 with 100 million yuan, were especially designated for those returning from abroad.[65] Grants administered by SEdC became easier for returnees to obtain after 1989 but remained small in amount, averaging 30,000 to 50,000 yuan according to press reports.[66] Provinces and municipal governments are also likely to increase research funds, but in smaller amounts. Shanxi province, for example, allocated US$ 200,000 annually to returned students for research beginning in 1989.[67]

### Recruiting Scientists: CAS Efforts

CAS sent over 7,500 of its personnel as visiting scholars and graduate students from 1978 to 1991, approximately 50 percent of whom had returned by 1991. In addition to the 400 to 900 sent by CAS each year, the CAS education bureau estimated that another 200 to 300 left its various institutes each year for self-financed foreign study. The return rate was quite high (over 90 percent) during the first three years of the program due to the fact that 80 percent were sent as short-term visiting scholars and most were older scientists. Between 1983 and 1988, a higher proportion of those sent by CAS were in the graduate student category (64 percent). These were probably mostly younger, with lower rank, and with weaker ties to their institutes. Although CAS planned for 40 percent of those sent to be trained in the United States, actual placements accounted for 60 percent of the total. The changing composition of the pool of CSS and the conditions for scholars in the United States were major factors in the increasing tendency of CAS personnel to stay abroad.[68]

In 1985, faced with the retirement of aging scientists and the delayed return of hundreds of its best people, CAS implemented a preferential policy toward "top-notch scholars" returning from studies abroad. This trial policy, including research funding, promotion, and housing priorities, was the first attempt to actively induce scholars to return.[69] But adding a stick to the carrot, CAS also began to replace staff who did not return on time from abroad.[70] CAS also established sixty-two postdoctoral research stations as part of the national initiative announced in 1984. Despite these measures, delayed return continued to be prevalent. One survey by CAS found that 80 percent of students it had sent to the United States wanted to stay for postdoctoral work.[71]

With a large proportion of scientists in the thirty-six to forty-five age bracket overseas, research at institutes was hampered. Research in some fields was almost completely dependent on foreign-trained scientists.[72] Then, worsening the situation, the flow of returnees to CAS institutes dropped dramatically following the June 1989 government crackdown.

In the early 1990s, CAS established several new initiatives aimed at attracting more scholars to return. In 1991, it began to hold a series of symposia for young scholars from within China and from abroad. Using funds from a Hong Kong foundation, CAS established the K. C. Wong Scientific Research Award to support at least ten researchers each year starting in 1991. In 1992, CAS specially allocated $500,000 annually to support research by outstanding scholars return-ing to work in a CAS institute for at least six months.[73] Other initiatives announced in 1993 included provisions for various short-term visits for schol-ars wishing to run seminars, to set up research bases, to attend summer sessions, and to participate in meetings.[74]

According to an official interviewed in 1992, one of the greatest problems for CAS in attracting personnel was its housing shortage, consequently, in the competition between institutions for highly qualified scientists, often the unit with the best housing was successful.

### Luring to Shenzhen and other Special Economic Zones

The rapid development in Shenzhen, a special economic zone (SEZ) across the border from Hong Kong, led to increased demands for highly trained personnel. Expertise was needed particularly in the fields of international trade and finance, which account for a very small part of government-sponsored students. As early as 1985, a team was sent to the United States and Canada by the Shekou district of Shenzhen to recruit students to work there.[75] In 1988, the Shenzhen SEZ issued regulations to recruit students from overseas by offering preferential treatment. The "temporary provisions" included freedom of entry and exit, multiple exit visas, free choice of employment, flexibility with job transfers, quota waivers for professional titles, housing subsidies, family resi-dence permits, patent rights, and freedom to run enterprises and invest capital. In 1992, Shenzhen sent more recruiters, including the mayor, to the United States along with central government representatives. According to press re-ports, forty-four returned to work in Shenzhen, and additional returned stu-dents had transferred from other work units in China.[76]

Other SEZs, such as Zhuhai (near Macao) and the Pudong zone of Shanghai, followed Shenzhen's lead in appealing to new returnees and those still abroad to fill positions in S&T, foreign trade, and management areas. Zhuhai's policies promised easy transfer, funding, business opportunities, job opportunities for family members, and special housing and appliance arrangements.[77] In contrast to the reluctance of most institutions to grant special treatment to returning CSS, the SEZs were able to grant preferences because of their highly mobile and rapidly expanding work forces and their competitive personnel structure.

In 1993, Shanghai also sent representatives from its Service Center for Returned Scholars from Abroad to the United States to recruit CSS by offering short-term residence permits, job titles, and permission to establish enterprises.[78] The enthusiasm by the Chinese government for these efforts by the SEZs and Shanghai was an indication that if the policies proved successful in recruiting students, similar policies might be implemented nationally.

### Political Pulls and Pushes

Since patriotism was one of the strongest pulls on students to return, the government's loss of goodwill and political legitimacy in the eyes of most students was very damaging. Following both the demonstrations by students in Hefei, Shanghai, Beijing, and elsewhere in December 1986 and January 1987 and the ousting of Secretary-General Hu Yaobang, Chinese students in the United States responded with strong support. The culminating action was the drafting and circulation of a petition and open letter to the Chinese government signed by 1,000 students.[79] The Chinese government responded to the increased activism abroad with surveillance and suppression. Yang Wei, a student who had returned to Shanghai from the United States, was sentenced to two years in prison for "inciting antirevolutionary propaganda," for involvement in the 1986–1987 demonstrations, and for acting as a liaison for the "reactionary" China Alliance for Democracy.[80]

Within months, SEdC issued new directives to "strengthen political investigation" of candidates for state-sponsored study abroad, thus supplementing Document No. 107, the comprehensive regulations on study abroad which had been approved just weeks before the outbreak of demonstrations. In the new directives, the government made clear its view that because of lax selection and control some of those studying abroad were "opposed to the four cardinal principles" of the Communist Party and were infected with "corrupt bourgeois ideology."[81]

The prodemocracy protests of 1989 and the subsequent suppression had a tremendous impact on virtually every Chinese person studying abroad. It would be difficult to overestimate the alienation and hostility they felt toward the Chinese government and the Communist Party. One of the early actions taken by Chinese students on most foreign campuses was to form new, democratically elected organizations and denounce the officially sanctioned bodies. These new groups soon formed federations just as students in Beijing were forming the Autonomous Federation of Students. In the United States, the Independent Federation of Chinese Students and Scholars (IFCSS) became the major national organization and established an elaborate electronic media network linking Chinese students and scholars worldwide.

After the protests and suppression of Spring 1989, the government not only lost the allegiance of tens of thousands of students overseas but also lost control over the network of CSS organizations through its embassies and consulates. Similarly, the SEdC, already distrusted by CSS because of attempts to impose various restrictions on study abroad, enjoyed little or no respect abroad. In response to the widespread political activism and opposition of CSS groups internationally, the party resorted to nonofficial channels, propaganda, and bureaucratic regulations for political persuasion and control.[82] Rumors of sharp restrictions of the outflow of students and punishment for activists abroad were rampant. Internal documents from a conference of education consular attachés held by SEdC in March 1990 display the antagonistic attitude of some government leaders toward the students and their foreign hosts. The document called the problem of China's exchange students "an international struggle and a fight against the brain drain." The United States was described as "holding our overseas students as hostages" and using the student issue as "a heavy bomb to pressure us."[83]

## CRAFTING POLICY CHANGES FOR THE 1990s

Serious internal debate concerning the entire study-abroad policy and the treatment of CSS overseas appears to have continued unresolved until 1992. A conciliatory tone toward students abroad was set by Deng Xiaoping in 1991: "We should welcome them with open doors." But Deng acknowledged that advocacy of political leniency was not accepted by some others in the leadership.[84] In 1992 during his much-heralded southern tour, Deng elaborated his views: "We hope that those studying abroad will come back. All overseas students may return and enjoy proper arrangements, regardless of their previous political attitude. This policy toward them must remain unchanged. They should be told that it's better to return home if they want to make their contributions."[85]

In an attempt to demonstrate the spirit of conciliation, to improve relations with CSS internationally, and to encourage more to return, the State Council issued a policy document welcoming all students to return, and SEdC sent recruiting teams to the United States and eight other countries in 1992.[86] There was general acceptance and enthusiasm for the policy direction and strong support for continuation of the study-abroad program. However, study-abroad policy was very much in a state of flux. In August 1992, Li Tieying, chair of SEdC, stated that in the future most support for study abroad would be through loans rather than stipends. He explained that the government remained committed to maintaining the program but wanted to avoid losing money as well as personnel.[87] A sterner tone was set by Jiang Guanzhong, deputy director of MOP, who acknowledged that brain drain was a universal phenomenon but warned that "those tending to stay abroad pose a threat to the stability of the scientific and technological ranks at home."[88]

Because the United States has been the recipient of approximately half (100,000) of the total number of government-sponsored and self-financed CSS, the especially low return rate from the United States was particularly troubling to the Chinese government. The response of the U.S. government to the June 4, 1989, tragedy further lessened China's hopes that most would return. In 1990, President Bush signed an executive order extending the visas of Chinese nationals until 1994 and waiving the two-year, home-country residence requirement. At least 53,000 Chinese nationals became eligible to apply for permanent U.S. residency status (green card) on July 1, 1993, under the Chinese Student Protection Act of 1992. With newly acquired green cards in hand, more Chinese returned to China for short visits, according to a Chinese embassy official in Washington in 1993, but few chose to resettle permanently. Although thousands of students completed doctoral programs in the United States, relatively few had returned to China by 1994.[89]

Are there new paradigms emerging from the developing policy? It seems so. Some open recruitment and opportunities for job mobility are the beginning of a marketplace for employment which has never existed before under the Communist Party in China. The rapidly developing connections between government institutions and the private sector, especially in the coastal areas and SEZs, is beginning to create niches for research and development (R&D) that may be able to attract more students.

It is too early to be sure, but current policies appear to be leading to a much more internationally connected and open system, at least for the academic elite. The invitation for students to return regardless of past political activities, guaranteed free entry and re-exit, the right to keep foreign passports, and the freedom to work both in China and abroad or in joint ventures are all significant changes in this direction. These have been combined with a range of structural and institutional changes such as the development of postdoctoral centers and open labs, increased funding for research, and more flexible personnel policies. The responses to the unintended consequences of a bold but shortsighted policy may, in fact, have led policy makers toward a more creative and systemwide approach to development policy.

## NOTES

1. See David M. Lampton, "Chinese Politics: The Bargaining Treadmill," *Issues and Studies* 23, no. 3 (March 1987): 11–41; Kenneth Lieberthal and Michel Oksenberg, *Policy Making in*

*China* (Princeton, N.J.: Princeton University Press, 1988); David M. Lampton, "The Implementation Problem in Post-Mao China," in *Policy Implementation in Post-Mao China*, ed. D. M. Lampton (Berkeley: University of California Press, 1987), 3–25.

2. *Zhongguo jiaoyu nianjian* (China Education Yearbook), *1949–1981* (Changsha: Hunan jiaoyu chubanshe, 1982), 666; Stewart Fraser, "China's International, Cultural, and Educational Relations: With Selected Bibliography," *Comparative Education Review* (February 1969): 60–84; and Leo A. Orleans, *Chinese Students in America* (Washington, D.C.: National Academy Press, 1988), 20–21.

3. Discrimination against returned scholars from the Soviet Union persisted into the 1980s and prompted government attention such as detailed in 1980 Communist Party Doc. 5 in *Zhishi fenzi zhengce wenjian huibian* (Collection of documents on policies towards intellectuals) [hereafter, *ZFZWH*] (Beijing: Laodong renshi chubanshe, 1985), 719–22.

4. R. P. Suttmeier, *Science, Technology, and China's Drive for Modernization* (Stanford, Calif.: Hoover Institution Press, 1980), 56.

5. Huang Shiqi, "Contemporary Educational Relations with the Industrialized World: A Chinese View," in *Chinese Education and the Industrialized World*, ed. Ruth Hayhoe and Marianne Bastid (Armonk, N.Y.: M. E. Sharpe, 1987), 228.

6. Deng Zhiduan, "China's Brain Drain Problem: Causes, Consequences and Policy Options," *Journal of Contemporary China* 1, no. 1 (1992): 8–9.

7. *China Exchange Newsletter* [hereafter *CEN*] 6, no. 5 (October 1978): 2.

8. *Beijing Review* [hereafter *BR*] (March 24, 1978): 13.

9. Joseph Needham, "Science Reborn in China," *Nature* (August 31, 1979): 835.

10. Leo Orleans, ed., *Science in Contemporary China* (Stanford, Calif.: Stanford University Press, 1980), 561.

11. *CEN* 6, no. 5 (October 1978): 3; see also *Chinese Education* [hereafter *CE*] 12, no. 1 (Spring 1988): 25.

12. *Xinhua*, January 4, 1980, Foreign Broadcast Information Service [hereafter *FBIS*], January 9, 1980, pp. L4–5; see also "Report of the State Council Scientific and Technical Cadre Bureau on the 1981 Plan for Selection of Personnel to Study Abroad," in *ZFZWH*, 724–27.

13. The second session of the Fifth National People's Congress in June 1979 was the scene of the first open debate on study-abroad policies. See *CEN* 7, no. 4 (August 1979): 1–2.

14. Premier Hua Guofeng told a West German banker that China planned to send 40,000 students overseas; Hong Kong, Agence France Press, October 3, 1978, FBIS, October 4, 1978, p. A25. Japan alone was targeted to receive 10,000 students at first, which was later scaled down to 2,000; Kyodo News Service, FBIS, October 13, 1978, p. A7.

15. Study Abroad Book Series Editorial Committee, Li Changfa and Gao Guangwen, chief eds., *Zhongguo liuxue shicui* (Collected History of China's Study Abroad Programs) (Beijing: Zhongguo youyi chubanshe, 1992), 303; *Zhongguo jiaoyu nianjian, 1949–1981*, 667.

16. Leo A. Orleans, "Chinese Students and Technology Transfer," *Journal of Northeast Asian Studies* 4, no. 4 (1985): 3–25.

17. Doc. 068 (September 4, 1979) in *ZFZWH*, 714. Although the government published statistics of the numbers of students and scholars sent abroad, it considered quotas as a secret and thus systematically deleted these figures from published official reports and documents such as Doc. 305 (December 25, 1980) in *ZFZWH*, 727; and Doc. 278 (October 19, 1981) in *ZFZWH*, 770. A 1984 directive set 3,000 as the maximum that could be sent each year under government sponsorship because of budget limitations, Doc. 38 (April 20, 1984) in *Renshi gongzuo wenjian xuanbian* (Selected documents on personnel work) [hereafter, *RGWX*] no. 7 (Beijing: Laodong renshi chubanshe, 1984), 206–7.

18. Committee on Scholarly Communications with the People's Republic of China (PRC), "Notes on Student Exchanges with China," (photocopy, November 1978).

19. "Quality Should Be the Main Concern in Sending Personnel Abroad," *CE* 23, no. 2 (Summer 1990): 89–90 (translation from *Shijie jingji daobao*, November 30, 1987).

20. *1989 Educational Statistics Yearbook of China* (Beijing: China Statistics Press, 1990); *BR* (December 27, 1993): 23 (translated from *Renmin Ribao*, Overseas Edition, October 29, 1993). *BR* published the figure 110,000 for the number of domestic doctorates which I assume to be a printing error.

21. Doc. 278 (October 19, 1981) in *ZFZWH*, 768–70.

22. *Zhongguo jiaoyu nianjian* (China Education Yearbook), 1949–1981, 667; 1982–1984, 301; 1988, 385–86; 1989, 330; 1990, 382.

23. See Denis Simon, "Implementing China's S&T Modernization Program," in *The Implementation Problem in Post-Mao China*, ed. David M. Lampton (Berkeley: University of California, 1987), 362–67; *CEN* 8, nos. 5–6 (October-December 1980): 7.

24. *Xinhua*, December 22, 1979, FBIS, January 7, 1980, p. L6.

25. *CEN* 6, nos. 3–4 (June-August 1978): 2.

26. State Council [hereafter SC] Doc. 115 (July 16, 1981), in *ZFZWH*, 745.

27. *CEN* 8, nos. 5–6 (October-December 1980): 7.

28. *Xinhua*, November 29, 1984, FBIS, November 30, 1984, p. K8.

29. SC Doc. 107 (December 13, 1986), in *RGWX*, no. 9: 463–74 (translated in *CE* 21, no.1 [1988]: 35–48).

30. *Zhongguo jiaoyu tongji nianjian* (Statistical yearbook of Chinese education) (Beijing: Renmin jiaoyu chubanshe, 1990), 110–11.

31. Author interview, Yan Yongping, November 1992.

32. Doc. 133 (August 18, 1983), in *ZFZWH*, 799–807.

33. SEdC Doc. (October 24, 1986), in *Jiaoyu fagui quanshu* (The Complete Laws and Regulations for Education) [hereafter *JFQ*], (Haikou: Nanhai chuban gongsi, 1990), 1309.

34. Doc. 6 (December 9, 1988), in *RGWX*, no. 11, 335–37; *Renmin ribao* [hereafter *RMRB*], June 1, 1993, p. 4.

35. Doc. 068, in *ZFZWH*, 711–18.

36. A Chinese Academy of Science (hereafter CAS) official stated that living expenses average $6,000, and an official from Jiangsu province estimated total costs at $8,000. China's English-language newspaper gave a range of $5,000 to $10,000 for visiting scholars studying for six months to a year; *China Daily* [hereafter *CD*], April 11, 1990, FBIS, April 12, 1990, pp. 40–41. China spends $15,000 for a graduate student to study in a two-year program, according to another report; *BR* (December 3, 1990): 33–34. A study of Chinese students and scholars (CSS) in the United States found annual support ranging from $5,000 to $15,000, monthly stipends from $400 to $760, and some receiving only airfare; see Carol Strevy, *Financial Status of Students/Scholars from the People's Republic of China on U.S. Campuses* (New York: Institute of International Education, 1989), 16.

37. Leo Orleans, "Chinese Students: An Emerging Issue in US-Chinese Relations?" *CEN* 16, no. 3 (1988): 3–7.

38. *CD*, March 31, 1992, p. 3, in Joint Publications Research Service (JPRS) CST-92-009, p. 127. Other news reports misinterpreted CAS figures of 7,500 staff, 5,500 visiting scholars, and 2,000 graduate students to mean a total of 15,000 personnel, thus double counting personnel; *Chronicle of Higher Education*, April 8, 1992, p. A44; *CEN* 20, no. 2 (1992): 31. See also *Xinhua*, December 1, 1993, FBIS, December 2, 1993, p. 25; interview, Yan Yongping, November 1992.

39. See *CEN* 9, no. 3 (1981): 12; *CEN* 10, no. 3 (1982): 1.

40. Ruth Hayhoe, *China's Universities and the Open Door* (Armonk, N.Y.: M.E. Sharpe, 1989), 124.

41. Doc. 20 (March 31, 1982) in *ZFZWH*, 774–77.

42. Doc. 101 (July 16, 1984) in *ZFZWH*, 788–92.

43. SC Doc. 107 (December 13, 1986).

44. SC Doc. 185 (December 26, 1984) in *RGWX*, no.7: 215–18.

45. The official gave an estimate of 170,000 persons, including both government and privately sponsored study abroad, but excluding those in language schools (primarily in Japan and Australia). Subtracting the 70,000 who went via government sponsorship yielded the 100,000 figure for the self-financed category.

46. *Xinhua*, May 20, 1991, FBIS, May 24, 1991, pp. 19–20.

47. See *CE* 12, no. 1 (Spring 1988): 73–103; JPRS CST-85-003, p. 23 (January 28, 1985); JPRS CST-85-005, p. 10 (February 20, 1985); JPRS CST-86-005, pp. 11–12 (February 11, 1986); JPRS CST-86-008, pp. 1–5 (March 1, 1986).

48. SC Doc. 185; *CE* 21, no.1 (Spring 1988): 25–28.

49. See Stanley Rosen, "The Role of Chinese Students at Home and Abroad as a Factor in Sino-American Relations," in *Building Sino-American Relations*, ed. William T. Tow (New York: Paragon House, 1991), 162–202.

50. Paul Pedersen, "The New China Syndrome: Delayed Return as a Viable Alternative to the 'Brain Drain' Perspective," National Association of Foreign Student Affairs (NAFSA) working paper 30 (1992), ERIC Doc. 356708.

51. Deng Zhiduan, "China's Brain Drain Problem: Causes, Consequences and Policy Options," *Journal of Contemporary China* 1, no.1 (1992): 13–24; Lan Shi, "Also on the Question of Foreign-trained Chinese Students," *CE* 23, no. 2 (Summer 1990): 69–74 (translated from *Shijie jingji daobao* [hereafter *SJD*], December 5, 1988, p. 13). In the same issue of *CE*, see also, Zhang Weiguo, "Set Your Sights Far to Appreciate the Scenery—An Interview with Members of the Visiting and Report-back Delegation of Chinese Students Abroad," pp. 77–79 (*SJD*, September 26, 1988, p. 15); and Yao Chun and Shen Gang, "Why Not Come Home, Chinese Students Abroad?—A Survey of the Situation of Shanghai Students Trained Abroad Between 1978 and 1985," pp. 56–62 (*SJD*, April 7, 1986), p. 8.

52. On the Taiwan experience, see Shirley Chang, "Causes of Brain Drain and Solutions: The Taiwan Experience," *Studies in Comparative International Development* 27, no. 1 (Spring 1992): 27–43; and "Taiwan's Brain Drain: A Case Study" (unpublished master's thesis, Pennsylvania State University, May, 1988), ERIC Doc. 293419.

53. *BR* June 10, 1991, p. 28; *CD*, October 19, 1992, p. 3.

54. Doc. 115 (July 16, 1981) in *ZFZWH*, 743–51.

55. *Xinhua*, December 29, 1993, FBIS, December 30, 1993, pp. B1–2.

56. Ruth Hayhoe, "Educational Exchanges and the Open Door," *CE* 21, no.1 (Spring 1988): 12. See article by Hua Xue, pp. 73–81, in same issue, as an example of the *Shenzhou xueren's* attempt to highlight the successful utilization of returnees.

57. *BR* (March 13, 1989): 23–24.

58. *RMRB*, October 23, 1992, p. 4; *CD*, January 24, 1992, FBIS, January 29, 1992, p. 40; FBIS, March 13, 1992, pp. 25–26 (*Xinhua*); *Xinhua*, April 18, 1992, JPRS CAR-92-027, p. 33; *CD*, May 22, 1993, p.1.

59. *BR* (January 20, 1992): 10; FBIS, January 16, 1992, p. 32 (*Xinhua*).

60. *CEN* 13, no. 1 (March 1985): 28; *CEN* 14, no. 1 (March 1986): 27–28; *RMRB*, July 13, 1985, p. 3.

61. *CEN* 15, nos. 3–4 (September 1987): 22.

62. *BR* (March 13, 1989): 25–26. After June 4, 1989, some postdoctoral students who had left China for research or to attend conferences failed to return on time prompting stricter regulations on travel; see Ministry of Personnel [hereafter MOP] Doc. No. 16 (December 27, 1989) *RGWX*, no. 12: 623–24.

63. *CD*, October 19, 1992, p. 3.

64. *Liaowang Overseas*, March 31, 1988, pp. 4–6, FBIS, April 15, 1988, pp. 27–30; *CD* March 16, 1989, p. 1; FBIS, February 21, 1992, p. 23 (*Zhongguo xinwenshe*); *RMRB Overseas Edition*, January 16, 1993, p. 1.

65. *CEN* 17, no.1 (March 1989): 23.

66. The 30,000 yuan average was reported in *CD*, May 22, 1993. Twenty million yuan was distributed among 400 returned scholars according to *CD*, January 24, 1992, p. 1, FBIS, January 29, 1992.

67. FBIS, March 28, 1990, p. 35 (*Xinhua*).

68. Interview, November 1992.

69. *BR* (June 10, 1991): 25.

70. *BR* (March 13, 1989): 28.

71. *CD*, March 16, 1989, p.1.

72. *BR* (May 6, 1991): 11; and *BR* (June 10, 1991): 25.

73. "Welcome to the CAS—Financial aid to visiting scholars and students studying abroad for working and conducting academic exchange in the CAS," (Bureau of Education, CAS, n.d.); *CD*, March 31, 1992, JPRS CST-92-009, p. 127.

74. *Xinhua*, December 1, 1993, FBIS, December 2, 1993, p. 25.

75. *CEN* 13, no. 3 (1985): 45.

76. *Xinhua*, February 12, 1989, FBIS, February 13, 1989, pp. 68–69; *Xinhua*, April 2, 1992, FBIS, April 3, 1992, pp. 4–5; Hong Kong AFP, April 7, 1992, FBIS, April 7, 1992, pp. 2–3; *Zhongguo tongxunshe*, April 27, 1992, FBIS, April 29, 1992, p. 68; *Xinhua*, May 12, 1992, FBIS, May 13, 1992, p. 11; *BR* (June 8, 1992): 35–36; *BR* (January 3, 1994): 24.

77. On Zhuhai, see *Shenzhou xueren*, 1992, no. 1, p. 21; On Pudong, see *China Exchange News*, Summer 1992, p. 31; FBIS, April 2, 1992, p. 62.

78. *BR* (September 13, 1993): 26 (trans. from *Zhongguo funubao*, May 21, 1993); "Shanghaishi guli chuguo liuxuerenyuan huiguo lai shanghai gongzuode ruogan guiding" (Regulations on encouraging personnel studying abroad to return to China and work in Shanghai), pamphlet, n.d.

79. Che Liao, "Chinese Students in the U.S. Support Domestic Student Movement," *China Spring Digest* (January/February 1988): 54–57.

80. *China Spring Digest* (January/February 1988): 10–15; FBIS, December 21, 1987, p. 15 (*Xinhua*).

81. SEdC, Doc. No. 210 (April 11, 1987) in *RGWX*, no.10: 340–42.

82. Two groups of university professors were sent by the government to visit students in Europe and Japan in the fall of 1989; *Zhongguo jiaoyu nianjian, 1949–1981*, 1990, p. 383.

83. Stanley Rosen, "The Role of Chinese Students," pp. 188–89. (Cites documents in *Pai Hsing* [Hong Kong], May 16, 1990, JPRS CAR-90-067, August 31, 1990, pp. 17–23. A translation of the same document by Shi Heping appeared as "Beijing's China Card," *Harper's* [September 1990]: 28–31.)

84. *Ching pao* (Hong Kong), September 5, 1991, pp. 47–48, FBIS, September 12, 1991, pp. 25–56.

85. Deng Xiaoping, "Gist of Speeches Made in Wuchang, Shenzhen, Zhuhai, and Shanghai, January 18–February 21, 1992," *BR* (February 7, 1994): 16.

86. *CD*, August 21, 1992, p. 1; *CD*, October 19, 1992, p. 3.

87. *Shenzhou xueren*, January 1993, p. 4.

88. *Zhongguo tongxunshe*, Feb. 25, 1992, FBIS, Feb. 27, 1992, p. 41.

89. From 1982 through 1992, a total of 6,346 People's Republic of China citizens received doctorates in science and engineering from universities in the United States. The numbers increased steadily during this period, with 4,557 earning degrees (72 percent) from 1990–1992; *Selected Data on Science and Engineering Doctorate Awards, 1992* (Washington, D.C.: National Science Foundation, 1993), 53–58.

# 7

## INTENDED CONSEQUENCES, UNINTENDED MEANS: THAILAND'S ACCELERATED RURAL DEVELOPMENT POLICY

*Fred R. von der Mehden*

Public policies often have unintended or negative consequences because they were inadequately planned, poorly implemented, or insufficiently funded, or because the conditions under which they were formulated changed. The reverse also occurs: policies have sometimes achieved desired results by departing from their implementation plans. This chapter assesses the Accelerated Rural Development (ARD) policy that was initiated in Thailand in 1964 to promote rural economic growth. It was seen by many people within and outside the Thai government as a means of decentralizing authority and developing better relationships between villagers and the central government.

ARD was envisioned as a megapolicy—it crossed sectoral boundaries, adopted an innovative approach to an important development problem, and employed a new organizational structure both to integrate planning and implementation and to generate large amounts of resources to promote rural development. The policy succeeded, but not for the expected reasons. ARD was never implemented along the lines originally proposed even though it generated many of the changes envisioned by its creators.

### THE DEVELOPMENT OF ARD

ARD emerged from the conditions of its time and from several government-supported rural development programs that preceded it. In 1956, the Royal Thai Government (RTG) established a community development program managed by the Ministry of Interior (MOI). Although its implementation was hampered by poor planning and by badly trained and ineffective staff, its goals were not unlike those of ARD. The community development program sought to increase local incomes through community action, to develop marketing facilities, to strengthen ties between the central government and villages by developing new patterns of communication, and to strengthen local governments.[1]

In 1962, the RTG's National Security Command (NSC) created a Mobile Development Unit program in Sakon Nakhon, Kalisin, and Nakhon Phanom.[2] Although it was not carefully planned and became mired in bureaucratic procedures, the mobile development units did have some success. They were expected to develop in three stages. In the first forty-five days, village headquarters composed of 120 people would be created to develop civic action projects in areas that were vulnerable to communist influence. A second phase of six months or less would be devoted to more intensive activities but with a reduced number of military to allow greater local initiative. In the third phase, the program would be transferred to an undefined group of local authorities. By 1967, however, the final stage had yet to be attained in the original units.

The framework for ARD emerged from the Northeast Development Program announced by Prime Minister Sarit in 1962 to counter the growing communist insurgency in the region. It was expected to spend about $300 million by 1967. Prior to the death of Sarit in December 1963, the Cabinet had appointed the Committee for Coordination and Operational Planning (CCOP) that worked with other government agencies and the NSC to initiate a new development program for the northeast region. The northeast provinces of Loei, Nong Khai, Nakhon Phanom, Sakon Nakhon, Ubol, and Udorn were chosen first because of their isolation and reported insurgency activities. At the same time, the United States Operations Mission (USOM) that administered the U.S. foreign aid program in Thailand was creating its own rural development program that would eventually be coordinated with RTG efforts. The project was delayed by Sarit's death, but his successor, Marshal Thanom Kittikachorn, revived it as the ARD program in 1964. Initially, the funding amounted to a little over $5 million, with more than 60 percent coming from the RTG and the rest from USOM.

ARD was conceived in response to the special conditions in northeast Thailand and the perceived dangers of communism in Southeast Asia. Northeast Thailand is a large plateau with inconsistent rainfall and poor soil. When ARD's programs began, the region had fifteen provinces and about nine million people, or about 30 percent of the Thai population. It was generally considered to be the poorest region in the Kingdom. About 95 percent of the population owned their own land and did not, therefore, have the tenancy problems that existed in central Thailand, but farmers in the northeast earned less than two-thirds of the income of their Central Plains counterparts. Income in the northeast averaged $43 to $50 a year, with a rich farmer seeing $100 in cash annually.[3] In addition, the region's population was increasing and putting additional pressure on the land.

Even prior to the perceived growth of communist influence in the region during the 1960s, the northeast was viewed by many Thai government officials in Bangkok as a haven for dissidents. Vietnam's Ho Chi Minh had lived in the area for a short time, and, as early as the 1930s, locals were arrested for allegedly cooperating with local and foreign communists.[4] During World War II, the Free Thai movement had been active in the region, and, after the war, northeast political leaders were constantly being charged with leftist or communist sympathies. Perceived ethnic differences and alleged discrimination by people from the Central Plains who led the RTG worsened a tense situation. Opposition leaders from the area faced arrest and even death from a Thai government that saw them as subversives.[5]

The perceived dangers of communism increased in the early 1960s with the growing conflict in Vietnam. The threatening rhetoric emanating from the People's Republic of China (PRC), which was in the initial throes of the Cultural Revolution, further worried Thailand's leaders. These worries were exacerbated by the growing number of supposedly communist-inspired incidents in the northeast. In 1962, the Voice of the People of Thailand was broadcasting from Laos, and a clandestine radio station in southern China began operations later. In 1964, the PRC announced the formation of the Thailand Independence Movement that called for the overthrow of the Bangkok regime. That same year the Thai Patriotic Front was formed, and the following year the two organizations reportedly merged. A year later the Chinese foreign minister, Chen Yi, announced that Thailand was a target for liberation, and, shortly thereafter, the Red Guard-run *Radio Peking* began to attack the Thanom-Praphat government and its alliance with the United States.

Meanwhile, insurgency was increasing in northeast Thailand. The first guerrilla attack on RTG forces took place on August 7, 1965, in Nakhon Phanom. Attacks were followed by insurgent propaganda sessions in villages, assassinations of village leaders and informers, and occasional raids on RTG military units. In 1967, the *New York Times* reported that 1,700 armed insurgents and 15,000 active sympathizers were in northeast Thailand.[6] The following year, the RTG estimated that there were 2,000 communist insurgents and 10,000 village sympathizers in the area.[7] Figures were, of course, unreliable—many incidents were not verified or simply involved banditry. But the combination of rhetoric from neighboring communist states, rumors of arms purchases abroad by communists and their sympathizers, and the increase in incidents of insurgency all raised the specter of Thailand as "another Vietnam." The Thai and U.S. governments began to seek ways of countering the growing threat of communism in the Kingdom, particularly in the northeast. In part, the perceived solution was to adopt traditional military counterinsurgency measures, including an expansion of the RTG army and police presence in the region.

Many of the staff in USOM, however, wanted to address the underlying social and economic problems that made the rural population vulnerable to insurgency. The U.S. aid program had long been involved in rural development programs in Thailand. From 1951 through 1953, it had provided $260 million in grants and $54 million in development loans.[8] In the mid-1960s, many other U.S. officials saw rural development as one more means of supporting U.S. efforts in the ongoing Indo-China war. The U.S. Embassy regarded foreign aid largely as a means of paying the rent for air bases in northeast Thailand. As U.S. involvement in Indo-China increased, Washington emphasized the need to establish more air bases in Thailand for search-and-rescue missions, for maintenance of the Royal Lao Air Force and planes under contract to the Central Intelligence Agency, and for other military operations in Indo-China. Officially under Thai sovereignty, but operated by the U.S. military, airfields were built or expanded in places such as Korat, Ubol, Udorn, and Nakhon Phanom. Ultimately the number of U.S. forces either based in the northeast or providing logistical support reached 35,000 men.

These operations were not directed toward insurgency in Thailand but supported U.S. military operations in Indo-China. Some of the aid, however, would slow the growing insurgency and the spread of conflict to Thailand. This was particularly true of police and local militia programs. While much of U.S. foreign aid for the improvement of the Thai police was not directed toward insurgency-prone rural areas, efforts were made to expand and improve the efficiency of the police presence in these areas. USOM also provided support to Thai village militia programs in insurgency areas and even carried out evaluations of their results after the RTG could not agree on how they were to be done. Thus, in 1967, of the $49.8 million that the United States gave in aid to Thailand, $17.1 million was allocated to civil police, $1.6 million for police development programs in remote areas, $781,000 for village radios, and $109,000 for support of village security units.[9]

Although it was ostensibly a rural development program, ARD was also designed to counter insurgency. One of its five objectives was to increase government surveillance over vulnerable areas by coordinating ARD programs with military police commands and by closely observing the activities of the local population.[10] The military and police saw important security elements in ARD's funding of rural road networks.

ARD began in 1964 in six *changwad* (provinces) in the northeast region— Ubol, Nakhon Phanom, Sakon Nakhon, Udorn Thani, Nong Khai, and Loei— all of which were considered provinces with existing or potential insurgency activities. By 1969, ARD covered twenty-two *changwad* and was then extended to other areas in the Kingdom. By 1975, ARD programs were in forty-one provinces—sixteen in the northeast, eleven in the north, nine in the south, and five in the central region. During this period, ARD's budget rose to 715 million baht. U.S. aid to ARD also increased annually until it became the largest component of U.S. foreign assistance to Thailand. From 1964 to 1975, the United States provided ARD with 1.2 billion baht, of which 167.3 million went to experts, 116.9 million was paid to contractors, 34.4 million was used for training, and 917.3 million went to purchase equipment.

## Coordination

Thailand's bureaucrats—like others in Southeast Asia—had considerable difficulty coordinating their activities among ministries and even among departments within the same ministry. Within the powerful MOI, for example, even when Marshal Praphat was its head, conflicts arose regularly over policy and the allocation of funds. Overt antagonism often emerged among various departments. Historically, rural development in Thailand suffered from this lack of coordination. To ameliorate this problem, ARD was to be placed outside the normal administrative structure. In 1963, the Sarit government had formed CCOP to develop ARD. At the end of 1965, the CCOP was replaced by the Central Committee for Accelerated Rural Development (CARD) under the leadership of General Praphat. CARD was initially composed of high-level representatives of government agencies concerned with rural development. These representatives would provide general policy guidance. This structure on the Thai side was reflected in USOM where, in 1962, a Rural Affairs Coordinating Committee had been formed to discuss possible programs to deal with the increasing problems of rural insurgency.

The most innovative national administrative change was the formation of the Office of Accelerated Rural Development. Initially the program had been put under the Department of Local Administration (DOLA) in the MOI and NSC. NSC was to choose *changwads* to be included in the program, and DOLA was to implement projects. After a year, however, ARD was shifted to the prime minister's office in order to reduce traditional ministerial conflicts. The office of ARD was to coordinate and administer the ARD program under the direction of Prasong Sukhum, a U.S.-trained civil servant. It was to be independent of old rivalries, capable of bringing into its ranks competent officials from other departments, and protected by the legitimacy of its location in the prime minister's office.

## Decentralization

ARD was also decentralized in order to achieve better coordination. At the provincial level, this rural development program was to be supervised by the governor, who would provide the overall authority for its implementation through a deputy governor in charge of ARD in that province. Within general guidelines formulated by CARD, each province was to develop its own plans in cooperation with other provincial administrative units and local authorities. The governor would take responsibility for ARD's financial operations in the province and could use ARD funds to encourage coordination. RTG and USOM planners believed that the provincial administrators would know more about local needs, and their participation would enable ARD to deal more effectively with local problems. In theory, the district officer was to assess villagers' views and pass them up to the provincial authorities or provincial legislature (*sapha-tambon*).

Some USOM officials believed that this aspect of ARD would help counter insurgency in that decentralization would further democratize the Thai political system. Granting more power to governors who would make decisions with local participation would help weaken the highly centralized Thai bureaucracy. Some in the USOM, perhaps naively, saw in the governor a representative of local interests who would promote greater pluralism in the Thai government. This was not a novel perception; in fact, in the early 1950s, the governors themselves argued for more power by claiming that democratization was associated with decentralization because the latter would bring government closer to the people.[11]

## Public Works

ARD's main objective was to develop a rural road network to bring peasants living in more isolated villages into contact with the outside world. A USOM study undertaken in the mid-1960s had found that during the rainy season a majority of villages in one part of the northeast could not be reached even with four-wheel-drive vehicles. The new roads would open markets for the peasants and make dissemination of agricultural innovations easier. But they could also help to suppress communist activity by making it easier for government forces to move into isolated areas and increase the surveillance capacities of local authorities. The rural roads would also provide access for district and provincial authorities to villages and extend programs that would increase the economic and social well-being of the rural people. ARD received funds for agricultural development projects such as sericulture and swine raising, agribusiness, and water resources development. But ARD was to be the means, the United States hoped, for promoting cooperation among Thai government ministries to improve education, agriculture, and community development in villages along these roads. The interministerial representation on CARD would be reflected in an integrated rural development program supported by several ministries under ARD's general leadership working through the provincial governors.

## Winning Loyalty

One of the main arguments for the creation of a rural development program in northeast Thailand in the early 1960s, as noted earlier, was to counter communist insurgency. One of ARD's primary goals was "winning the loyalty of the villagers for the Thai Government by eliminating grievances and demonstrating that the government can function and act in the people's interest."[12] By meeting the villagers' "felt needs," ARD was supposed to change both their attitudes and their behavior toward the RTG and the insurgents.[13] This hope was at the core of the "other war" strategy. Accordingly, ARD's provincial, district, and local planning processes were to be implemented by collaboration among representatives of all levels of government who would develop appropriate local projects. In addition, USOM supported a village democracy program that was intended to educate and encourage the villagers to identify and promote their local needs.

## ARD IN ACTION: THE FIRST DECADE

U.S. support for ARD was discontinued in the mid-1970s after the war in Vietnam ended. ARD then became almost entirely a Thai government program. How did ARD perform during its first full decade of operation in achieving its three goals of coordination, decentralization, and integrated rural development during a time when the United States was pulling out of Indo-China and reducing its support of counterinsurgency programs in Southeast Asia? Some progress was made toward each of these goals, but not necessarily in the ways envisioned by ARD's original planners.

### Coordination

During the early years, ARD was to introduce a new era of cooperation among ministries of the Thai government. But neither U.S. academics nor technicians in the field paid much attention to ARD after 1975. Initially, CARD was formed to coordinate ministries at the national level, but funds were also provided to the provincial governor for promoting local cooperation. Among the central ministries, however, traditional bureaucratic divisiveness continued. Funds that were allocated through ARD were used to extend older departmental projects that were rarely integrated with others. Attempts to plan and implement ARD projects at the provincial level were resented by officials at other levels of the Thai government who considered these new practices a usurpation of their traditional roles.

Tensions were exacerbated by actions of both the MOI and its head, Marshal Praphat, who was the second most powerful figure in Thailand in the late 1960s and was viewed by other officials of the RTG as having imperial bureaucratic ambitions. ARD was now perceived to be simply another MOI program. Its director, General Chamnarn Yuvapurna, was considered a protegé of Praphat even though he was also a knowledgeable and aggressive supporter of rural development. The MOI during this period was challenging the authority of the Ministries of Education and Agriculture by attempting to transfer some of their programs to its own organization. Relations with the Ministry of Agriculture became so bad during ARD's early years that USOM had difficulty funding agricultural projects because the U.S. was viewed as supporting MOI and *changwad* administration.

In modern times, the provincial governor has been responsible to the Office of the Undersecretary in the MOI and formally appointed by the King. Before ARD was created, the governor had only DOLA staff, including the deputy governor (*Palad Changwad*), who supervised DOLA officials in the province; the provincial clerk (*Cha Changwad*), whose staff maintained records and correspondence; the chief financial officer (*Samiantra Changwad* or Keeper of the Official Seal); the local inspector in charge of supervising local government; and the governor's private secretary. The extent of the governor's actual powers at the time was open to some dispute. The governor certainly maintained authority over DOLA officials at the provincial and district levels, including the *Nai Amphur*. As the provincial representative of the MOI, he supposedly had some authority over the police and community development departments. But the trend toward increasing specialization of services and better education of technical personnel placed the governor—in fact, if not in law—more and more in the position of a general manager concerned with overall supervision and control and gave technical personnel more independence, particularly in such strong agencies as education and public health.[14]

How much power each governor really had depended on the personality and capabilities of the individual holding the office. A competent governor with a strong personality could successfully manage conflicting personnel and provide some degree of coordination. But it was the hope of USOM and the MOI that ARD would increase the authority of the governor. An ARD deputy governor was added to his staff to supervise the planning and implementation of the provincial ARD program. The governor became the provincial ARD director and was ultimately responsible for projects in his area. More than 5,000 ARD personnel were added to the original twenty-seven ARD *changwads*, each having an engineering staff headed by a graduate engineer. An average of $1.2 million in construction equipment was provided to each province under the control of the governor's staff.

In ARD's initial years of operation during the mid-1960s, serious problems arose that could not be solved, even by the end of the decade. While ARD funds were channeled through the governor, individual departments also received support, and this gave technical departments some degree of independence. But the variety of organizations with ARD funds, in addition to the departmentally based ARD projects, often left the governor's staff inadequately informed about ARD activities and weakened its ability to coordinate programs in the province. It took some time before the central administration of ARD was firmly established. In this sense, decentralization meant that there was little supervision of provincial programs. Also, as ARD geared up its operations, provincial officials were frequently away for meetings in Bangkok or for training.[15] This division of responsibility only exacerbated a perennial problem in isolated provinces where senior staff tended to "go home" to Bangkok on weekends. Many of the ARD staff were young, urban, college-educated civil servants and contract workers with little departmental loyalty or provincial or local experience. This further added to bureaucratic tensions.[16]

### Integrated Rural Development

ARD was planned as an integrated rural development program that would encompass a wide range of activities, but the most easily measured output of the ARD program was always the number of kilometers of all-weather road constructed.[17] Thus, it should not be surprising that this component of ARD always received the most attention. By 1969, ARD had built and repaired about 1,735 kilometers of road and 1,293 service tracks and village access roads. In addition, it undertook thirty-six land-clearing projects, constructed and repaired 1,307 shallow wells, made 181 water storage ponds, and built 115 small dams. By 1971, it had extended more than 3,700 kilometers of roads connecting about 3,000 villages, which still put the ratio of roads to population in the northeast significantly lower than in other Southeast Asian countries such as Malaysia, Vietnam, and the Philippines. The pace of construction increased as ARD resolved some of the problems of planning, construction, and maintenance that had plagued its early years. By 1975, ARD was maintaining 4,900 roads in the northeast and 10,000 roads in the north.

## ARD'S DEVELOPMENT, 1970–1993

By 1970, ARD's budget was increased markedly, and the program expanded in personnel, provinces covered, and projects undertaken. ARD also went through important changes in its goals and administrative structure.

### ARD Expansion

From the original six northeastern provinces designated in 1964, ARD was extended to twenty-two provinces by 1970 and forty-two provinces by 1975. In 1978 and 1979, fourteen more provinces were added, primarily in the central region, and in 1982, Mukdahan, which had previously been part of Nakhon Phanom, received its own ARD program. In 1989, ARD was further extended to fifteen more central and southern provinces, and, in 1991, the government made it a national program covering the entire Kingdom except for Bangkok.

During these years, ARD's budget grew substantially, more than doubling in some years. As democracy took hold in Thailand in the 1980s, politicians saw ARD as a means of meeting constituents' demands for infrastructure improvements in their districts. In some years, ARD received more funding from

Parliament than its administrators sought. In 1992, for example, Parliament's amendment increased ARD's budget by 1.9 billion baht ($76 million). As ARD extended into more provinces, more politicians were interested in seeing its activities increased, and more legislators attempted to influence the way ARD projects were developed.

The size of the ARD staff also grew significantly, increasing to 13,215 in 1993. The characteristics of senior staff also began to change. The early reliance on foreign engineers waned as more Thai engineers were trained. The initial pattern of hiring young social science university graduates also gave way to hiring engineers and other technical personnel.

All of this was occurring at the same time that U.S. aid to ARD was in sharp decline. When U.S. aid ended, ARD turned to support from other nations and international organizations. In its initial ten years of operation, the preponderance of non-Thai funding was from the United States, ultimately totaling 1,236,391,000 baht ($61.8 million). This support came in the form of training, equipment, contractors, experts, and administrative assistance, all of which ended as Thailand lost its strategic significance to the United States during its withdrawal from Indo-China. No other country was to provide as much financial support to ARD as did the United States, but as U.S. aid was phased out in the mid-1970s, other donors came forward. The World Bank provided loans, and other governments supported training, equipment, infrastructure, experts, and projects. Aid came from Germany, Israel, Australia, Italy, Canada, Japan, and the United Kingdom. Ultimately, the total amount of aid from these sources was higher than that given by the United States from 1964 to 1975, but unlike U.S. aid, this support tended to be more for specific projects or for specific geographic areas in Thailand. For its part, ARD was to become a model for development and provided some training in road building and water resource improvement for personnel from other Third World countries, especially Africa.

ARD's goals also changed over the years. The initial emphasis on counterinsurgency declined as the perceived domestic dangers from communism diminished and the U.S. role in ARD ended. According to Thai sources, the decline in counterinsurgency rhetoric came in the mid-1970s as U.S. involvement came to a close. By the early 1980s, the RTG declared victory over the domestic communist insurgency, and an ARD publication printed for foreigners made only passing reference to what had been learned about dealing with rural insurgency.[18] Security goals were not entirely eliminated, however, and are still cited as a justification for ARD activities in some parts of the country where military facilities are located as well as for road building in national parks.

Beginning in 1982 during the period when Prem Tinsulanond was prime minister, ARD was given the ambitious mission of ending rural poverty. By the 1990s, however, the program was still allocating the largest part of its budget to road building, despite the government declaration that water resources improvement and development of rural economic and social infrastructure were to be among its highest priorities. Rural road construction was to remain ARD's greatest success. By 1993, there was almost no major village in the north or northeast that could not be reached by motor vehicle throughout the year. And even when road construction was essentially completed, ARD turned the bulk of its attention to improving and maintaining existing roads.

A variety of other ARD programs such as aid for farmer training, the provision of tools and equipment, creation of cooperatives, and support for agribusiness projects with bank credit received lower priority for funding. Livestock promotion, occupational training, village fisheries, irrigation, and experiments in setting up rural stores selling goods at controlled prices fared little better in ARD's budget. ARD did supply personnel and equipment for royal projects initiated by the king, largely in provinces with royal palaces such as Sakon Nakhon, Hua Hin, and Chiangmai. Some of these projects were subsidized from royal funds, but others were supported by ARD.

Training was an important program for ARD. In the beginning, it was necessary to train Thais in engineering, administration, and accounting. Special educational facilities were established, or cooperative arrangements were made with other institutions. For example, engineering education was developed in cooperation with the College of Technology at Korat, training in staff development with the Mass Communication Organization, training in management with the Management Training and Productivity Center, and organization development with the Bangkok Metropolitan Office. Local youth programs were particularly important because they allowed ARD to give strong emphasis to leadership as well as to occupational and community development training. ARD also supported a six-month training program for village and subdistrict (*tambon*) health workers.

Relationships between ARD and local, provincial, and national levels of the bureaucracy were developed throughout the program's history. ARD initially sought to develop its policies in consultation with various national ministries and to decentralize and integrate rural development programs at the provincial and district levels. But ARD never met the goals envisioned by USOM. Coordination and decentralization problems plagued all of ARD's relations with other ministries.

### ARD as Facilitator

Any assessment of ARD must ask a final question: What was the major accomplishment of the ARD program in rural Thailand? Clearly, ARD did not develop into the integrated rural development program initially envisioned by either the Thai government or USOM. But it did become a successful builder of rural roads and an active participant in the country's efforts to improve village water resources. There have been significant changes in the initial *changwads*

covered by ARD in the northeast and north: major improvements in communications, electricity, goods available at the local level, housing, drinking water,
mechanization of agriculture, health, and education. These positive changes,
however, have been accompanied by low levels of economic growth for the
farmer and by debt, single cropping, and a lack of employment opportunities
in the region. In spite of improvements, interviews with village leaders in 1993
revealed widespread complaints of low incomes, a lack of sufficient agricultural
water, and heavy debts to commercial and agricultural banks and money
lenders. Many leaders noted difficulties in obtaining proper land ownership
documents. Although income had increased, the basic needs of villagers had
also changed as Thailand modernized—rural people sought not only basic
necessities but also televisions, modern houses, and mechanical plows. Television stimulated new appetites for the appurtenances of modern life that were
difficult to satisfy with the incomes generated largely from single crop farms in
the northeast. And many of the villages still lack sufficient water for drinking
and agriculture as well as adequate health facilities. Yet, on balance, the positive
changes in life styles and amenities between 1966 and 1993 are readily apparent.

Clearly, there were often important variations in how programs were administered at the provincial and district levels. Many of the changes that are now
taking place began only in the past decade, and the bureaucracy is still not
moving at a consistent pace in meeting demands. Yet, ARD has been a facilitator
of integration and decentralization. In 1966, a cost-benefit study of roads
prepared by the USOM Research Division noted that although roads were
important for development, they were "only part of an important mix, including land, labor, markets, supervised credit, and the establishment of public
services. The existence of transportation facilities will not guarantee the establishment of public services; but if this is an avowed objective of the government
and important human resources are committed to the program, roads will help
get more 'mileage' from these resources."[19]

That analysis found that increased governmental activity at almost every level
came with improved roads. More villagers visited the district office, *amphur*
officials had one less excuse not to go to the villages, and the work load increased
for the *amphur* administration. Similarly, a 1970 study of ARD road impacts
reported "a substantial increase in government services, in the mobility of
officials, and in the expansion of government facilities where new roads were
opened."[20]

It was not until Prime Minister Prem took action in the early 1980s, however,
that there was significant pressure from Bangkok to coordinate ARD programs
at the provincial and district levels, and it was during the 1980s that democracy
began to take hold in rural Thailand. Recent administrations have continued to
push for integration and decentralization. For example, in 1993, Prime Minister
Chuan Leekpai reemphasized the desirability of decentralization and the need
for provincial officials to work with local representatives.[21] But few of these

efforts would have been successful without the rural road network established by ARD. In the 1960s, poor roads made travel to and from the villages and districts difficult, and ministerial policies did not encourage official coordination or interaction with villagers. And even if there had been policies to bring integrated development projects to the villages, it would have been extremely difficult for officials to reach most rural areas. Before the road network was extended by ARD, it took village leaders two to three days to visit a district office; the same journey now takes less than an hour. Because of inadequate roads, district agriculture officers did not visit villages. As roads were extended and improved, the Ministry of Agriculture hired more local personnel and expected its officers to visit villages regularly to provide technical advice, to help develop the local economy, and to collect social information. This information was put on computer and fed into the development index used by provincial authorities to establish priorities for village and *tambon* projects.

All of these changes have had an homogenizing effect on rural Thailand by diminishing local cultural loyalties and reinforcing the sense of being part of a single Thai culture. This is not the kind of political, progovernment, anticommunist loyalty sought by the initial advocates of ARD, but roads and electricity have strengthened economic and political interaction with the rest of the Kingdom.

## CONCLUSIONS

ARD accomplished many of its goals, but not always in the ways its designers intended. It was a program that transcended sectoral boundaries, that facilitated coordination and integration of ministerial programs, and that helped to decentralize more decision making to the local and provincial government levels. There have been important positive changes in rural living conditions since the ARD program began. Success in achieving those goals can, of course, be attributed to rapid national economic growth and more stable political conditions in Thailand. But without the ARD road network, the disparities in income and wealth between the Bangkok metropolitan area and the rural regions of Thailand would undoubtedly have been wider and the accomplishments in transforming rural living conditions would have been weaker. In addition, ARD became a model for projects in other countries. ARD, as it was implemented, produced significant side effects that went well beyond those of the road-building projects that ultimately dominated the program. It brought improvements in local economies, communications, and education as well as the provision of public services. These results were what ARD's originators had hoped for, but not what observers expected as it developed in its early years as a road-building program.

Thus, as Montgomery observed of other megapolicies adopted by governments in Asia and the Pacific Basin, the side effects of ARD policies outweighed its direct effects.[22] Montgomery notes that "as megapolicies fade into history, their repercussions are often unexpected, dispersed, and relatively remote from their original objectives"; this was particularly true of ARD.

## NOTES

1. Joint Thai-U.S. Military and Development Center, *Public Administrative Environment in Nakhon Phanom* (Bangkok: Joint Thai-U.S. Military and Development Center, 1967), 4.5.24.

2. Lee Huff, "Mobile Development Unit Follow-Up" (Bangkok: Joint Thai-U.S. Military Research and Development Center, 1964).

3. Kenneth Young, "Thailand: The Northeast," *Asia* 6 (Autumn 1966): 7–8.

4. Charles Keyes, "Isan: Regionalism in Northeast Thailand," data paper no. 65, Cornell University Southeast Asia Program, Ithaca, N.Y., 1967, p. 22.

5. David Wilson, "Thailand and Marxism," in *Marxism in Southeast Asia*, ed. Frank Trager (Stanford, Calif.: Stanford University Press, 1959), 81.

6. Unsigned article, "Power Struggle in Thailand Slows Drive on Rebels," *New York Times*, October 6, 1967, p. 14.

7. See Robert Muscat, *Thailand and the United States: Development, Security and Foreign Aid* (New York: Columbia University Press, 1990).

8. Orlin Scoville and James Dalton, "Rural Development in Thailand: The ARD Program," *Journal of Developing Areas* 9, no. 1 (1974): 54.

9. United States Operations Mission [hereafter USOM], *The US/AID Program in Thailand* (Bangkok: USOM, 1968), 5.

10. United States Operations Mission, *Accelerated Rural Development Agreement: Project Agreement no. 163–7030* (Bangkok: USOM, 1967), 8.

11. Fred Riggs, *Thailand: The Modernization of a Bureaucratic Polity* (Honolulu: East-West Center, 1966).

12. United States Operations Mission, *Evaluation Report: Joint Thai-USOM Evaluation of the Accelerated Rural Development Project* (Bangkok: Thai-American Audio Visual Service, 1965), 166.

13. For an analysis of the indicators of counter-insurgency and modernization associated with the ARD project, see Robert E. Krug, Paul A. Schwarz, and Suchitra Bhakdi, "Measuring Village Commitment to Development," in *Values and Development: Appraising Asian Experience*, ed. Harold Lasswell, Daniel Lerner, and John D. Montgomery (Cambridge, Mass.: MIT Press, 1976), 104–32.

14. See Frederick Horrigan, *Local Government and Administration in Thailand: A Study of Institutions and Their Cultural Setting* (Ph.D. diss., Indiana University, 1959).

15. John Limbert, *Accelerated Rural Development for the Changwads of Loei and Udon* (Bangkok: TOAID A–628, 1965), 11.

16. Scoville and Dalton, "Rural Development," 63.

17. United States Operations Mission, *Non-Capital Project Paper: Accelerated Rural Development* (Bangkok: USOM, 1969), 7.

18. Office of Rural Development, *Accelerated Rural Development* (Bangkok: Ministry of the Interior, 1982), 2.

19. United States Operations Mission, *A Cost-Benefit Study of Roads in North and Northeast Thailand* (Bangkok: USOM Research Division, 1966), quote at 36.

20. J. Dalton, *Goals and Work of ARD's Research and Evaluation Divisions-Annex C* (Bangkok: Office of Accelerated Rural Development, 1970).

21. Unsigned article, "PM warns officials not to waste funds in rural budget," *Bangkok Post,* June 4, 1993, p. 17.

22. John D. Montgomery, "Beyond Good Policies," see Chapter 1.

# 8

# AGRO-INDUSTRIAL DEVELOPMENT
# POLICIES IN KOREA, 1910–1970

*Vijaya Ramachandran*

The combination of decisions that produced Korea's rapid industrial growth began with several decades of investment in agriculture. Korean support of the agricultural sector evolved into a general approach that went far beyond the traditional role of government. That role emerged from policy experiments in the agricultural sector and spread to other sectors, such as transportation, communications, and, eventually, industrial production. Early expectations about the role of government in promoting private enterprise changed drastically during the period of Japanese colonial rule and continued its course during the period following the Korean War. Between 1910 and 1938, the government created new organizations to administer agricultural policy, made substantial investments in infrastructure and productive inputs, and established new institutions whose structure was replicated in other sectors as development proceeded. In the end, the agricultural policies formulated to increase production during the Japanese colonization of Korea via intensification of land use became the prototype of agricultural growth in the rest of East Asia. The replicability of the Korean approach is also relevant for other developing countries that are land scarce and labor rich.

Repeated policy experiments have shown that industrialization without adequate development of the agricultural sector has resulted either in a low or negative growth rate or in a highly skewed income distribution in which a large majority of the population is unable to participate in the process of economic development.[1] From the beginning of Japanese colonization in 1910, investments in agriculture have aimed at increasing food production. The infrastructure investments associated with that goal contributed eventually to general economic growth. They proved to be vital, not only for raising rural incomes but also for enabling the transformation into an industrialized economy.[2] Such a rise in agricultural productivity appears to be essential to an industrial takeoff, no matter what part of the world is under consideration.

It was once thought that South Korea was an exception to this rule. A major study of the South Korean economy undertaken by the Council on East Asian Studies at Harvard University concluded in 1980 that the Korean government had not invested significantly in agriculture during the first stage of the development process and, consequently, that rural Korea's development policies differed from those of many other developing countries. It is, in fact, true that after independence there was no agricultural revolution that preceded development in the other sectors of the Korean economy. Contrary to the prevailing wisdom on the linkages between agricultural growth and industrialization, it appeared that agriculture had benefited from the industrial and export boom rather than the reverse. There was thought to be growth in the agricultural sector only as a consequence of growth in manufacturing and not vice versa. Consequently, Korean agricultural policy was considered a significant departure from the accepted paradigm to develop agriculture in order to industrialize. The authors conceded that although agriculture was given some attention, farm policies during the fifteen-year period from 1945 to 1960 were subordinated to the government's concern with industry and general economic stability. Subsequent to this analysis, a general consensus gradually emerged that Korea had industrialized without substantial growth in the agricultural sector.

In historical perspective, however, this view is misleading. In fact, a megapolicy involving simultaneous development of several sectors had begun to emerge even before independence.[3] Indeed, the Korean case exemplified a massive effort of land intensification in Asia and might be regarded as a prototype for the model of East Asian growth that includes new technology and intensified labor use as key elements. What needs to be explained is not how Korea ignored agriculture in the development process but how a combined set of policies integrating rural and industrial investments and institutional changes emerged over a period of decades.

## THE COLONIAL PERIOD, 1910–1940

The Japanese colonizers placed a high priority on institutional, technical, and economic policies to promote agriculture. The magnitude and scope of Japanese investment in Korea clearly reveals that Japan intended its annexation of the Korean peninsula to be permanent. Immediately after full annexation of the Korean peninsula, the colonial office undertook land reform. It completed a cadastral survey that enabled a complete evaluation of size and value of farm holdings, permitted private ownership status of land, and implemented a new system of taxation. The goal of this exercise was to ensure that Korea provided a steady supply of food to Japan. Consequently, various Korean and Western scholars have described it as exploitative; one scholar even refers to the colonial period as a "useless inheritance."[4] However, the actual effects of colonization were quite complicated. The demand for rice from Tokyo became even stronger after the Japanese Rice Riot of 1918, which was caused by poor harvests and high rice prices in Tokyo. After this event, the colonial government in Korea made a massive investment in the agricultural sector in order to provide food to Japan, and the process of agricultural development began in earnest.

Colonial investment in the agricultural sector in Korea proved to have far-reaching effects. Although the goal was to increase food supply to Japan, the colonial government made several important changes in the agricultural sector that were beneficial to the local population. Colonial investments were made in three major sectors: investment in inputs; investment in infrastructure, including roads and irrigation systems; and investment in new technology, such as multiple cropping techniques and new seed varieties. The effects of these investments were to increase production, particularly of rice, and to create a much-needed source of food for the Japanese population. Subsequently, these investments would have high payoffs for the process of industrialization as well.

A new system of private property rights implemented by the Japanese government proved to be far superior to the preexisting feudal system. Japanese landlords took over ownership but rented land to Korean farmers, and a system of property rights came into being that lowered risk for both Japanese landlords and Korean farmers. Tenants paid rent in order to cultivate land, while landlords paid taxes to the government; reasonable and stable rates were observed in both situations. Landlord-tenant disputes were resolved by law, and the dissipation of rent for the purchase of political patronage no longer occurred. Tenancy of the land became widespread; as much as 54 percent of agricultural land was cultivated by tenant farmers by the early 1930s. Tenancy rates reached almost 60 percent by the end of the colonial period. Although land ownership was highly skewed (less than 3 percent of the population owned two-thirds of the land), and much of the land was owned by Japanese landlords, the new system resulted in an increase in rice production; provided greater incentives for tenant farmers than the old system of arbitrary use charges; lowered risks associated with production by establishing stable rental rates; and, with the assistance of government investment in infrastructure, encouraged landlords to invest in fertilizer and new technology for use by tenant farmers. Most importantly, these actions significantly transformed the expectations of the population regarding the role of the government in serving agricultural development. These expectations remained unchanged after the Korean War and became critical to the South Korean government's efforts to control the process of rapid industrialization.

Colonial investment emphasized growth in infrastructure (see Table 8.1). Investment in irrigation and roads as a fraction of total expenditure was between

Table 8.1
Output and Expenditure, 1910–1938

|  | 1910–1919 | 1920–1929 | 1930–1938 | 1910–1938 |
|---|---|---|---|---|
| Infrastructure expenditure as a percentage of revenues | 0.30 | 0.39 | 0.43 | 0.37 |
| Infrastructure expenditure as a percentage of total expenditure | 0.37 | 0.43 | 0.47 | 0.43 |
| Terms of trade (percentage of agriculture to manufactured goods) | 0.83 | 0.80 | 0.88 | 0.84 |
| Value of rice exports* (growth rate in percentage) | 72.53 (11.7) | 150.32 (8.37) | 294.06 (26.43) | 156.46 (9.30) |
| Volume of rice production** (growth rate in percentage) | 77.26 (2.83) | 88.06 (1.43) | 116.01 (8.06) | 93.57 (4.0) |
| Value of land tax*** | 506.78 | 734.70 | 7052.15 | 3167.11 |

*Notes:* * Value of rice exports is in million yen in 1934 constant prices.
     ** Volume of rice production index is based on 1934 = 100.
     *** Value of land tax is in 1000 yen in 1934 constant prices.

*Sources:* The main source of data is a collection of statistics on colonial Japan: Toshiyuki Mizoguchi and Mataji Umemura, eds., *Basic Economic Statistics of Former Japanese Colonies, 1895–1938* (Tokyo: Toyo Keizai Shinposha, 1988). Other data are taken from the dissertations of two scholars of Korean economic growth: Sung Hwan Ban, *The Long-Run Productivity Growth in Korean Agricultural Development, 1910–1968* (Ph.D. diss., University of Minnesota, 1971); and Sang-Chul Suh, *Growth and Structural Changes in the Korean Economy, 1910–1940* (Cambridge: Council on East Asian Studies, Harvard University, 1978). These data are fairly accurate given the emphasis on good recordkeeping by the colonial government.

35 and 50 percent, indicating clearly that one of the priorities of the colonial government was to create an infrastructural base in rural areas. Although a system of land taxation was put into place soon after full annexation occurred, land tax revenues as a percentage of irrigation investments rarely exceeded 10 percent, indicating that investment in rural areas greatly exceeded any taxation of these areas. Tax revenues rose only toward the very end of the colonial period as war preparations began in Tokyo. As a fraction of government revenues, investment in irrigation and roads was between 30 and 43 percent for the entire colonial period. During this time, area under irrigation rose from under 10,000 hectares to over 160,000 hectares, and average annual growth in irrigated land area was around 18 percent.

These policies were not accidents of casual, unrelated decisions. The colonial government was aware of the scarcity of arable land and invested in land intensification soon after annexation, with the goal of creating a permanent and effective source of supply of the japonica variety of rice for consumption in Japan. Institutions of property rights and taxation were designed from the outset to realize this goal, as were substantial investments in inputs and infrastructure—the costs of which greatly exceeded land revenues.

The investments made after the Japanese Rice Riot of 1918 resulted in very rapid development of the agricultural sector. The pattern of expenditures and output for each of the three decades of colonial rule shows that expenditures in the rural sector were very high; rice production and exports grew rapidly, at 4 and 9 percent per year respectively.

Growth was highest in the last decade of colonization as various investments in infrastructure and agricultural inputs (particularly fertilizer) were put into place. Rice production grew in the colonial period at an average annual rate of 4 percent a year; the majority of growth occurred in the last decade of colonial rule as returns from various investments in inputs and infrastructure were realized. Rice exports, growing at 26 percent a year as Korea became a critical food source for Japan, also increased in the last decade. War preparations in the last years of colonial rule only increased this dependence on Korean rice.

Data on inputs indicate that investments were high in the first and second decades of colonization and resulted in high growth rates for the third decade (see Table 8.2). The average annual growth rate of fertilizer consumption and irrigation greatly exceeded the growth of land area under cultivation and reflected an overall drive toward intensification of land use. Nonrice crop production increased rapidly as well, registering a growth rate of 3.65 percent per year for the period 1927–1938. In terms of regional variation, much of the growth in production occurred in the southern part of the country known as the Korean Rice Belt; this area had a much warmer climate than the north, and a high percentage of its production was paddy rice.[5]

Price policies also contributed to positive outcomes, but not in the fashion usually associated with exploitative urban-based policies. The terms of trade do not show any significant discrimination against agricultural production. This highlights a curious aspect of Korean agricultural policy: the pursuit of agricultural growth through cost reduction rather than incentive creation through price policy. Some scholars have argued that price discrimination in the agricultural sector has led to little or no development in this sector in Korea. The data show us, however, that this is not the case. Rather, terms of trade fluctuated a great deal, and price policy was simply not one of the key determinants of growth. The pattern of terms of trade shows that the price index of agricultural goods to manufactured goods did not reveal a constant preference for agriculture until the last few years of colonial rule. This reflects the goal of the colonial governments to create a cheap yet abundant source of rice for Japan. The correlation between the terms of trade and rice production is weak or negative and suggests that other factors were more important in affecting food supply than rice prices.

Table 8.2
Inputs, 1910–1938

|  | 1910–1919 | 1920–1929 | 1930–1938 | 1910–1938 |
|---|---|---|---|---|
| Fertilizer consumption* | 778.44 | 7861.10 | 38872.89 | 15552.61 |
| (growth rate in percentage) | (24.05) | (27.06) | (14.19) | (21.96) |
| Multiple cropping index** | 116.53 | 132.24 | 139.97 | 129.68 |
| (growth rate in percentage) | (2.77) | (0.79) | (0.33) | (1.28) |
| Irrigated area*** | 14877.33 | 61776.9 | 148693.8 | 74639.6 |
| (growth rate in percentage) | (31.44) | (19.80) | (2.87) | (18.1) |
| Area under cultivation**** | 4458.6 | 4582.4 | 4835.9 | 4624.1 |
| (growth rate in percentage) | (0.77) | (0.22) | (0.70) | (0.55) |

*Notes:* * Value of fertilizer consumption is measured in constant 1934 prices in million ton.
     ** The multiple cropping index is set to 1910 = 100.
     *** Irrigated area is measured in hectares.
     **** Area under cultivation is measured in thousand hectares.

*Sources:* See Table 8.1.

Investments in inputs, indicated by growth rates in fertilizer consumption and multiple cropping, greatly exceeded any efforts to increase the area of land under cultivation. There was a sharp rise in production as fertilizer consumption increased from very low levels in the early colonial period to relatively high levels as domestically manufactured fertilizer became available to farmers. The correlation of fertilizer consumption, irrigation, and multiple cropping with production and exports was very strong. In particular, the correlation between investment in irrigation and production was high (around 0.8) as was the correlation between fertilizer consumption and production. Irrigated land increased steadily during the period of colonization, growing at an average annual rate of 18 percent. The value of fertilizer consumption in constant (1934) prices increased from under a million yen to over 38 million yen by the end of the colonial period with an average annual growth of around 22 percent. Consumption of domestic fertilizer increased rapidly as a nitrogen fertilizer plant built by the Japanese in North Korea went on line in the last decade of the colonial period. Evidence suggests that the Japanese government strongly encouraged farmers to use chemical fertilizers as well as traditional organic fertilizers.[6]

Other aspects of land intensification compounded the effect of increased use of fertilizer. The use of multiple cropping techniques increased steadily during the colonial period with an average annual growth rate of 1.28 percent. Infrastructure investments were also an important element of the emerging policy. The Japanese colonization period foreshadowed modern Korean agricultural policies. Between 1910 and 1930, the Japanese colonial government focused on creating a steady source of rice for Japan by investing in irrigation systems that were technically superior to those in Japan and in a major fertilizer plant in North Korea that would provide a source of domestically produced nitrogen fertilizer.

The combination of infrastructure and input investments produced striking results, accounting for over 70 percent of the increases in production. The combination of inputs derived through principal component analysis is statistically significant in explaining production, yield, and exports (see Table 8.3). The included variables account for between 55 and 91 percent of variance in the dependent variables. The weights attached to each input in the principal components analysis show the relatively greater importance of irrigation and fertilizer consumption in explaining the growth of rice production and yield.

In short, economic growth in the agricultural sector began early in the twentieth century. It was during this period of colonization that the stage was set for economic expansion and for the creation of an industrial economy. Through investments in several sectors and changes in property laws, the

Table 8.3
Estimations of the Cobb-Douglas Production Function Using Principal Component Analysis

| Dependent Variable | Principal Component | Terms of Trade | $R^2$ | F | N |
|---|---|---|---|---|---|
| Production | 0.08** (7.38) | | 0.66 | 54.51 | 29 |
| Yield | 0.06** (6.17) | | 0.57 | 38.08 | 29 |
| Exports | 0.24** (16.61) | | 0.91 | 275.96 | 29 |
| Production | 0.08** (6.88) | 0.02 (0.13) | 0.64 | 26.27 | 29 |
| Yield | 0.06** (5.85) | -0.02 (0.21) | 0.55 | 18.39 | 29 |
| Exports | 0.24** (15.48) | 0.10 (0.55) | 0.91 | 134.57 | 29 |

*Notes:* The principal components for production, yield, and exports are as follows:
    Production: (0.02*area)+(0.52*irrigation)+(0.78*fertilizer)+
      (0.04*multiple cropping)+(0.35*time)
    Yield: (0.52*irrigation)+(0.78*fertilizer)+(0.04*multiple cropping)+(0.35*time)
    Exports: (0.02*area)+(0.52*irrigation)+(0.78*fertilizer)+(0.04*multiple cropping)+(0.35*time)
    All variables are expressed in logarithmic terms. The constant terms are suppressed. For a description of the variables, see notes in Tables 8.1 and 8.2. The *t*-statistic for each coefficient is reported in parentheses. ** Indicates that the coefficient is significantly different from zero at the 1 percent level of confidence.

*Sources:* See Table 8.1.

government transformed its role from one of distant governance into one that was critical in providing several important inputs to growth. The expectations of the population regarding the government's role in the economy were significantly changed. These expectations helped shape the role of government in modern Korea.

## MODERN KOREA, 1954–1970

There is a strong sense of continuity between agricultural growth in the colonial and post–Korean War period. Although sixteen years passed before the resumption of growth in the agricultural sector, many of the multisectoral investment policies made by the colonial government were maintained by the new South Korean government. Expectations regarding the role of government also remained unchanged. However, diminishing returns were beginning to set in. As the data show, investment levels remained quite high but the returns were not as great as those realized during the colonial period. The general conclusion suggested by the data is that by the time industrial expansion began, the Korean agricultural sector had reached maturity. This conclusion challenges the argument that there was no growth in the agricultural sector prior to industrialization. Rather, the data suggest that the returns to investment were maximized about two decades prior to industrial takeoff. However, in terms of institution building, the role of the government remained unchanged. Many agricultural sectors were controlled by the government in a manner similar to that under colonial rule.

Under the auspices of the Ministry of Agriculture and Fisheries, a system of disseminating information and technology was put into place. Irrigation associations and farmers' clubs were formed and contributed even more to dissemination efforts. The irrigation associations became a forum not only for diffusing technology but also for exerting control on the agricultural production process.

The post–Korean War system was dominated by government ministries assigned to the task of agricultural growth. The National Agricultural Cooperative Federation was the sole supplier of inputs, such as fertilizer and credit, while the Office of Rural Development was in charge of agricultural research. Irrigated land increased by about 85 percent between 1954 and 1970. Maintenance of the irrigation system was not very good, but crop losses were small because there was not much need for the efficient use of water.[7] Irrigation associations were formed along the lines begun by the Japanese in the 1930s. This number grew over 4 percent per year, with over 800 associations in existence by 1970. These associations served as an important channel of communication for disseminating inputs. They decreased the amount of control that individual farmers had over the production process because association heads, in close collaboration with ministry officials, made most of the decisions on the adoption of inputs, new technology, the supply of agricultural credit, and new methods of cultivation. In many ways, the policy-making process was very similar to that of the colonial government. As in the colonial period, it involved multisectoral efforts in technology, communications, infrastructure, and finance to speed up the growth process. Also, the government retained control of a significant portion of economic activity through a very large bureaucracy that was the only source of inputs and financial services. The expectations generated by the colonial government regarding the role of the government in the economy were crucial to public acceptance of a government-led market economy in the postwar era. Finally, the types of organizational innovation introduced during the colonial period were continued by the postwar government. Various ministries closely controlled the process of economic development in a manner similar to the colonial government.

The only major change to occur in the postwar period was in pesticide consumption. The decision to increase pesticide use was probably made for two reasons: the returns to fertilizer consumption were already maximized, and pesticide had been underutilized and would increase yield further. Whatever the reason, pesticide production and consumption increased drastically; consumption grew almost 18 percent per year. Simultaneously, irrigated land area expanded, and agricultural credit grew rapidly, at around 16 percent per year. Fertilizer consumption, already at a high level, remained steady at around 30 kg/hectare. The number of farmers' clubs increased almost 5 percent per year while membership in these clubs grew 13 percent. These clubs were the main vehicle for the government to disseminate information about new technology and cultivation practices; the bureaucracy that administered the agricultural sector was able to maintain close contact with individual farmers through farmers' clubs.

In general, growth in production was not as rapid as that during the colonial period. The yield per paddy increased about 2 percent per year while production grew at less than 3 percent. Upland rice yields grew at the rate of 4.54 percent per year, but the amount of land under cultivation in upland areas was minuscule (about 15,000 hectares) compared to total land cultivated. Cultivated land area did not expand significantly, increasing at the rate of 0.69 percent per year. There is no doubt from the data that growth in the post–Korean War period was not as high as the early phases of agricultural growth.

The overall conclusion suggested by the data is that growth did occur in the agricultural sector after 1954, but most of the expansion that usually precedes industrialization occurred much earlier, that is, during the period of colonization. Thus, the Korean case is not an anomaly among industrialized countries with regard to development of the agricultural sector, rather, it represents an extraordinary effort by a colonial government to get agriculture moving.

## CONCLUSIONS: KOREA AND THE EVOLUTION OF A MEGAPOLICY

The four elements critical to a megapolicy were all present in Korea's policies of agricultural development. The intersectoral dimension manifested itself in the simultaneous efforts to introduce new technology, revise the tax system, improve roads and irrigation systems, and provide new channels of communication between the government and the Korean population. Of the four elements, the organizational innovation that occurred is perhaps the most significant. The government became a significant player in the economy, and the kinds of institutions that it created in order to do this survived the Korean War and became an integral part of modern Korea. The government-led market economy as described by several scholars of modern Korea was an extraordinary result of organizational innovation that became a trademark of East Asian growth. Along with this organizational innovation, new expectations emerged about the role of government in the process of economic development. These expectations became crucial for government-led efforts to industrialize in the postwar era.

The potential for replicability of the Korean experience in other settings cannot be ignored. For countries that are just beginning the process of agro-industrial transformation, the policies followed by the colonial government and the postwar government are extremely important. The multisectoral investment policies and the role of government need to be explored in greater detail because of their relevance to newly industrial countries.

The final lesson from the Korean experience is that it does not represent a case of industrialization without prior development of agriculture. For countries which are yet to realize a sustainable positive growth rate in the agricultural sector, the Korean case does not provide an example of leapfrogging over agricultural development. Rather, it provides an example of agricultural growth that occurred several decades before industrial takeoff but nonetheless had a strong influence in the creation of a source of food supply to the modern industrial economy. Agricultural growth in Korea occurred through simultaneous expansion of investment by the government in various sectors. The role of the government as a provider of technology and other goods transcended the traditional role of government up until the period of agricultural expansion. The new role of government became the norm, not just for agricultural development but also for industrial growth. Other governments in East Asia pursued similar policies over time, however, the Korean case stands out as the first experiment to transform the role of government in order to drastically increase its participation in the process of economic growth.

Korea's integration of agricultural and industrial decisions emerged over time as a coherent megapolicy. Both sets of policies consist of a series of decisions that include infrastructure investments, organizational and institutional arrangements, and technical and resource inputs. This policy may not have been recognized as a unified effort at the outset, but, in retrospect, its coherence makes it a prototype applicable in other developmental contexts.

## NOTES

1. For a discussion of the consequences of industrialization without sufficient development of the agricultural sector, see Jagdish Bhagwati and T. N. Srinivasan, *Foreign Trade Regimes and Economic Development: India* (New York: Columbia University Press, 1975).

2. For a detailed discussion of the role of agriculture in economic development, see C. Peter Timmer, "The Role of the State in Agricultural Development," in *Agriculture and the State: Growth, Employment and Poverty in Developing Countries*, ed. C. Peter Timmer (Ithaca, N.Y.: Cornell University Press, 1991); John M. Staatz and Carl Eicher, "Agricultural Development Ideas in Historical Perspective," in *Agricultural Development in the Third World*, ed. Eicher and Staatz (Baltimore: Johns Hopkins University Press, 1984); and C. Peter Timmer et al., *Food Policy Analysis* (Baltimore: Johns Hopkins University Press, 1983).

3. A megapolicy involves four key elements: complexity, as indicated by an intersectoral dimension; organizational innovation; expectational creativity or the generation of new claims on government; and universality or the possibility of replication in other settings.

4. Alice Amsden, *Asia's Next Giant: South Korea and Late Industrialization* (London: Oxford University Press, 1989).

5. Kenneth Kang, "Agricultural Transformation Under Colonial Rule: The Case of Korea," unpublished manuscript, Harvard University, 1994.

6. Ibid., 3.

7. For a description of the irrigational system administration in Korea, see Robert Wade, *Irrigation and Agricultural Politics in South Korea* (Boulder, Colo.: Westview Press, 1982).

# 9

# FROM MARX TO MARKETS: CHINA'S ECONOMIC REFORMS AS A MEGAPOLICY

*Shang-Jin Wei*

The Chinese economic reforms that began in 1979 pulled the country from the verge of economic collapse and put it well on the road to economic development. Pre-reform China was plagued by rigid central planning, a poor work ethic, extremely low productivity, and a scarcity of goods including daily essentials. The reforming China is moving quickly toward a market economy, with the work ethic improving, productivity increasing, and goods and services in more abundant supply. With a double-digit growth rate for the last decade, China now is one of the fastest growing economies in the world.

The reform launched in 1979 qualifies as a megapolicy. It involved the welfare of 1.2 billion people, or over one-fifth of the world's total population. It required not just a simple fix of the old planning system, but a major overhaul. Market mechanisms and institutions had to be created for external trade, agriculture, industry, distribution systems, and banking. And because all sectors of the economy were involved, the sequencing and packaging of policies and programs had to be worked out. Finally, the economic reforms undertaken in China in the post-Mao era had virtually no precedent. There were no textbook examples or well-worked-out models that the country could follow in transforming the economy from a centrally planned to a market-oriented system. Indeed, the abundant Western advice now available to Eastern Europe and the former Republics of the Soviet Union was not available to China when it began its reforms.

This chapter describes the evolution of the Chinese economic reform policies, and it should be noted that the economic reforms in China truly evolved. A fundamental characteristic of the Chinese experience was its trial-and-error approach. At the initial stages of reform, both government and Communist Party leaders emphasized the need to experiment. In addition to experimentation, some vision regarding the coordination of the various sectors was also an important factor in the success of this megapolicy. The most important lessons may be in the sequencing and packaging of programs that allowed the government to coordinate this multisector shift in economic policies.[1]

Several basic lessons of China's experiences are evident:

1. In order to undertake a large-scale multisector reform, a series of small steps with continuous experiments along the way is not a weakness but an efficient means of attaining ultimate goals. The process of attracting foreign investment in China is a good illustration. An immediate and widescale opening of China to foreign investment was deemed risky, both economically and politically, at the start of the reforms. Instead, four small and isolated areas were chosen to test the usefulness and tolerability of foreign capital on Chinese soil. Only when its merit was proven, was foreign capital allowed in other regions of the country.

2. Reforms involve redistribution of power among various interest groups and arouse opposition from various segments of society. Sometimes, a big-bang approach to reform may not be politically feasible. In this case, a gradual or sequenced approach may circumvent political opposition and push the reform forward. The order in which China's economy was reformed—agriculture first, industry and commerce later, and the financial sector last—may be partially responsible for China's relatively smooth transition.

3. At any given point in time, different components of a reform program interact with each other. If two components reinforce each other, then the chance of success for this stage of reform is enhanced by the simultaneous implementation of these two components. On the other hand, if one component retards the progress of the other component, the probability of successfully implementing the entire reform is hampered by the simultaneous implementation of those two components. The packaging of the open-door policy and domestic economic reforms in China appears to have reinforced each factor.

This chapter explores the trial-and-error feature of the Chinese experience focusing on the open-door policy and then turns to the sequencing and packaging of the reforms.

## POLICY REFORM THROUGH SUCCESSIVE APPROXIMATION

Almost the entire Chinese reform process can be characterized as a series of trial-and-error changes or experiments. In the phrase often attributed to Deng Xiaoping, China's reform is like "walking across a river by feeling for stones under the water." The lengthy process of developing a securities market and a market-oriented fiscal system, for example, involved a series of experiments. The cautious small steps were not always forward moving, nor were they necessarily coherent, but they generally and cumulatively moved towards an open market system of resource allocation.

The experimental nature of the Chinese economic reforms was reflected in many local projects. In 1979, the central government wanted to reform the fiscal arrangements between the central and provincial governments. The traditional arrangement was that the central government took all of the revenues from local governments and then reallocated the expenditures to the provinces according to the needs of each locale as specified by a national plan. This left the local governments and local enterprises little incentive to raise more tax revenues or to increase production. The central government knew something needed to be done (such as revenue sharing between the central and local governments) but was unwilling to uproot the old system overnight. To test the viability of the new idea, two provinces, Fujian and Guangdong, were singled out. They were requested to turn over a fixed amount of tax revenue to the central government every year and were allowed to keep the remainder. There were problems with this arrangement, but relative to the old system, it produced miraculous results. Because the two provinces now have a claim to the remaining tax revenue, each has a great incentive to stimulate locally controlled enterprises to improve their productivity and profitability. The two provinces, particularly Guangdong, are among the fastest growing regions in China over the last fifteen years. When the merit of the new system proved itself in these two provinces, the central government began to implement a modified and improved version nationally.

Another example of the experimental evolution of Chinese economic reforms was the development of financial markets. Financial market reform lagged behind other sectors. Because well-functioning financial institutions such as banks and stock exchanges could be easily observed in Western market economies, the question was not what needed to be done, but at what speed. Instead of demolishing the monolithic state-owned banking system and establishing security markets overnight, the government approved a series of small measures. First, in the mid-1980s, the single centralized People's Bank was decentralized into one central bank and four specialized banks. The aim was to let the specialized banks behave like commercial banks in a market economy. Second, two stock exchanges and a bond market were established. The performance of these exchanges was closely monitored, and, after a period of trial, government leaders decided that the degree of speculation in these exchanges was beyond their tolerance levels. Requests to establish exchanges in other regions were denied. But the two existing stock exchanges in Shanghai and Shenzhen were allowed and, indeed, encouraged to develop further.

A third example of the gradual evolution of Chinese economic reforms has been the experiment with the use of international capital markets. The government issued debt instruments several times in hard currencies. Moreover, starting from the early 1990s, some Chinese companies' stocks began to be listed on the New York Stock Exchange as part of an explicit experiment by the Beijing government. The financial components of the overall economic reforms are still continuing to evolve and have a long way to go before financial institutions in China begin to operate like those in mature Western market economies. For one thing, high entry barriers still prevent private banks from being established and competing with the state-owned specialized banks. But the earlier experiments provided useful insights to further reform in the financial sector.

### Evolution of the Open-Door Policy

Perhaps one of the most daring and systematic reforms in China was its external trade policies.[2] This aspect of the reforms, often referred to as the open-door policy, was one of the most important components of China's policy for economic transformation. The pre-reform trade regime from 1949 to 1978 was best characterized as an extreme version of import substitution or a "closed-door" policy. Foreign investment was virtually nonexistent. Trade with the rest of the world was limited. China's economic strategy emphasized self-reliance (*zili gengsheng*), an approach that forced China to rely almost exclusively on its own resources and savings to develop the economy.

Imports of foreign technology were considered—when they were considered at all—as a temporary expedient. A government official in charge of trade policies in 1955 claimed that the purpose of importing was "to lay the foundation of China's industrial independence, so that in the future China can produce all of the producer goods it needs and will not have to rely on imports from the outside."[3]

There were three key characteristics of the pre-reform trade regime: (1) state trading corporations monopolized every transaction involving exports or imports, (2) no linkages existed between domestic and world market prices, and (3) foreign exchange was strictly controlled. Since 1979, this isolationist trade policy has been gradually liberalized. Although each step in the liberalization policy may, in and of itself, seem timid and incomplete, the series of steps contributed to overall economic reform.

First, there was a decentralization of trade decision making from 1979 to 1984 in which the branches of the state trading corporation were made more independent. Provincial authorities and line ministries were allowed to set up their own trading corporations. Although there was a proliferation of trading corporations, the decentralization was still limited because most imports needed centralized approval by the Ministry of Foreign Economic Relations and Trade (MOFERT). After four or five years of experimentation with limited decentralization, the government further decentralized the system in 1984 and 1985.

At the beginning of 1984, the foreign exchange sharing system between the center and provincial governments (as opposed to between the center and the enterprises) was formalized. Most provinces were allowed to keep 25 percent of the foreign exchange they earned for their own use. Fujian, Guangdong, Tibet, and Inner Mongolia were allowed to keep more. Exporting firms were allowed to keep half of their foreign exchange earnings. Next, the principle of nonexclusion was introduced in 1984 for import control. Before this, no goods could be imported unless they were explicitly approved. In reality, all imports had to obtain approval from MOFERT. Since 1984, many institutions were allowed to import goods without approval from MOFERT unless the goods were on a list of restricted imports. Effectively, 35 percent of imports were exempted from central approval. Finally, local trading corporations and importing and exporting firms were given full responsibility for their own profits and losses.

It would be an oversimplification to think that the Chinese trade regime was on a monotonically liberalizing path. In fact, there were several reversals. Beginning in 1985, the government resorted to old methods of administrative control to combat the problem of trade deficits. Although it did not completely reverse the reforms, several steps were taken by the government to slow them down and to backtrack: (1) the number of goods on the list of restricted imports was increased, (2) export licensing was introduced, (3) the right of local enterprises to use their retained foreign exchange was restricted, and (4) all import licenses were deliberately granted more slowly. Some goods, such as televisions and automobiles, were banned outright.

## From Special Economic Zones to the Pudong New Area

While foreign investment was courted by the government, it was not allowed on a national scale. For a while, only a small number of rather isolated areas (cordoned off with barbed wire) were open to foreign investors. In August 1980, the Beijing government declared four cities—Shenzhen, Zhuhai, Shantou, and Xiamen—as special economic zones (SEZs). The authorities in SEZs could make investment decisions largely independent of the state economic plans. They could adopt special tax concessions and less restrictive regulations on foreign exchange. Special land use regulations were adopted in order to attract foreign investment. For foreign-invested or foreign-managed firms, there was a two-year tax holiday followed by another three-year period of low tax rates. After the initial five years, joint ventures with foreign participation would pay only 15 percent taxes, compared with 33 percent for foreign firms outside the SEZs and 55 percent for domestic state-owned firms.

The establishment of the SEZs was a curious event from the viewpoint of pure economic efficiency. The four sites were close to Hong Kong and Taiwan and far away from the center of the country, and it was not clear why foreign investment should be severely restricted geographically. Only after the success of the SEZs in attracting foreign capital was apparent did the government gradually proceed with opening up other parts of the country to foreign investment. In 1983, the government declared the entire island of Hainan—about the same size as Taiwan—a special area open to foreign investment. The apparent success of the SEZs also encouraged the government to adopt a more receptive attitude toward foreign investment in the older industrial cities. In 1984, fourteen cities along the Pacific Coast opened to foreign investment. Local administrators in these cities were authorized to take limited steps to deepen reforms, encourage exports, and extend some of the preferential treatment accorded to an SEZ. But the extent of the new reform policies in industrial cities in general, and in Shanghai in particular, remained timid and conservative compared with the SEZs.

Foreign-invested firms brought in new capital, foreign exchange, technology, and managerial talents not only to their own enterprises but also to domestic firms in the same cities.[4] As a consequence of the different applications of open-door and reform policies in different parts of the country, Shanghai lagged behind other regions in the nation. Its dominant position as the number one exporting city in the country was taken over by Shenzhen in the mid-1980s. Its distinction as having more industrial output than any other city and province in the nation was lost to other provinces with bolder reform measures.

The lesson from this experience is that China's economic reforms were undertaken gradually because of government leaders' uncertainty about their success. They saw overambitious one-stroke-to-completion policy reforms as too risky. An experimental approach reduced the overall cost by incrementally moving toward the ultimate objectives. In the long run, whether a reform is completed in one week or five years is inconsequential. What is important is that it will be sustainable over a long period of time.

## SEQUENCING AND PACKAGING REFORM: POLITICAL FACTORS INFLUENCING ECONOMIC POLICIES

Large-scale economic reforms can easily be killed by powerful political opposition. This was potentially true when seeking to abolish the practice of comprehensive central planning in China. The reforms had to be implemented by the same bureaucrats whose livelihood had depended for so long on making and carrying out central plans. Yet, the very same reforms threatened to diminish the power of bureaucrats whose jobs were to control the implementation of central plans under the old system. Why did politics in China not undermine the economic reforms as it appears to have done in Russia, Ukraine, and some other transitional societies later? One hypothesis is that the particular sequencing of reforms in various sectors was partly responsible for the reform policy's success.

China's overall reform program is best characterized as a gradual or sequential process even though the exact sequence of sectoral reforms did not necessarily result from a blueprint at the outset. Thus, in retrospect, it seems that even if a sequential approach was less efficient economically compared to a one-stroke or big-bang approach, it may have been more effective politically. Indeed, for large-scale reforms that involve many sectors, a big-bang approach simply may not be politically feasible. A well-designed sequential reform may circumvent or ameliorate political problems.[5]

The reforms started in agriculture in 1979 and were only applied to foreign trade a year or two later. It was four or five years after the initiation of the whole economic reform program that attempts were made to restructure enterprise. Recently, the country has launched into banking and security market reforms and is actively planning changes in exchange rate policies. Throughout the last decade, one observes steady increases in the political support for the reforms.[6]

The farmers' support for the first stage of reform was politically crucial. Although the reform was not subject to a referendum, the top leaders would have been uneasy had there been widespread discontent with changes in the agricultural sector because China remains primarily an agricultural society. When the urban industrial reforms started almost five years later, the agricultural sector would have lost because of increases in the prices of fertilizers, tractors, and other inputs produced in the urban sector. Thus, the sequencing of reforms to build political support and to mitigate adverse consequences was a critical factor in the success of China's economic transformation policies.

Perhaps no less important was the appropriate packaging of reforms across various sectors to enhance the attractiveness of the overall reform strategy. Government leaders realized that the careful packaging of reform programs could maximize their success in each sector while at the same time using advances in one sector to improve the chances of success in other sectors. In contrast, an ill-designed package could complicate the execution of the entire reform program because failure in one component of reform might hamper progress in the others. An illustration of the impact of packaging is the interaction between the open-door policy and the effort to expand the nonstate industrial sector. Borrowing terminology from mathematics, the first type of packaging is "superadditive," and the second type is "subadditive." If packaging components of reform make the entire policy more likely to succeed than if an individual component was carried out independently, the package exhibits superadditivity. If the components contradict each other so that the combination is more difficult to carry out than the individual component, the package exhibits subadditivity.

The open-door policy and the domestic market reforms in China constituted a superadditive package. These two key components of the Chinese reform were implemented in parallel. Logically, the two could have been carried out separately, like the halfhearted reform attempts in Hungary and other Eastern European countries during the 1970s and early 1980s. Domestic reforms were implemented, but governments did not open the country up to foreign investment. On the other hand, both Taiwan and South Korea adopted open trade regimes long before they enacted serious domestic market reforms such as financial liberalization.

## CONCLUSIONS

This chapter highlights three lessons from the Chinese economic reform experience. First, when contemplating large-scale reforms that do not have precedents, reform advocates should be aware that an experiment-based approach that builds in flexibility is more cost-effective than either the rigid execution of a preconceived detailed plan or doing nothing until a perfect plan is formulated. A good example of this experiment-based approach was the evolution of the Chinese policy toward foreign investment in state-owned firms that started in four isolated SEZs and eventually spread to developed industrial centers such as Shanghai.

Second, sequencing matters. Given the ultimate goal, effective sequencing of segments of a reform may help lower political resistance. Careful sequencing could push forward a reform program that otherwise would have been undermined by political opposition. The Chinese sequence—agriculture first, foreign investment and trade second, and industry and financial market reforms later—was politically wise in China's particular situation. Political resistance may have been much greater had China tried to implement the reforms in all sectors at the same time.

Finally, packaging matters. Policy makers need to know what parts of the reforms can be executed simultaneously. Effective packaging raises the probability of success for individual policy components, while ineffective packaging may make individual components unnecessarily more complicated. An example of two mutually enforcing reforms in China was the parallel pursuit of the open-door policy that attracted foreign direct investment and the domestic reforms that established and expanded township and village enterprises outside the control of the central government.

Although China's conditions are unlikely to be identical to those in other transitional economies or developing countries, these three lessons are still useful. There is a Chinese proverb that advises, "A stone from another mountain can be used to sharpen the jade (of this mountain)."

## NOTES

1. It should be noted that the Chinese experience contrasts sharply with the predominant advice from the West for the transition economies. See, for example, the eloquent exposition by David Lipton and Jeffrey Sachs, "Creating a Market Economy in Eastern Europe: The Case of Poland," Brookings paper on Economic Activity, 1 (1990): 75–147; and David Lipton and Jeffrey Sachs, "Privatization in Eastern Europe: The Case of Poland," Brookings paper on Economic Activity, 2 (1990): 293–341.

2. The discussion in this subsection is based partly on Nicholas Lardy, *Foreign Trade and Economic Reform in China, 1978–1990* (Cambridge, England: Cambridge University Press, 1992); Shang-Jin Wei, "Open-Door Policy and China's Rapid Growth: Evidence from City-level Data," National Bureau of Economic Research (NBER) working paper 4602 (1993); and Shang-Jin Wei, "Foreign Direct Investment in China: Source and Consequences," working paper, Kennedy School of Government, Harvard University, n.d.

3. Lardy, *Foreign Trade and Economic Reform*, p. 16

4. Shang-Jin Wei, "Open-Door Policy"; and Shang-Jin Wei, "Gradualism Versus Big Bang: Speed and Sustainability of Reforms," unpublished, Harvard University, 1993.

5. The interaction between politics and economics can be examined more rigorously. Based on a framework developed by Raquel Fernandez and Dani Rodrik, "Resistance to Reform: Status Quo Bias in the Presence of Individual-Specific Uncertainty," *American Economic Review* 85, no. 5 (December 1991), Shang-Jin Wei formalized this idea in a mathematical model, "Open-Door Policy." For a different analysis, see Charles Wyplosz, "After the Honeymoon: On the Economics and the Politics of Economic Transformation," unpublished, Institut Européen d'Administration des Affaires (INSEAD), 1992. For a discussion on the sequencing issue based purely on economic criteria, see Sebastian Edwards, "The Sequencing of Economic Reform: Analytical Issues and Lessons from Latin American Experience," *The World Economy* 13 (1990): 1–14; Rod Flavey and Cha Dong Kim, "Timing and Sequencing Issues in Trade Liberalization," *The Economic Journal* 102 (1992): 908–24; and Ronald I. McKinnon, *The Order of Economic Liberalization: Financial Control in the Transition to a Market Economy* (Baltimore: Johns Hopkins University Press, 1991).

6. For more detailed discussion, see Alan Gelb, Gary H. Jefferson, and Inderjit Singh, "Can Communist Economies Transform Incrementally? The Experience of China," in *NBER Macroeconomic Annual 1993*, ed. Olivier J. Blanchard and Stanley Fischer (Boston: MIT Press, 1993); Peter Harrold, "China's Reform Experience to Date," World Bank discussion papers, China and Mongolia Department, no. 180 (1992); Gary H. Jefferson, Kang Chen, and Inderjit Singh, "Lessons from China's Economic Reform," *Journal of Comparative Economics* 16, no. 2 (June 1992); Justin Yifu Lin, "Rural Reforms and Agricultural Growth in China," *American Economic Review* 82, no. 1 (1992): 34–51; John Mcmillan and Barry Naughton, "How to Reform a Planned Economy: Lessons from China," *Oxford Review of Economic Policy*, 1992; Dwight H. Perkins, "China's 'Gradual' Approach to Market Reforms," Harvard Institute for International Development, unpublished, 1992; Shang-Jin Wei and Peng Lian, "Love and Hate: State and Non-state Firms in Transition Economies," Harvard University Kennedy School of Government, Faculty Research Working Paper Series R93–40 (1993); Shahid Yusuf, "The Rise of China's Nonstate Sector," World Bank, unpublished, 1993; and Gang Zou, "Enterprise Behavior Under the Two-Tier Plan/Market System," University of Southern California, unpublished, 1992.

# 10

# ENERGY CONSERVATION AS A MEGAPOLICY: THE CASE OF CHINA

## Lin Gan

China has experienced dramatic economic changes over the past two decades as the result of its 1979 open-door policies and the economic reforms of the 1980s and early 1990s. During the 1980s, energy and environmental issues began to influence the course of this economic transformation. The resultant policies brought fundamental changes in social behavior, values, and structures; helped transform science and technology (S&T) development policy; and contributed to changing government decision-making processes.[1]

Two concerns have dominated the thinking of planners and policy makers in China. The first was how to balance economic development, energy supply, and environmental protection; the second was how to choose a technological path that served societal interests and objectives while at the same time responding to the political interests and power of the parties involved in policy making. The energy policies that emerged in China can be explained only by describing the interactions among the most important institutional actors who were involved in making or shaping critical decisions.

This chapter examines the dynamics of policy interaction between the government and other institutions in formulating energy policy and choosing the most appropriate technological paths to energy conservation. Conflicts among participants from different educational backgrounds and professional disciplines strongly influenced political decisions and the development of alternatives to the conventional supply-oriented policies.

China's experience shows that patterns of technology choice, innovation, and transfer were determined largely by institutions seeking to adjust their relationships. Energy conservation policy resulted from compromises to resolve basic conflicts between economic growth and environmental protection as major development objectives.

## THE SETTING FOR POLICY INNOVATION

China's rapid economic growth came as a result of the economic reforms adopted since 1979. Gross domestic product (GDP) grew during the 1980s at an average annual rate of 9.5 percent, and China achieved one of the highest economic growth rates in the world.[2] In early 1992, the Chinese government increased the pace of economic transition from a Soviet-style planned economy to a market-oriented system and called its combination of planned and market mechanisms a "socialist market economy." By the mid-1990s, the government expected the annual economic growth rate—stimulated by joint ventures and foreign investments, especially in small- and medium-scale rural industries and private enterprises—to reach 12 percent. This rapid economic growth brought dramatic changes in sectoral policies, particularly for energy and environmental management.

From the early 1980s, energy played an increasingly important role in determining the pace of China's economic growth. Development of the energy sector was considered a strategic area of policy making because energy shortages blocked the growth of industrial production and constrained economic output.[3] Although the energy sector experienced continuous growth in the 1980s at an average annual rate of 5.5 percent, energy production lagged far behind the needs of industry.[4] The Chinese government then began to increase energy supply, particularly through investment in electric power generation. During the 1980s, government investment in the electric industry grew substantially.[5] From 1991 to 1995, it invested heavily in the construction of coal-burning, large, hydroelectric and nuclear power plants in order to meet pressing energy demands.[6]

Meanwhile, China suffered from severe inefficiencies in energy use: one dollar of production output in China consumed four to five times more energy than was required in major industrial countries.[7] During the 1980s, it became obvious that gross national product (GNP) and production growth depended on increasing energy supplies. Eventually, planners challenged the conventional policy of increasing energy production to satisfy demand, and energy conservation gained ground. Policy makers began to pay more attention to energy conservation, environmental protection, and the development of energy-saving technologies.[8]

Energy policy in China changed drastically after 1979 and 1980 when the government was just awakening to the seriousness of the problem. A second stage followed from 1980 to 1983 when more detailed and diversified energy policies dealt with serious energy crises and environmental problems. During the third stage in the evolution of energy policies from 1983 to 1988, the government strengthened the institutions required to implement them. The fourth stage, from 1988 to 1991, called for careful assessment and recalibration of energy policies and technological choices. During a fifth stage beginning in 1991, the government began to adjust, refine, and integrate its energy and environmental policies.

## The Period of Awakening, 1979–1980

In the 1960s and throughout most of the 1970s, China's economic strategy was dominated by the Maoist ideology of economic self-reliance. Chinese leaders thought that an energy crisis such as that experienced in the West during the early 1970s could never happen in a nation that depended almost solely on domestic energy supplies. At the time, macroeconomic policies gave little support to conserving energy resources either in production or in consumption. This policy, of course, simply worsened the energy crisis that constrained economic development in later years.[9]

The late 1970s and early 1980s produced severe energy shortages that required government action. In addition, the government became increasingly concerned about the economic costs of pollution that cost billions of yuan in environmental damage.[10] The period of learning forced government leaders to admit mistakes and consider alternative options for the future.

During the early 1980s, scientists and energy and environmental policy experts called attention to the energy crisis and environmental challenges. The State Science and Technology Commission (SSTC) conducted a series of national symposia held from 1979 to 1982 that were attended by influential energy experts and government leaders. The State Council's awareness of the need for energy conservation had developed in the late 1970s as energy demands increased and energy shortages became more serious. In 1980, the government began to set annual targets for energy saving and proposed financing, technology, and implementation measures. One important stimulus was the report "The Year 2000 in China" which attempted to forecast trends in fifteen sectors, including energy and the environment.[11] This research project, proposed by the Technology and Economic Research Center, a key think tank in the State Council, was later included in the Sixth Five-Year Plan for 1980–1985 as a priority project.[12]

This process of consciousness building was marked by lively debates. The supply-oriented policy was backed by many conservative leaders at the State Planning Commission, but some think tanks provided independent advice on the energy crisis and pushed the government to establish a conservation policy.[13] At this phase of policy formation, Zhao Ziyiang, the former chairman of the Communist Party, backed those advocating conservation. His support was crucial in swaying opinion among many party and government leaders.

## The Period of Policy Formulation, 1980–1983

The second phase of the energy policy's evolution brought a dramatic shift in the government's agenda. The efforts made by some energy experts and environmental officials in the earlier years altered the perceptions of top leaders about the relationships among economic development, energy, and the environment. A systems approach was developed to integrate economy, energy, technology, and environmental issues in public policy making. This framework encouraged policy makers to give energy conservation higher priority in economic development plans. In 1980, the State Council sought "to put energy exploitation and conservation in an equal position, and energy conservation as a priority in the short run."[14] Environmental protection was, for the first time, included in the national Five-Year Plan. The government adopted a policy to "harmonize" economic and social development with environmental protection and energy technology. This policy approach created a framework for the energy conservation actions that were implemented later.

Serious attempts to review energy technology options started in 1983. A resolution of the State Council prompted the SSTC, the State Planning Commission (SPC), and the State Economic Commission (SEC) to organize a large-scale technology assessment program. More than 2,000 experts and government officials examined technology policies in thirteen sectors, including energy and environmental protection. This comprehensive review was the first effort in China to incorporate a large, systematic, cross-sectoral technology assessment in a national policy.

In the early 1980s, energy conservation policy focused on projects that could yield quick economic returns. Improved technologies, mostly of domestic manufacture, were introduced to upgrade low-efficiency industrial boilers and to create comprehensive waste heat utilization systems. Investments were made in co-generation (the process of supplying both electric and steam energy from the same power plant), district heating, coal gasification, and coal-washing and separation technologies to attain higher energy efficiency. These projects provided economic returns within one or two years.

## The Period of Policy Strengthening, 1983–1988

The third phase of policy making involved regulatory enforcement and institutional strengthening at the national level. The SSTC played a central part in shaping energy conservation policy. In 1983, Yang Jun, the former vice director of the SSTC, submitted the report "To Strengthen the Conversion of Coal and Its Comprehensive Utilization" to the State Council stressing that "if we are to realize the strategic objectives put forward by the 12th Congress of the Communist Party, the efficient use of coal and its economic and rational utilization will have a historical significance, and should be considered as an important decision making for economic development in China." This initiative received a positive response from the leaders of the State Council. In the same year, a new organization, the Special Planning Office for Coal Conversion and Comprehensive Utilization, was established under the S&T Leading Group of the State Council. This organization initiated coal-related S&T policies and took a leading role in policy debates and technology assessments. Important policy research was also carried out at the National Research Center for Science and Technology for Development (NRCSTD), supported by the SSTC.

The SSTC had been actively involved in organizing energy policy research from the late 1970s. From that time on, the primary motivation for energy policy research was the need to overcome energy shortages through technical means. The Department of Resources Saving and Comprehensive Utilization took a leading role in formulating energy conservation policies and in following up to ensure implementation. In 1983, about 200 energy experts and government officials met to discuss energy technology policy assessment and presented the report "Main Points of Energy Technology Policy" that was included in China's Blue Book on technology policy in 1985. This was the first government effort to assess systematically alternatives for developing energy-saving technologies. Its main thrust was to assign energy conservation an equal priority with energy exploitation and production.

Efforts to strengthen environmental management at that time were seen as cost-effective efforts to implement energy conservation policies. The State Council and the environmental protection agencies adopted new environmental regulations. For instance, Stipulation of Coal Burning Smoke Pollution Prevention Technology Policy, issued in 1984, had a profound impact on the development of district heating, coal gasification, and the dissemination of coal briquettes in urban areas.[15] In the same year, the National Environmental Protection Agency (NEPA) was separated from the Ministry of Construction to become an independent institution under the State Council, under which it received more power to enforce national environmental regulations.

Provincial and regional environmental protection agencies were strengthened in 1985, and more than 800 counties established environmental protection units. The strengthening of environmental management regulations also led to behavioral changes in energy production and consumption and in enterprise management. Meanwhile, more than 200 energy conservation technology service centers that had been established nationwide began to develop a network of technical support units for large- and medium-scale state-owned enterprises to provide monitoring, consultation, policy advice, information dissemination, demonstration projects, and training for energy conservation.

In the mid-1980s, the government strengthened energy conservation policies by (1) disseminating energy-saving technologies such as co-generation in power production and small cement industrial energy technology innovations, (2) importing advanced energy technologies from industrialized countries (more than seventy state-organized key technology transfer projects were involved), and (3) shifting from single-technology innovations to systems innovations in order to improve the efficiency of the entire energy network. It also began investigating higher energy intensive industrial technology and equipment and monitoring energy production and consumption patterns nationwide.

New technologies for energy conservation were also introduced. The main policies included the Energy Conservation Technology Policy that was issued in 1985, and Technology Standards for Appraising Rational Use of Electricity in Industrial Enterprises and the Notice for Disseminating Energy Conservation Technology Measures, which were promulgated in 1987. In 1986, the State Council established Provisional Regulations for Energy Conservation Management, a comprehensive energy conservation policy. The highest government policy-making body, the State Council, held regular meetings to discuss and promote energy conservation. Institutions such as the Energy Conservation Department were established or strengthened at the national level and within provincial and local governments. State enterprises formed energy conservation units to implement the policy. Management controls for energy conservation were made part of the management responsibility system in manufacturing industries. These control measures played a vital role in achieving energy-saving targets in state enterprises.[16] Economic incentives were used later to complement the management enforcement system.

From 1986 to 1988, twenty-nine sectoral technology policies for energy conservation were introduced by the Ministry of Chemical Industry, the Ministry of Textiles, the Ministry of Urban Construction, and other agencies. Financial support was provided mostly through the SSTC to journals and newspapers to disseminate information and build awareness about energy conservation.

### The Period of Policy Assessment, 1988–1991

During the fourth phase, the government and other institutions began to identify new technologies for energy conservation. The importance of technology advancement and innovation gained ground in the minds of many government officials as they became aware of the limits of command and control. Control measures had limited efficacy because outdated energy technologies (for example, many boilers were still operating at 1950s and 1960s levels) were the main causes of inefficiency.[17] To develop a new set of energy technologies was seen as a logical extension of previous policies. Many scientists and government officials considered new technologies as a more cost-effective way to reach energy conservation objectives and to improve environmental quality. Important research projects were initiated to study policy options for advanced clean coal technology development.

The attitudes of many leaders of the energy industry also began to change. The Ministry of Energy had been deeply concerned with supply and demand issues and with finding ways of overcoming energy shortages. Its technology assessments had focused primarily on how to upgrade production technologies, but it made little real effort to support the development of clean coal technologies.[18] Now the Ministry of Energy began to express interest in energy policy research and sponsored demonstration projects aimed at disseminating new energy technologies, equipment, and products, including improved coal combustion, renewable energy, and rural energy conservation technologies.

The influence of technical knowledge and expertise continued to grow. As the complexity of energy and environmental matters increased, policy makers sought advice from sectoral experts and technical advisers. The influence of technical experts was exercised through different channels: think tanks, advisory committees, nongovernmental academic organizations, and personal advice.[19] The NRCSTD of the SSTC, for example, became an important source of scientific knowledge. NRCSTD became actively involved in energy technology assessment. It had been providing policy advice since the early 1980s, but researchers involved in such activities usually had their training in natural sciences. Many were now bringing insights into the linkages among environment, energy, and management sciences. Their vision of useful research began to focus on long-term policy options for S&T development in China.

One example of this research was the project on Strategies and Policies for New Coal Utilization Technology Development in China that was conducted in 1987 and 1988. Based on quantitative research methods, the reports suggested options such as coal-burning, $SO_2$-reduction technologies, and coal gasification and liquefaction technologies. The policy recommendations focused on the environmental aspects of energy production and use and urged the government to strengthen the regulatory measures in existing environmental policy.[20]

Despite the government's official policy to promote clean coal technology, however, capital investments in coal washing and separation facilities declined drastically during the late 1980s and early 1990s.[21] From 1987 to 1990, capital investment in coal washing and separation dropped from 4.2 percent to 1.3 percent—from 253 million yuan ($44.4 million) to 100 million yuan ($17.5 million)—of total investment in the coal industry. In the same period, investment in coal production increased by about 71 percent from 5.7 billion yuan ($1 billion) to 9.8 billion yuan ($1.7 billion).[22]

Other problems arose from the deficiencies in energy policy. The coal production plans set up by the former Ministry of Energy did not take into account the quality of the coal produced but only considered the quantity. Coal-washing capacities could not be fully utilized in low-quality coal, and the large quantity of $SO_2$ contained in raw coal was emitted through direct combustion, which led to acid rain problems, particularly in the southwestern and northeastern regions of China.[23] At the same time, China was importing large quantities of sulphur from abroad for medical and chemical production uses.[24] Clearly, this policy represented a conflict in values between production-oriented and environment-oriented institutions.

### The Period of Policy Adjustment, 1991–1995

The fifth phase in the evolution of energy policy has been a period of adjustment during the nationwide shift to a market-oriented economy and the demise of central planning. Among the responses to changes in the economic system were the creation of new institutions such as the Energy Conservation Investment Corporation in the SPC and the search for technical knowledge for decision makers. The rapid transition to a market-oriented economy created uncertainty among leaders of government institutions, who began to investigate options for energy conservation in the future. The Ministry of Coal, for example, sponsored a research project on the "Coal Industry under the Transition toward a Market Economy"; the State Economic and Trade Commission (SETC) began a study of "Energy Conservation under the Regulation of a Market Economy"; and the SSTC and the SETC jointly sponsored the project "Clean Coal Technology Plan in China."[25]

The SSTC was also active in promoting clean coal technology assessment. In 1991, it organized an international conference, Environmentally Sustainable Coal Technology Policy Choice, and followed up by participating in international conferences on clean coal technology policy in India and Germany. These activities were related to the growing concern about reducing $CO_2$ (carbon dioxide) emissions in China. All of this work culminated in the Energy Conservation Law drafted by the SPC and the Ministry of Energy.

In 1992, the State Council introduced the "National Medium- and Long-Term S&T Development Guidelines" in which clean coal technology research and development (R&D) was listed as a high priority and targeted as a medium-term objective, with large-scale industrial applications foreseen as the long-term goal.[26] The emerging clean coal technology policies have several characteristics: they (1) demand technical knowledge from several sectors; (2) aim to achieve multiple objectives including energy efficiency improvement, environmental pollution control and prevention, and greenhouse gas emissions reduction; (3) stimulate institutional innovation in new forms of R&D cooperation; and (4) generate new expectations for long-term energy-environment systems development and management.

As a result of these decisions, science and technology has a more important impact on China's policy than ever before. The State Council decision to respond to international calls to promote sustainable development led in 1992 to the introduction of ten policy measures in which clean energy technology development was given a high priority. Although similar measures had been taken before, the lack of economic incentives and regulatory controls had clearly handicapped technological R&D.

As a result of the dissemination of knowledge and scientific findings, government leaders became increasingly aware of the interrelationships among the economy, energy, environment, and technology. This expansion of consciousness is partly related to the United Nations (UN) sponsored World Summit on Environment and Development held in Rio de Janeiro, Brazil, in 1992. The preparation for the UN Summit and the signing of the Conventions on Climate and Biodiversity obliged the government to take action. The United Nations Center for Environment and Development (UNCED) translated the concept of sustainable development into sectoral policy recommendations. The preparation for implementing Agenda 21 projects gave the government an opportunity to test a sustainable development strategy promoted by the United Nations Development Program.[27]

Key officials like Qu Geping, former director of the NEPA, became involved in environmental management and played a crucial role in disseminating knowledge about sustainable development in China.[28] Their influence was reflected in the government's policies for energy technology assessment and selection and in the incorporation of environmental objectives in energy sector management and planning. As a result of these policies, many new organizations were established in China to deal with issues of environmental protection and natural resources management. The influence of these environmental advocates was seen not only in central government institutions and R&D organizations but also in regional and local government institutions. The sustainable development concept began to shift government policy away from the traditional growth-oriented path that had tended to treat sectors separately toward one that emphasized the need to transform the entire society. The convergence of integrated energy management and environmental protection policies was, clearly, part of that transition.

## THE IMPACTS OF ENERGY CONSERVATION POLICIES

After the energy conservation policy was adopted, a variety of instruments were used to implement it at the national, regional, and local levels. They included (1) strengthening management control mechanisms, (2) increasing regulatory enforcement, (3) disseminating energy conservation propaganda, (4) providing financial incentives, (5) supporting human resources development, (6) promoting energy-saving and clean technology development, (7) encouraging the development of renewable energy technology, and (8) promoting structural change in the industrial sector.

Strengthening management controls has been the primary tool to promote energy conservation. National and regional plans integrated energy conservation projects and programs to ensure funding and key resources needed for project implementation. Different levels of government and enterprise established personal responsibility systems to ensure project implementation; industrial policies restricted high-energy-intensive, small-scale industrial development. The government also organized demonstration projects to disseminate energy conservation technologies at the local level.

The government adopted new regulations and strengthened enforcement. From 1979 to 1990, twenty-eight regulations were issued by the State Council, the SPC, the SEC, and various ministries. More than 600 energy standards were introduced in twenty-five sectors. Propaganda strengthened the call for energy conservation. In October 1991, the SPC organized a national campaign, Energy Conservation Propaganda Week, and selected sixty-three large state-owned enterprises as the demonstration units for energy conservation. Mass media were mobilized to communicate to the general public information about the importance of the energy conservation policies.

Financial resources were mobilized to fund energy conservation projects, including low-interest loans and tax deductions or exemptions for producing energy-saving equipment and products and for importing energy-efficient technologies. From 1980 to 1990, investments in energy conservation at the state, provincial, and enterprise levels totaled 20 billion yuan ($3.7 billion) and resulted in 50 Mtce (million tons of coal equivalent) of energy-saving capacity annually.

From the late 1980s to the early 1990s, demonstration projects were conducted for technologies that could be used by state enterprises. As part of the shift toward a market-oriented economy in 1992, the government-rationalized energy prices came closer to market value.[29] Government institutions such as the SPC seemed prepared to give up some of their control over energy prices and to relinquish their monopoly on energy-resources distribution, with the expectation that energy conservation measures would pay off.

China's energy conservation policies also brought substantial improvements in efficiency. Energy consumption per 10,000 yuan of GNP was reduced by 30 percent from 1980 to 1990, and some 280 million tons of coal were saved. The average annual rate of energy savings reached 3.6 percent by 1990.[30] The majority of the twenty-five industrial sectors experienced a decline in energy consumption per unit of GNP production (toce/100 million yuan) from 1985 to 1990.[31] Key industrial technologies, such as the innovations adopted in the iron and steel and chemical industries, included energy-saving efforts, as a result of which particles released into the atmosphere were reduced by 5 Mt and $SO_2$ emissions declined by 5.5 Mt annually.

The use of coal gas in urban residential areas reduced the use of individual stoves in residential buildings. Tianjin, the third largest city in China, increased coal gas dissemination 55 percent from 1985 to 1989 and significantly reduced urban air pollution caused by direct coal burning for cooking.[32] District heating systems influenced urban planning and the construction industry and generated new concepts and standards for apartment building design and technical innovations in the construction industry.

From 1981 to 1990, the implementation of energy conservation policies led to innovation and advancement in industrial technology in more than 1,000 large projects, about 300 of which were state sponsored. Large-scale technology innovation took place in such energy-intensive industries as chemicals, construction, cement, and iron and steel. Projects on district heating and industrial-waste heat utilization in urban areas yielded widespread social and environmental benefits.

Energy conservation policy also had an impact on the behavior of industry leaders. Many industrial enterprises, particularly large state-owned companies, were, for a long time, reluctant to embrace technological change because of disincentives and market competition. Prompted by energy conservation policies, many industry managers are slowly coming to accept the rationale for investing in energy-saving technologies and end-use efficiency.[33] Structural changes are now being made that will have a profound impact on the industrial sector for years to come.

## CONCLUSIONS

Energy policy in China evolved rapidly over the past two decades.[34] The main features of the evolution of energy conservation policy in China can be summarized as follows: (1) it was a policy response to an urgent crisis; (2) there was a strong influence of S&T expertise and R&D policy analysts in sectoral policy making; (3) there has been an increasing integration of environmental protection concerns into energy policy planning and management; (4) there is a growing dependence of sectoral policy makers on S&T development and support; (5) an alternative paradigm for energy systems development is emerging even though it is still in its initial stages; and (6) sectoral biases and institutional conflicts of interests are the major obstacles to reaching energy conservation objectives.

The impacts of China's energy conservation policies have been diffused into every aspect of society, but the policies themselves were mostly developed and implemented in a top-down manner. Actions have been taken by the central government and disseminated to and implemented at lower levels. It is also evident that nongovernmental organizations (NGOs) have had little influence on energy conservation policies. It is interesting to note that China's move toward energy conservation had little to do with the influence of the mass media, the general public, or NGOs, which are still very weak in China. These influences were limited by strict government controls that have historical roots in the totalitarian regime. In this regard, China differs from many other developing countries, such as India, where nongovernmental organizations and the mass media play highly visible roles in shaping the government's response.

The process of energy policy making has always been shaped by conflicts (less intensive in the 1990s than in the 1980s) over whether to emphasize energy conservation or energy production.[35] Some policy makers have argued that conservation policies were no more successful than supply-oriented policies because of the government's strong support for the expansion of energy production. Zhu Chengzhang, a high-level official at the former Ministry of Energy, has argued that although the government's official policy was to give energy exploitation and energy conservation equal priority, "the results were not satisfactory. Energy exploitation still took a dominant position, even though in principle energy saving was a priority. This situation is a continuation of the traditional ways of managing the national economy."[36]

The validity of this argument is supported by an examination of the government's investments in energy. From 1985 to 1990, the government invested 300 billion yuan ($52.6 billion) in energy sector development, but only about 4.7 billion yuan ($0.8 billion) was invested in technical innovation for energy conservation, and 11.4 billion yuan ($2 billion) for capital construction in energy-saving facilities. The overwhelming majority of investments were used to increase energy supplies.[37]

Despite some constraints on the full implementation of China's energy conservation policies, the impacts have been important. The concept of megapolicies provides a useful framework for understanding the complex public policy-making process in which energy conservation decisions have been made. Social learning has been an important component of the process, from defining problems to implementing policy proposals.

Important forces in shaping energy conservation policy were scientific knowledge and technical expertise. One example is the coal combustion technology feasibility studies conducted by a research group at NRCSTD. Prominent technical, management, environment, and information-management experts were consulted on the most cost-efficient coal combustion technologies for future research and development.[38]

Other important sources of influence were the advisory committees of experts whom the government invited to assist sectoral managers. These committees were particularly important in state industrial organizations that generally lacked access to expert knowledge and the capacity to interact across sectoral boundaries. And because decision making in technical fields became increasingly complex, government agencies also began to seek external expert knowledge in formulating sectoral policies. In 1990, for example, the former Ministry of Energy invited thirty-four prominent experts from a variety of disciplines to establish an advisory committee on strategic issues of energy sector management.[39]

Although the concern for global environmental problems was not the primary force shaping China's energy conservation policies in the 1980s, it was an important factor. Particular attention has been focused on the potential growth of $CO_2$ emissions and the impacts of climate warming on national ecosystems.[40] This fact partly explains China's positive response to calls for dealing with global environmental problems in international forums during the 1990s.[41]

## NOTES

1. Andrew Jamison and Erik Baark, *Technology Innovation and Environmental Concern: Contending Policy Models in China and Vietnam*, discussion paper, no. 187 (Lund, Sweden: Research Policy Institute, 1990).

2. World Bank, *World Development Report 1992: Development and the Environment* (Washington, D.C.: The World Bank, 1992): 220.

3. Lin Gan, *Global Warming and Options for China: Energy and Environmental Policy Profile*, WP–90–52 (Laxenburg, Austria: International Institute for Applied Systems Analysis [IIASA], 1992), 12.

4. World Bank, *World Development Report 1992*.

5. Department of Industry and Transportation Statistics, National Statistics Bureau, ed., *Zhongguo nengyuan tongji nianjian: 1991* (China energy statistics yearbook) (Beijing: China Statistics Press, 1991), 29.

6. Cheng Jinping, "China Decided Priorities for Coal Production," *Renmin Ribao* (*People's Daily*), March 8, 1991, p. 1; Li Xianguo and Song Zhenlu, "China's Energy Strategy Moving toward the West," *Renmin Ribao*, February 10, 1992, p. 1.

7. Ministry of Energy, Planning Section, "Major Problems of the Energy Industry in the 'Seventh-Five Year Plan' and the Prospects for the Next Ten Years," in *Zhongguo nengyuan yanjiu wenji* (Selected works of the China energy research) (Beijing: China Energy Editorial Department), 46.

8. In October 1992, the Development Research Center of the State Council and the National Environmental Protection Agency (NEPA) jointly organized the International Conference on Economic and Environmental Sustainable Development in China. It was a high-level meeting in which governmental ministers, distinguished scholars, and international experts participated. After the conference, an International Consultant Committee for Economic and Environmental Sustainable Development was established to provide policy advice to the government. See National Environmental Protection Agency (NEPA) and the Secretariat of the State Environmental Protection Commission, *Chixu fazhan de zhanlue gouxiang* (Strategic thinking for sustainable development) (Beijing: China Environmental Science Press, 1991).

9. Qu Geping, *Zhongguo de huanjing yu fazhan* (Environment and development in China) (Beijing: China Environmental Science Press, 1992), 2.

10. According to Dr. Qu Geping, the economic costs of environmental pollution accounted for 69 billion yuan and ecological deterioration accounted for 26 billion yuan annually, which was about 14 percent of GNP in the early 1980s. See Qu Geping, *Zhongguo de huanjing guanli* (Environmental management in China) (Beijing: China Environmental Science Press, 1989), 147.

11. The study involved more than one thousand environmental experts and covered thirteen important areas of environmental protection. See Qu Geping, ed., *2000 nian zhongguo de huanjing* (China's environment by the year 2000) (Beijing: Economic Daily Press, 1989).

12. In 1985, this center was reorganized, together with the Economic Research Center and the Price Research Center of the State Council, into a new policy advisory body, the Economic, Technology and Social Development Research Center of the State Council.

13. In 1980, thirteen policy alternatives were suggested to the government to solve the energy crisis, and energy conservation was the key component.

14. State Science and Technology Commission (SSTC), *Technology Policy in China: Energy,* Blueprint, no. 4 (Beijing: SSTC, 1985): 1–4.

15. Qu Geping, *Zhongguo de huanjing guanli,* 247.

16. Department of Economic and Trade, State Council, ed., *Quanguo jieneng xianjin qiye jingyan huibian* (Collection of the experiences of the advanced energy conservation enterprises in China) (Beijing: China Economics Press, 1992).

17. Ibid., 33.

18. Department of Policy and Legislation, Ministry of Energy, ed., *Nengyuan zhengce yanjiu wenji* (Collected works on energy policy research), vol. 1 (Beijing: Ministry of Energy, 1991).

19. Think tanks (for example, S&T policy research institutions) were established mostly in the late 1970s and the early 1980s as a response to the concern for integrating science and technology research and development into public policy making. It was commonly referred to as "soft science" research in China, that is, research focusing on interdisciplinary or cross-sectoral issues of national policy problems. The main differences between think tanks and the scientific community is that think tanks are much more concerned about long-term strategic issues and cross-sectoral matters; the scientific community is more concerned with basic research despite the fact that the Academy of Sciences also takes long-term views on development issues, mostly on S&T forecasting.

20. Ma Chi, "Some Thoughts on Developing New Coal Utilization Technologies in China," in *Nengyuan zhengce yanjiu: 1984–90* (Energy policy research: 1984–90) (Beijing: National Research Center for Science and Technology for Development [NRCSTD], 1990).

21. Technical processes to reduce ash content of coal can reduce the burden on transportation systems and increase coal combustion efficiency. Thus, coal washing and separation can serve two objectives: energy-efficiency improvement and environmental protection.

22. *Zhongguo nengyuan tongji nianjian: 1991,* 27.

23. According to an interview with a governmental official at the SSTC conducted by the author in April 1994.

24. Qu Geping, *Zhongguo huanjing wenti ji duice* (China's environmental problems and countermeasures) (Beijing: China Environmental Science Press, 1989), 197.

25. The State Economic and Trade Commission (SETC) is a relatively new organization established in 1993. It was originally the State Economic Commission (SEC) that merged into the State Planning Commission (SPC) in 1988. Its organizational structure has been readjusted several times because of conflicting mandates and division of labor with the SPC.

26. SSTC, *Zhongguo kexue jishu zhengce zhinan* (China S&T policy guideline), S&T White Book, no. 5 (Beijing: S&T Document Press, 1992): 39.

27. China organized an international round-table conference held in Beijing in July 1994. The purpose was to attract foreign investment and grants for the selected first group of sixty priority projects for Agenda 21, in which energy conservation was highlighted.

28. Qu Geping, *Zhongguo de huanjing yu fazhan.*

29. Pu Hongjiu, "The Necessity of Reforming the State Controlled Coal Prices," in *Nengyuan zhengce yanjiu wenji* (Collected works on energy policy research), vol. 2 (Beijing: Ministry of Energy, 1992): 7.

30. Shen Deshun et al., "The Strategic Position of Energy Conservation Policy in China," in *Shichang jingji yu zhongguo nengyuan fazhan zhanlue* (Market economy and China energy development strategy), ed. Qiu Daxiong et al. (Beijing: Nuclear Energy Press, 1992), 28.

31. *Zhongguo nengyuan tongji nianjian: 1991,* 246.

32. *Ziyuan heli liyong shouce* (Handbook of rational use of the resources) (Beijing: China S&T Press, 1991), 433.

33. *Quanguo jieneng xianjin qiye jingyan huibian.*

34. This can be seen from the priority projects developed by the government under the Agenda 21 plans.

35. Zhu Chengzhang, "The Level of Energy Consumption and the Potentials for Energy Conservation in China," in *Shichang jingji yu zhongguo nengyuan fazhan zhanlue*, 32.

36. Zhu Chengzhang, "The Current Situation in the Energy Policy and Reform in China," in *Shichang jingji yu zhongguo nengyuan fazhan zhanlue*, 136.

37. Mao Yushi, "Several Basic Theoretical Questions in Energy Policy Research in China," in *Nengyuan zhengce yanjiu wenji* (Collected works on energy policy research), vol. 2 (Beijing: Ministry of Energy, 1992): 91.

38. *Zhonguo jishu zhengce: Nengyuan* (Technology policy in China: Energy) Blue Book, no. 4 (Beijing: SSTC, 1985): 16–23.

39. *Zhongguo nengyuan tongji nianjian: 1991*, 19.

40. China established the State Climate Change Committee in 1987 to coordinate climate related R&D activities. The SSTC played a major role in assessing the potential impacts on climate change. See *Climate*, S&T Blueprint, no. 5 (Beijing: S&T Document Press, 1990).

41. Dr. Qu Geping stated four reasons why China paid more attention to the global environmental problems and debates: (1) If the global mean temperature rose, China would experience more natural disasters that could consequently reduce crop production. This would be a serious threat to national stability because of China's huge population and the need for agricultural products. (2) If the sea level rose, many of the low land areas along the long coastline would be flooded. This could bring severe damage to the agricultural and industrial base which constitutes the most important part of China's industrial regions. (3) The health of China's more than 1.1 billion population would be very vulnerable to ozone layer depletion, and China may receive the largest proportion of the health effects due to its huge population. (4) The consciousness-building process on global environmental problems will lead to changes in human behavior and attitudes, economic readjustment, and S&T development, such as the development of innovative new energy technologies and products. These changes will, in turn, provide new opportunities for China, and China shouldn't miss these opportunities in the efforts to proceed with its modernization plan. See Qu Geping, *Zhongguo de huanjing guanli*, 179–80.

# 11

# JAPAN'S OFFICIAL DEVELOPMENT ASSISTANCE TO CHINA: A BILATERAL MEGAPOLICY

*Quansheng Zhao*

Since 1972 when China and Japan normalized their bilateral relationship, economic cooperation between the two countries has remained one of the most important factors in maintaining stability in the Asia-Pacific area. Chinese and Japanese policies for promoting trade, foreign investment, joint ventures, technology transfer, and personnel exchanges deserve study because they are ushering in a new period of Asian history. Although the 1972 Sino-Japanese rapprochement and the 1978 Sino-Japanese Peace and Friendship Treaty laid foundations for the rapid development of bilateral relations, it was not until 1979 that China received any Japanese official development assistance (ODA). At that time, Beijing signed an agreement with Tokyo accepting a government loan. Since then, Japan has remained the largest ODA donor to China among all of the members of the Development Assistance Committee (DAC) of the Organization for Economic and Cooperative Development (OECD), and China has ranked among the top recipients of Japanese ODA.[1]

The emergence of this important set of economic and political relationships raises interesting policy questions. Why did Japan decide in the late 1970s to deliver a major aid program to China? Why after decades of isolationism did China decide to welcome foreign advisors and capital assistance from Japan? What problems did the resulting program address, and in what sense were its component parts the result of compromises among international and domestic forces in the two countries?

This chapter examines Japan's ODA to China to illustrate how an important set of bilateral policies emerged in the two countries. The extent to which each country is pursuing policies for its own purposes requires a thorough analysis of what Robert Putnam has called "two-level games." Putnam argues that the foreign policy-making process can be best understood as one in which decision makers are viewed as actors who play at both international and domestic politics. Analysts use the concept of "win-set" to explain how international and domestic factors influence foreign policy decisions. Policy makers seek that set of possible international agreements that would "win" by gaining majority approval among domestic constituencies. According to Putnam, any successful agreement must fall within the domestic win-sets of each of the parties to the accord. Thus, agreement is possible only if those win-sets overlap. The larger each win-set, the more likely they are to overlap. Conversely, the smaller the win-sets, the greater the risk that negotiations will break down.[2] To study this two-level game, one must pay special attention to the impact of both international bargaining and domestic social and institutional influences on the choices of policy makers.

Using the two-level-game framework, this chapter focuses on a series of actions that lay at the nexus of international and domestic factors affecting decisions in two countries that produced a fairly coherent series of foreign aid policies since 1979.

## JAPAN'S ODA TO CHINA AS A GREAT POLICY

Japan's ODA to China can be regarded as a megapolicy as Montgomery defines it in Chapter 1. As he observes, great policies transcend traditional sectoral boundaries and jurisdictions as defined in the conventions of government operations. Great policies require new organizational or procedural devices for their implementation; they generate new expectations that could not be met by normal programs; and they define new models of policy responses and suggest new paradigms of policy analysis.[3] In other words, megapolicies emerge from a transforming vision or a strategic notion.

In this sense, Beijing's decision to receive foreign aid and Tokyo's decision to provide large amounts of ODA to China appear to be megapolicies that fundamentally transformed the relationships between China and Japan. To better understand Japanese ODA to China, one needs to ask questions such as: What were the Japanese trying to do with their aid? What did they want China to become? What was China's vision of how it could achieve modernization by working with the Japanese donors? Was this an innovative strategy on the part of Japan or China or both? The following sections will address these questions by first looking at basic factors influencing aid and then separately examining foreign aid policy-making processes in both China and Japan.

## Magnitude of the Aid Policy

China was a latecomer in joining Japan's group of aid recipients. Despite the late entry, Japanese aid to China grew substantially throughout the 1980s and well into the 1990s (see Table 11.1). After 1978, Japan quickly became the largest aid donor to China. During the period from 1979 to 1984, Japan's ODA to China accounted for 45 percent of the total amount of external assistance received by China, including both bilateral aid from DAC members and multilateral aid from international organizations. During the same period, the International Monetary Fund was second (14 percent), with United Nations (UN) agencies third (12 percent), and West Germany fourth (9 percent) in the size of their aid to China.[4] Japan remained the top donor to China among DAC members in the 1980s and early 1990s (see Table 11.2).

China also became one of the largest recipients of Japanese aid. From 1982 to 1986, China was at the top of Japan's ODA list. From 1987 to 1992 (except 1991), China ranked second only to Indonesia.

From 1979 to 1995, there were three major packages of Japanese government loans to China. The first government-to-government loan was 350 billion yen (U.S.$ 1.5 billion) for China's five-year plan (1979–1984) pledged by Prime Minister Masayoshi Ohira on a visit to China in December 1979. This was followed by a 470 billion yen (U.S.$ 2.1 billion) package agreed to by Prime Minister Yasuhiro Nakasone in March 1984 for the five-year period 1985 to 1990. The third package was the 810 billion yen (U.S.$ 5.4 billion) covering 1990–1995 offered by Prime Minister Noboru Takeshita during his visit to Beijing in August 1988.

The substantial bilateral economic exchanges and government aid from Japan created an unprecedented degree of economic interdependence between the two countries. The economic exchanges between Tokyo and Beijing have had far-reaching political and strategic implications. As observers of international affairs have noted, Sino-Japanese relations "will assume increasing importance in Asia as both the U.S. presence and Soviet ambitions in the region fade in the post–Cold War era."[5] As long as China pursues its goal of economic modernization and its political future remains uncertain, Japan's aid diplomacy will continue to play a crucial role in Sino-Japanese relations both economically and politically.

## THE EMERGENCE OF JAPANESE ODA POLICY TOWARD CHINA

The foreign aid policies in Japan and China are products of quite different circumstances. An assessment of these policies must consider two phases of

Table 11.1
Japan's ODA Disbursements to China (US$ million)

| Year | Grant Aid | Technical Assistance | Loan Aid | Total |
|------|-----------|---------------------|----------|-------|
| 1979 | 0.0  | 2.6   | 0.0   | 2.6     |
| 1980 | 0.0  | 3.4   | 0.9   | 4.3     |
| 1981 | 2.5  | 9.6   | 15.6  | 27.7    |
| 1982 | 25.1 | 13.5  | 330.2 | 368.8   |
| 1983 | 30.6 | 20.5  | 299.1 | 350.2   |
| 1984 | 14.3 | 27.2  | 347.9 | 389.4   |
| 1985 | 11.6 | 31.1  | 345.2 | 387.9   |
| 1986 | 25.7 | 61.2  | 410.1 | 497.0   |
| 1987 | 54.3 | 76.0  | 422.8 | 553.1   |
| 1988 | 52.0 | 102.7 | 519.0 | 673.7   |
| 1989 | 58.0 | 106.1 | 668.1 | 832.2   |
| 1990 | 37.8 | 163.5 | 521.7 | 723.0   |
| 1991 | 56.6 | 137.5 | 391.2 | 585.3   |
| 1992 | 72.1 | 187.3 | 791.2 | 1,050.6 |

*Source: Wagakuni no seifu kaihatsu enjo* (Japan's Official Development Assistance), (Tokyo: Gaimusho, various volumes).

Table 11.2
Share of DAC Countries in Total ODA Received by China (US$ million)

| Year | Top Donor | Second Donor | Third Donor | Other Donors | Total Bilateral | Total Multilateral |
|------|-----------|--------------|-------------|--------------|-----------------|--------------------|
| 1990 | Japan 723.02 (51.1%) | Germany 228.94 (16.2%) | Austria 102.84 (7.3%) | 361.57 (25.5%) | 1,416.37 (100%) | 659.80 |
| 1991 | Japan 585.30 (50.1%) | France 138.46 (11.9%) | Germany 107.09 (9.2%) | 337.04 (28.8%) | 1,167.89 (100%) | 782.95 |

*Source: Wagakuni no seifu kaihatsu enjo* (Japan's Official Development Assistance), (Tokyo: Gaimusho, various volumes).

Japanese ODA to China: (1) the initial and mutually beneficial stage from 1979 to 1988, the first decade that China received ODA from Japan, and (2) the crisis-and-bargaining stage from 1989 to 1994, after the Tiananmen incident, when Japan decided first to suspend and then to resume ODA to China.

## The Initial and Mutually Beneficial Phase, 1979–1988

The first decade of Japan's ODA to China was considered by both countries as mutually beneficial. The key issues during this period revolved around Japan's decision to offer aid and China's decision to accept it.

### Chinese Policy Making

China's experience with Western intervention beginning in the mid-nineteenth century with the Opium War (1839–1842) made its leaders sensitive to issues of national sovereignty and foreign intervention. Two major reactions developed in China that have influenced thinking about foreign relations ever since: one was "antiforeignism," represented by the Boxer Rebellion of 1898 to 1901, which made Chinese leaders extremely hostile to any kind of foreign political, military, or economic presence in China; the other was "self-strengthening," a call by political leaders for China to resist foreign aggression through selective use of foreign ideas and goods. These reactions continued to manifest themselves during the era of the People's Republic.[6]

After the communist victory in 1949, officials in Beijing were suspicious of foreign loans. An exception was $1.5 billion in government loans from the Soviet Union and East European socialist countries from 1953 to 1960. In the 1960s and most of the 1970s, China firmly stuck to Mao's idea of self-reliance (*zili gengsheng*) that rejected economic cooperation with capitalist nations and isolated China from the capitalist world economy.

After normalization of relations between China and Japan in 1972, Tokyo, on several occasions, raised the issue of government loans as a form of economic cooperation. But these proposals were rejected unequivocally by Beijing.[7] As late as 1977, the Chinese leadership still insisted that China not allow any foreign interests or jointly managed companies to develop domestic natural resources or to accept any foreign credits. A *Renmin Ribao* (People's Daily) editorial, for example, claimed, "We never permit the use of foreign capital to develop our domestic resources as the Soviet revisionists do, never run undertakings in concert with other countries and also never accept foreign loans. China has neither domestic nor external debts."[8] The authoritative Communist Party journal *Hong Qi* (Red Flag) also emphasized that China "is an independent and sovereign socialist state" and would never allow foreign capital to invest in China.[9]

China's domestic and foreign policy changed drastically in late 1978, however, when paramount leader Deng Xiaoping announced the open-door and economic reform policies to promote modernization. For the first time, China showed a willingness to accept foreign aid. In September 1978, the government of China opened the first serious discussions of accepting Japanese ODA when China's Liu Xiwen, vice minister of foreign trade, met with Japan's Yoshihiro Inayama, president of the Japan-China Economic Association. A month later on a trip to Tokyo, Deng Xiaoping publicly confirmed China's willingness to accept loans.[10]

With this striking change in China's policy toward loans from a foreign government, Communist Party leaders had to find ways to legitimize the decision and to increase domestic support. After the death of Mao and the end of the Cultural Revolution, Chinese foreign policy shifted from promoting world revolution to emphasizing China's modernization and stability. Despite such fundamental changes in the beginning of the post-Mao era, there was still serious resistance in China to accepting foreign loans. This resistance arose from three major concerns. First, some Chinese leaders feared that capital inflows from major industrialized countries would jeopardize China's sovereignty. Second, a more widespread concern was that China's opening to Western countries would bring in capitalist ideologies. Third, political leaders worried that borrowing foreign capital would damage China's image and reputation as a no-debt country.[11]

To address these concerns, China's reform-minded decision makers, represented by Deng and then Premier Zhao Ziyang, first emphasized the importance of foreign loans for China's modernization. These leaders argued that accepting loans from foreign countries was essential for China to get access to cheap capital that it badly needed for economic development. Foreign loans and investments would offer China new sources of capital, advanced technology, advanced management skills, and access to international markets. Reformers argued that as long as foreign loans and investments conformed to the state plan and played a subordinate role in the domestic economy, they would not compromise China's sovereignty or independence. According to this school of thought, China was a fully independent and sovereign country that was not in danger of crumbling under pressure from outside, and China's socialist institutions could control foreign influences.[12]

To further reassure domestic constituencies, Chinese leaders repeatedly emphasized the importance of sovereignty and self-reliance. In September 1979, three months before the first loan agreement between China and Japan was signed, Vice Premier Gu Mu declared during his trip to Japan, "We will accept loans from all friendly nations as long as China's sovereignty is not impaired and the conditions are appropriate."[13] In late 1982, Premier Zhao Ziyang emphasized that "the aim of our foreign economic and technical exchange is of course to raise our capacity for self-reliance." In October 1984, Deng Xiaoping argued that economic cooperation and joint ventures with foreign countries would enhance self-reliance in the long run.[14] In fact, from the very beginning, the government made sure that China was in firm control of all major decisions on program planning as well as project selection, development, and implementation. Based on this principle, China would carry on extensive consultations and coordinate with aid-giving countries such as Japan.[15]

Officials in Beijing also felt strong pressures from the outside world. By the end of the 1970s, China's economic development was far behind the Four East Asian Tigers (Taiwan, Hong Kong, Singapore, and South Korea), three of which had large Chinese populations. All of these countries had developed their economies by integrating themselves into the world economy, and all had received foreign loans. These successful examples further encouraged Beijing leaders to look for foreign assistance.

Thus, both international and domestic pressures were creating an environment in which public opinion was becoming more favorable toward China receiving loans from Japan. Under changing international and domestic pressures, Japan's low-interest capital, advanced technology, and markets became increasingly attractive to China's leaders. Those bureaucrats who ran China's economic ministries also saw advantages to obtaining Japanese ODA. First, Japanese government loans had attractive conditions. These soft loans had longer payback periods and lower interest payments than the Chinese government could obtain elsewhere. Japan's government loans were repayable in thirty years at a little more than 3 percent interest with a ten-year grace period.[16] The conditions of loans that China could obtain from other channels, even in Japan, were much tougher. The most notable were short-term private commercial loans and Export-Import Bank loans. For example, in May 1979, the Export-Import Bank of Japan agreed to lend China $2 billion for fifteen years at 6.25 percent interest. Three months later, China obtained two commercial loans for a total of $8 billion at a higher rate and with shorter payment periods.[17] Second, although commercial loans were needed, Japan's government soft loans could more nearly satisfy China's seemingly insatiable demand for funds for large-scale infrastructure projects, such as railways, ports, and hydroelectric power plants, as fiscal crises repeatedly threatened China's key projects. Thus, Japanese loans came to account for 85 to 90 percent of China's total bilateral ODA. Third, as the first noncommunist government to offer government loans to China, Japan played a leading role for other industrialized nations. Western countries such as Belgium and Denmark as well as international organizations, including the World Bank, quickly followed in offering China assistance. A senior U.S. government official commented, "Very clearly, China's most important international relationship is with Japan."[18] Finally, Chinese economic bureaucrats gained valuable managerial skills and useful knowledge about how to approach the international financial community through its experience with the Japanese loan agencies.[19]

*Japanese Policy Making*

The international conditions and domestic pressures that Japan faced in the late 1970s were quite different from China's. As early as 1961, Japan had become a member of the DAC, a coordinating organization of the world's donors.[20] Japan's emphasis on foreign aid made it, by 1989, the world's largest foreign aid donor. Because of economic and geopolitical considerations, Japan extended most of its assistance to Asia (71 percent in 1980, 68 percent in 1985, and 65 percent in 1992).[21]

As noted earlier, soon after the normalization of relations with China in 1972, Japan offered to provide ODA, but Beijing was not ready to accept outside assistance from any country until late 1978. Both international and domestic factors explain Japan's enthusiasm to provide aid to China.

First, in the 1970s, ODA reflected a country's international status. As a DAC member, Japan was sensitive to its status within the group—it ranked fourth in the group as early as 1968 and then contended for second place with France. Although Japan's total foreign aid spending rose rapidly, the ODA percentage of gross national product (GNP) remained low. Prior to 1978, Japan's spending on foreign aid remained at about 0.25 percent of GNP, far below the UN guideline of 0.7 percent for industrialized countries.[22] To improve its international standing, Japan was pressed to increase its aid spending. In July 1978, Japanese Prime Minister Takeo Fukuda pledged to double Japan's ODA funds in three years. Thus, Japan viewed China as a new and appropriate recipient of this increased ODA budget. By successfully including China in the list of less developed countries (LDCs) drawn up by DAC's Statistics Commission, Japan was able to include its aid to China in its ODA contribution.[23] Although still low, Japan's ODA as a percentage of GNP increased to 0.30 in the 1980s and 1990s.[24]

A second factor influencing Japan's aid policy toward China was economic competition with other industrialized countries. Although trade with China in the late 1970s was less than 5 percent of Japan's total trade, China was economically important to Japan. For years, Japan, alternating with Hong Kong, was China's leading trade partner and accounted for about 25 percent of China's total foreign trade. Eventually, bilateral trade increased rapidly. In 1993, China emerged as Japan's second largest trading partner after the United States.[25] However, Japan's leading position in the China market was constantly challenged by other industrialized countries. From the Japanese perspective, large-scale projects normally had "high-feasibility" status and received better publicity in the international community and were, therefore, more desirable.

China's first loan request was for a package of eight infrastructure construction projects that included three hydroelectric power plants, three railroad lines, and two ports. When China began to explore loan possibilities for these projects in the summer of 1979, Tokyo was well aware of the competition from the Western countries. For example, there were several private commercial loan offers from France ($7 billion), Great Britain ($5 billion), Sweden, and Canada. The Japanese also knew of U.S. Vice President Walter Mondale's promise of $2 billion Eximbank credits to China when he visited Beijing in 1979.

The Japanese government understood that these project loans would be a convenient and useful way to enhance Japan's long-range economic position. They would allow Japan, as Chae-Jin Lee, a long-time observer of Sino-Japanese relations, pointed out, "to establish a firm foothold in China's economic infrastructure, and induce a spillover effect to other areas of Sino-Japanese economic cooperation." [26]

In the first aid package (1979), Japan agreed to provide government loans for six out of the eight proposed construction projects—all of the railroad and port projects were selected, but two hydroelectric power plant projects were dropped. This selection clearly reflected Japan's economic interests. The two ports, Shijiusuo and Qinhuangdao, were important for exporting coal to Japan. Two of the three railroad lines, the Yanzhou-Shijiusuo Railway and the Beijing-Qinhuangdao Railway, directly connected the two ports. Japan provided 62 percent and 100 percent of requested loan amounts respectively. On the other hand, the third railroad, Hengyang-Guangzhou Railway, was irrelevant to Japan's energy supply route and thus received only 16 percent of what China had requested. Two of the hydroelectric power plant projects (Longtan and Shuikou) were rejected by the Japanese because they conflicted with Japan's economic interests. The Longtan Hydroelectric Power Plant would have had the capacity to supply electricity to a large aluminum refinery with an annual production capability of 600,000 tons and make it a potential competitor with Japanese joint ventures in aluminum production in Indonesia and Brazil.[27] As one observer suggested, these examples demonstrate that the actual selection of projects reflected "the needs of the donor rather than the recipient, that is, it followed Japanese rather than Chinese economic priorities."[28]

Another important influence on Japanese aid policy was not only China's economic potential but also its strategic and political importance in Asia. Despite Prime Minister Nakasone's claim during an Upper House hearing on ODA in the National Diet that Japan would not bring strategic considerations into the distribution of its foreign aid, strategic considerations clearly influenced its aid policies.[29] Article 9 of Japan's postwar constitution renounces "the right of belligerency." As Nigel Holloway points out, Japan "cannot use military might in pursuit of its overseas policy."[30] This left economic cooperation as one of the only alternative means by which the Japanese government could exercise international influence over its Asian neighbors, particularly China.[31]

Japan's strategic goals underwent several changes after the 1960s. In the 1960s, ODA was used to promote Japan's exports. After the 1973 oil shocks, Japan's aid policy switched to securing supplies of raw materials, and China was clearly seen as an important source, along with Indonesia and countries in the Middle East. At the beginning of the 1980s, Japan tried to increase aid to strategically important countries such as Egypt, Pakistan, and Turkey, with which it did not already have close links. China's natural resources, in particular its energy resources, were considered to be strategically important for Japan. After the oil shocks of the 1970s, Japan became aware that political instability in the Middle East could jeopardize its supply of fuels from that region. With rich natural resources such as coal and oil, China was an ideal source from which Japan could diversify its energy supplies.

Japan's leaders were also well aware of international sensitivity to Japan's aid to China. To reduce other countries' concerns, the Ministry of Foreign Affairs in September 1979 released the Ohira Three Principles. These three principles were aimed at (1) assuring cooperation with the United States and other Western nations, primarily the European Economic Community (EEC), (2) easing fears that Japan might try to monopolize the China market by balancing aid to China with aid to other Asian countries, especially those in Southeast Asia, and (3) prohibiting loans to China's defense-related industries. The last principle was to deflect criticism from the Soviet Union, Vietnam, and South Korea.[32]

Although Sino-Japanese relations improved dramatically with the loan agreements, they were not entirely free of political friction. The most notable incidents centered on charges of revived militarism in Japan. In 1982, 1985, and 1986, large anti-Japanese demonstrations in Beijing and other major Chinese cities were inspired by Chinese leaders' sharp criticism of the Japanese government's revision of the description of Japan's behavior during World War II in school textbooks (known as the "textbook controversy") and by an official visit by Prime Minister Yasuhiro Nakasone to the Yasukuni Shrine to honor the war dead. Other problems included a territorial dispute over Diaoyu Island (*Senkaku*) and a controversy between China and Taiwan over ownership rights of a student dormitory in Kyoto. This controversy resulted in a Japanese court decision favoring Taiwan. During these frictions, Japan's political leaders pledged more large-scale soft loans to China. Japanese officials never admitted to any direct connections between the controversies and the loans, but clearly they were goodwill gestures to cultivate political ties with China.

Emotional ties toward China also played a part in formulating Japanese aid policy. Public opinion polls consistently ranked China second only to the United States as the most friendly nation. Because of cultural, historical, and geographical ties, Japanese emotions toward China were sometimes, as Swadesh De Roy suggests, "above reason."[33] There were also widespread feelings of regret among the Japanese, especially among the older generation, about Japan's behavior in China during World War II. Both nationalist leader Chiang Kai-shek in 1951 and communist leader Zhou Enlai in 1972 declined Japan's war reparations as goodwill gestures. Many Japanese felt that Japan could use government loans as surrogate reparations. As one experienced foreign banker in Hong Kong suggested, "Financially these loans make no sense. Politically they are really disguised reparations."[34]

To further promote the bilateral relationship and increase mutual understanding, Japan concentrated most of its grants to China on humanitarian projects and cultural exchanges. One of the most important projects was the

China-Japan Friendship Hospital in Beijing that cost 16.4 billion yen and accounted for 57 percent of all of Japan's grants to China from 1980 to 1985. Other smaller projects included a Sino-Japanese youth exchange center in Beijing (1985), a rehabilitation center in Beijing for the physically handicapped (1986), water purification facilities in Changchun (1986), forest resources restoration (1988), an experimental fishery station in Hebei Province (1988), a national library and a foreign language college in Beijing (1988), and preservation of the Dunhuang Mogao Cave on the historic Silk Road (1988).[35] A 1 billion yen grant to the Mogao Cave was pledged by Prime Minister Noboru Takeshita when he visited China in 1988; he indicated that the grant was to "appeal to the hearts of the Chinese people."[36] Economic assistance to China also came in the form of technical and training assistance. For example, in 1986, of the 10,000 "foreign experts" in China, about 40 percent were Japanese. A management training center funded by the Japanese was opened in Tianjin in 1986.

Japan's aid diplomacy and the efforts to appeal to the hearts of the Chinese people had been fruitful. U.S. journalists observed that despite problems surrounding the textbook controversy, the Japanese maintained better access to top leaders in China than did Western leaders and diplomats. For example, in 1984, Chinese Communist Party Secretary General Hu Yaobang invited visiting Japanese Prime Minister Yasuhiro Nakasone to a rare private family dinner.[37] In early 1985, Hu dined with Japanese Ambassador Yosuke Nakae three times in one week, whereas U.S. Ambassador Arthur Hummel, during his entire four-year posting, met with Hu only once. After signing the agreement transferring Hong Kong to Chinese sovereignty in 1997, British Prime Minister Margaret Thatcher proudly announced that Chinese officials agreed to receive a British trade delegation. But when the mission of 10 top British industrialists arrived in February 1985, they found themselves outdone by a visit of 100 members of the Japanese Chamber of Commerce. The Japanese delegation met with China's paramount leader Deng Xiaoping; the British did not. A Western journalist concluded, "No other country can compete with Japan for access in China."[38]

In sum, the first decade (1979–1988) of Japan's aid to China can be described as the initial and mutually beneficial stage. Despite different international and domestic influences on their policies, the two countries were able to cooperate economically through Japan's ODA. The overlapping win-sets in economic, political, and strategic interests that satisfied domestic constituencies in both countries largely explain the success of these policies.

## The Crisis and Bargaining Stage, 1989–1994

The second phase of Sino-Japanese economic cooperation policy began with the Tiananmen incident of June 1989 when Chinese military forces cracked down on the student-led prodemocracy movement and killed hundreds of demonstrators. This incident aroused worldwide protest and economic sanctions from Western industrial countries. This international crisis also led to changes in Japan's ODA policy toward China.

*Japanese Policy Making*

Japan's initial reaction toward the Tiananmen incident was cautious yet clear. Both Prime Minister Sousuke Uno and top foreign affairs officials deplored Beijing's armed suppression and called it "morally intolerable." In the immediate post-Tiananmen period, because of a lack of clear direction, Japanese aid officials followed a "case-by-case review" process for approving loans and grants to China.[39]

Japan also reacted to strong international pressures in the wake of the Tiananmen incident. Tokyo felt that it had no alternative but to join the economic sanctions imposed on China by Western industrial countries and put a hold on its government loans. Yet, the Japanese government was cautious. Instead of calling it a sanction, officials in Tokyo initially described the suspension of loan disbursements as a way of protecting Japanese aid officials in China from the violent military actions in Beijing.

Japan was the only Asian country that joined Western industrial countries' effort to impose economic sanctions against Beijing's military suppression of the prodemocracy movement.[40] One of the measures Japan took was to freeze its government loan of 810 billion yen ($5.4 billion) that had been scheduled for disbursement in April 1990. Other measures included the suspension of high-level government contacts and several scheduled economic and cultural exchange meetings, including the inauguration of an investment-promotion organization for China and a Sino-Japanese meeting on technology transfer. In addition to emphasizing basic democratic principles, Japan was also deeply concerned with its international obligations. Many observers believe that if Japan had not taken a tough stance on condemning China's military crackdown, Tokyo "might find itself internationally isolated."[41]

This international pressure slowed Japan's process of lifting economic sanctions and resulted in some confusion over when Japan should resume government aid to China. For example, a Japanese government source indicated in December 1989 that Japan would extend the 810 billion yen loans ($5.4 billion) once the World Bank lifted its freeze on new loans to China. Finance Minister Ryutaro Hashimoto then promised in early January 1990 that Japan would unfreeze the loan programs when Beijing lifted martial law.[42] Another possible release date, according to an official from Japan's Ministry of Foreign Affairs, was the resolution of the Fang Lizhi issue. Fang, a well-known dissident and physicist, took refuge in the U.S. Embassy in Beijing after the crackdown and remained there for more than a year.[43] Despite these announcements, Japan let several opportunities pass without lifting its loan freeze. Loans were not resumed when Beijing lifted martial law in January 1990 nor when the World Bank resumed humanitarian aid to China. Nor did they resume when Beijing released several hundred political prisoners in the first half of 1990, or when Chinese officials decided to allow Fang Lizhi to go abroad.

Despite its reluctance to resume the loans, the Japanese government avoided pushing China into further isolation. Immediately after the crackdown, chief spokesman for the Ministry of Foreign Affairs, Taizo Watanabe (referring to the Japanese military's behavior during World War II) emphasized that, "What the government is taking into account most is the fact that relations between Japan and China are naturally different from those between the United States and China." He also warned that Japan must be cautious because Beijing might launch a harsh attack against Tokyo's economic sanctions in order to distract domestic attention from internal political unrest. This view of the government was supported by many business leaders. For example, Bank of Japan Governor Satoshi Sumita advocated a "wait and see attitude" right after the Beijing crackdown.[44]

What concerned the Japanese government more were the signals from its Western partners, notably the United States. As late as July 1990, opinion in Washington was quite negative toward Beijing. Even though President George Bush extended China's most-favored-nation (MFN) status, the U.S. Congress was getting tougher in its policy toward China. U.S. lawmakers were determined to step up their efforts to limit loans to China by exercising their influence over the World Bank.[45] The Bush administration also held firm in its policy toward the Japanese loans. U.S. National Security Adviser Brent Scowcroft told a key Liberal Democratic Party (LDP) leader, former Japanese Foreign Minister Hiroshi Mitsuzuka, "not to restore the credits too quickly."[46] These pressures reinforced Japan's cautious policy toward China.

The United States had been ambivalent toward Japanese aid to China before Tiananmen. On the one hand, the United States itself was explicitly prohibited from extending ODA to China by the Foreign Assistance Act due to the fact that China was "a member of the international communist movement," and conservative lawmakers as well as the U.S. Commerce Department viewed Japan's aid presence in China suspiciously. They worried about U.S. competitiveness in the Chinese market as well as the human rights issue.[47] On the other hand, State Department and foreign aid officials had consistently encouraged Japan to take the lead in improving the West's relations with China. If foreign aid could help restore a moderate and open China, it would undoubtedly serve U.S. interests.[48]

While refusing to implement new loans, Japan lifted its freeze on ongoing aid to China in August 1989.[49] In October 1989, the World Bank resumed lending to China for humanitarian purposes, including a $30 million loan for earthquake relief and a $60 million credit for agricultural projects in February 1990.[50] Following the World Bank lead, the Japanese government, for the first time after the Tiananmen incident, released a new grant of $35 million in December 1989 for improving facilities at a Beijing television broadcasting station and a Shanghai hospital.[51]

From that time, the Japanese government frequently reminded government officials in the United States and other Western countries that it was not in their interests to impose heavy sanctions on China. Japan was also reluctant to criticize China openly at the July 1989 Paris Summit of seven major Western industrial countries.[52] "To isolate China will not be good for world peace and stability," Prime Minister Toshiki Kaifu claimed at a January 1990 news conference.[53] The prospect of a wealthy Japan facing an isolated, chaotic China had long been a nightmare for Japanese decision makers and prompted Japan to become a mediator between China and the Western world. A Japanese economic official put it this way: "Japan should take one step ahead of other nations in improving its relations with China. Japan can help create a climate for other nations to improve their relations with Beijing."[54]

Japan's decision to resume loans to China was made a year after the Tiananmen incident. At the Group of Seven Economic Summit held in July 1990 in Houston, Japanese Prime Minister Toshiki Kaifu announced that "Japan will gradually resume" its third package of government loans valued at 810 billion yen (U.S.$ 5.4 billion), thereby ending its economic sanctions against China.[55] This soft loan package to China was designed to last for five years, and about 15 percent (120 billion yen, or $0.8 billion) of the total amount was expected to be disbursed in the 1990 fiscal year.

Experienced observers of Asian affairs noted that while other world leaders were keeping their distance, Japan's leaders were moving quickly to restore friendly relations with Beijing after the uproar over Tiananmen began to subside and to speak for China's interests at the Group of Seven meeting in Houston.[56] Even though Japan's decision was understood by the United States and other Western economic powers, these countries did not immediately follow Japan's lead in changing their policies toward China.[57]

Japanese political leaders also faced strong domestic reactions toward the Tiananmen incident. Economic sanctions were frequently called for and received strong public support, not only from the ruling LDP and top government bureaucrats but also from opposition parties. Initially, LDP's Foreign Affairs Department Chairman Koji Kakizawa openly called for economic sanctions and said that Japan should make clear that it is a nation that respects the principles of democracy, freedom, and human rights. Even the Japanese Communist Party (JCP) Secretariat Chief Mitsuhiro Kaneko asked to "immediately halt economic assistance to China" because it is "paid for by the sweat of the Japanese people's brows." Japan's largest labor organization, the Japanese Private Sector Trade Union Confederation known as *Rengo* (with 5.4 million members), and the 4.5 million-strong General Council of Trade Unions announced that they would suspend all exchanges with China to protest Beijing's action.[58]

Later, however, opposition parties actively worked to restore Japanese aid to China. Whereas the Democratic Socialist Party (DSP) and the JCP remained uncompromised toward Beijing, the Japanese Socialist Party (JSP) and the

Clean Government Party (CGP) were ready to push for releasing the loans by the beginning of 1990. Secretary general of the JSP, Tsuruo Yamaguchi, visited Beijing in mid-May 1990 and met with President Jiang Zemin and Politburo Standing Committee member Song Ping. Yamaguchi promised that "JSP would continue to work hard to resume the third loan package."[59] At the end of May, President Jiang Zemin and Premier Li Peng met in Beijing with the visiting CGP delegation, headed by its founder and Honorary President Daisaku Ikeda, with whom they discussed bilateral relations.[60] An equally important factor was that Japan's business community began to complain that the loan freeze had seriously affected exports to China, and the business community wanted the government loans resumed.[61]

Domestic demands for resuming loans with China helped push the Japanese government toward releasing the disbursements two months prior to the Houston summit in July 1990. Prime Minister Kaifu met with the JSP Secretary General Tsuruo Yamaguchi before his eight-day visit to Beijing. Yamaguchi urged Kaifu to lift the freeze on loans. The prime minister told the JSP leader that there would be no problem in telling the Chinese leaders that "Japan will certainly honor its promise" in the $5.4 billion loans, but that there were "difficulties in resuming aid immediately."[62]

Japan's dual positions toward Tiananmen clearly reflected different international and domestic pressures. This complicated position was highlighted by a *Japan Times* editorial on the first anniversary of the Tiananmen incident. The editorial condemned Beijing's repressive policy but claimed that "outsiders' one-sided perceptions of China have played an excessively great role in isolating China in the international community" and stated that "it is time to try to pave the way for China's full-fledged return to the international community."[63]

This dual position inevitably produced a diplomatic dilemma and created confusion in Japanese policy toward China. For more than a year, Japan refused to restore the loans and argued that Tokyo's hands were tied by public opinion and international obligations.[64] Japan's action, in line with Western economic sanctions (including the suspension of World Bank loans worth $750 million), continued to sour relations between Japan and China.[65] It became increasingly clear that Japanese ODA to China was not only economically significant but also a crucial part of Japan's diplomacy toward China and directly affected overall bilateral relations. The controversy forced Tokyo to search for a balance among various options that would confirm Japan's continued support of the West and, at the same time, avoid pushing China into further isolation. Therefore, Japan needed to work on two diplomatic fronts—China and the West—in its post-Tiananmen policy.

After the resumption of Japan's ODA to China in the summer of 1990, bilateral relations between the two countries warmed up quickly. Political, economic, and cultural contacts reached high levels. According to one evaluation of the Japanese Ministry of Foreign Affairs, Japan's aid program to China was a "total success."[66] However, facing a changing post–Cold War international order and more diverse domestic demands at the beginning of the 1990s, Japan made noticeable changes in its ODA policy for China.

Beginning with an announcement by Prime Minister Toshiki Kaifu in April 1991 and confirmed by Prime Minister Kiichi Miyazawa in January 1992, the Japanese government adopted new ODA principles: Japan's ODA would hence-forth be provided in accordance with the principles of the UN Charter (especially sovereign equality and nonintervention in domestic matters) and the following four principles:

1. Environmental conservation and development should be pursued in tandem;

2. Any use of ODA for military purposes or for aggravation of international conflicts should be avoided;

3. In order to maintain and strengthen international peace and stability, full attention should be paid to trends in recipient countries' military expenditures, their development and production of mass-destruction weapons and missiles, their export and import of arms, and so forth; and

4. Full attention should be paid to efforts for promoting democratization, the introduction of a market-oriented economy, and any situation regarding the securing of basic human rights and freedoms in the recipient country.[67]

This new emphasis on environment, nonmilitary, and human rights issues would have far-reaching significance for Japan's ODA toward China in the 1990s. Beginning in 1992, the two countries started a series of negotiations for the fourth Japanese aid package. The extensive bargaining between China and Japan made it difficult to reach an agreement. While emphasizing that on human rights issues Japan would not push China as hard as the United States did, Tokyo would like to see China's military spending policy become "more transparent."[68]

But the controversy between the two countries did not center directly on such sensitive issues as human rights and military spending. Rather, the two sides concentrated on a seemingly technical issue—the length of the package. Japan's aid policy toward China was under extensive review in 1993 and 1994. The review focused on whether and how to change the previous preferential formula for Beijing under which Tokyo made an advance pledge of yen loans to cover a multiyear period.[69] In order to increase its control, Japan proposed that the previous pattern of five-year agreements be replaced by annual aid packages.[70] This proposal was strongly opposed by the Chinese side.

From the Japanese perspective, there were three reasons for the change. First, China was then the only Japanese aid recipient enjoying such favorable treatment; all other recipients were given annual aid pledges. Second, there were increasing public concerns about the growth of the ODA budget in Japan. Third, it was the normal practice for the Ministry of Finance to determine budget-related matters on an annual basis.[71]

There were, however, other considerations behind these changes. According to Akio Suzuki, staff director of the Japan-China Economic Association, this change reflected pressures from the United States. There had been frequent Japanese-U.S. consultations regarding Japan's China policy and its impact on China's human rights practices.[72] Another explanation was the conflict between political leaders and government bureaucrats: the politicians of the ruling LDP had been firm supporters of the long-term arrangement for yen loans to China, whereas the government bureaucracy was in favor of annual reviews. However, with the domestic chaos in Japanese politics in the early 1990s, particularly the LDP's loss of power in the summer of 1993, the influence of politicians significantly declined. Advocates of the short-term arrangement became stronger.[73] Japanese aid policy was largely driven by decisions of government agencies, including the ministries of foreign affairs, finance, international trade and industry, and economic planning.[74]

Given the strong domestic and international pressures on the two countries to continue their economic cooperation, however, observers expected them to reach a compromise toward the end of 1994 or early 1995 for Japan's fourth ODA package to China.

## CONCLUSIONS

Japan's ODA policy toward China has become an indispensable part of Sino-Japanese relations. The two stages of this innovative economic cooperation policy between the two Asian powers had significant policy implications. Clearly it transcended traditional sectoral boundaries and jurisdictions as defined in the conventions of government operations, required new organizational or procedural devices for implementation, and generated new expectations that could not be met by normal programs.

The policy created new economic, political, and diplomatic relations between China and Japan. The economic benefits to both countries are obvious. From the Chinese perspective, Japan's aid programs provided large amounts of less expensive capital than China could obtain elsewhere as well as advanced technology for China's modernization—in particular, its large-scale infrastructure construction projects. In addition, it also greatly enhanced China's position in the world economic system and in international markets. For Japan, the policy has not only ensured it of long-term raw materials but also enhanced its position in the China market. The degree of Japan's involvement in China's economic affairs as a result of its ODA policy cannot be matched by any other country. The large-scale aid programs have also enhanced Japan's international reputation as a leading foreign aid donor.

Equally important to both countries were the political and diplomatic impacts of the policy. For Beijing, Japan was the most understanding partner among industrial countries. Japan's ODA to China enabled Beijing to act more assertively when facing possible Western economic sanctions over political issues. The annual debate and human rights review in the United States over MFN treatment was regarded in China as a hostile challenge. One of the reasons that the annual review of MFN status did not improve China's human rights practices was that Japan and the European Economic Community (EEC) countries did not follow the U.S. lead. The close economic ties between China and Japan, and Japan's ODA in particular, enhanced China's bargaining powers in the international arena.

On the other hand, Japan also gained more leverage in its dealings with China. Aid diplomacy enabled Japan to use fully its advantageous economic strength. The unexpected political turmoil in China (the Tiananmen incident) and Japan's quick, yet cautious, reaction further demonstrated the importance of Japan's foreign aid to its political and strategic goals. Aid diplomacy served the functions of promoting Japan's international status and smoothing relations with neighboring countries—in this case, China. It also demonstrated that Japan had given priority to maintaining its role as a faithful partner to the West, particularly the United States. As a *Beijing Review* article points out, "By using its economic power, Japan seeks to become a political power."[75] One of the reasons behind Beijing's lifting of martial law in January 1990 was concern over negative international reaction and economic sanctions from Western countries. Japan was an important part of this concern. Even though Japan decided in July 1990 to gradually resume its government loan package, the fact that Japan imposed economic sanctions for more than a year demonstrates "Tokyo's increasing efforts to translate economic clout into [political] influence and participation."[76]

This comparative study provides a complicated picture of two-level games. Foreign policy making in both China and Japan can best be understood as a process in which decision makers must balance international and domestic politics. During most of the fifteen-year period between 1979 and 1994 as Japan's ODA policy toward China was evolving, Beijing and Tokyo faced different international pressures. But the overlap in interests between the two countries came largely from domestic pressures. As noted earlier, for policy makers to make successful international agreements, those decisions must fall within the domestic win-sets of each of the parties to the accord. Thus, agreement is possible only if those win-sets overlap. The mutual economic benefits from bilateral cooperation was a strong force in sustaining the Japan-China economic cooperation policy in both China and Japan. There were also strong bureaucratic and political interests within the two countries that wanted to maintain the momentum and to continue economic cooperation. Domestic political stability in China concerned decision makers in both Beijing and Tokyo and provided a strong motivation for officials in both countries to find a workable economic cooperation policy.

## NOTES

1. The Development Assistance Committee (DAC) consists of eighteen members, including all the European donors plus Japan, Australia, Canada, and the United States. According to DAC criteria, official development assistance (ODA) can consist of capital grant assistance, technical cooperation, capital subscriptions, government loans, or contributions to UN agencies and international financial institutions.

2. Robert Putnam, "Diplomacy and Domestic Politics: The Logic of Two-Level Games," *International Organization* 42, no. 3 (Summer 1988): 427–60.

3. See Chapter 1 this book, John D. Montgomery, "Beyond Good Policies."

4. Tasuku Okubo, *China and Japan: Financial Aspects* (Tokyo: Sophia University, 1986), 5.

5. *Far Eastern Economic Review* (August 23, 1990): 32.

6. For a detailed analysis of the impact of historical legacy to China's open policy, see Margaret Pearson, *Joint Ventures in the People's Republic of China* (Princeton, N. J.: Princeton University Press, 1991), 38–51.

7. Chae-Jin Lee, *China and Japan: New Economic Diplomacy* (Stanford, Calif.: Hoover Institution Press, 1984), 113.

8. *Renmin Ribao* (People's Daily), January 2, 1977, p. 1.

9. *Hong Qi* (Red Flag), March 1977; also see Robert Kleinberg, *China's "Opening" to the Outside World* (Boulder, Colo.: Westview, 1990), 1.

10. *Peking Review*, October 25, 1978, pp. 15–17.

11. Long Yongtu, general director, International Trade and Economic Affairs Bureau of the Ministry of Foreign Trade and Economic Cooperation of China, interview with the author, Beijing, January 4, 1994.

12. Margaret Pearson, *Joint Ventures*, 51–65.

13. *Beijing Review*, September 14, 1979, pp. 4–5.

14. *China Daily*, October 1984, p. 1.

15. Sun Yongfu, deputy director, Planning Division of the International Exchange Center of the Ministry of Foreign Trade, interview with the author, Cambridge, Massachusetts, March 19, 1994.

16. *Bangkok Post*, July 21, 1988, p. 28.

17. Allen Whiting, *China Eyes Japan* (Berkeley: University of California Press, 1989), 121–22.

18. Amanda Bennett, "Japan Excels in Relations with China: A Fact that Washington Finds Useful," *Wall Street Journal*, April 13, 1984.

19. Yu Zhensheng, deputy chief, Fifth (Japan) Division of the Foreign Financing Administration Bureau of the Ministry of Foreign Trade and Economic Cooperation of China, interview with the author, Beijing, January 7, 1994.

20. Philip Trezise, "U.S.-Japan Economic Issues," in *The United States and Japan*, ed. The Atlantic Council of the United States (Lanham and New York: University Press of America, 1990), 35.

21. See Robert Orr, "The Rising Sum: What Makes Japan Give?" *International Economy* (September/October 1989): 81; and *Wagakuni no seifu kaihatsu enjo* (Japan's Official Development Assistance), (Tokyo: Gaimusho, 1993).

22. Alan Rix, *Japan's Economic Aid* (New York: St. Martin's Press, 1980), 31–32.

23. Chae-Jin Lee, *China and Japan*, 120–21.

24. *Wagakuni*, various volumes; and *Japan Economic Institute Report*, no. 1B (January 5, 1990): 13.

25. "China Emerges as Japan's 2nd Largest Trading Partner in 1993," *Japan Times*, January 31–February 6, 1994, weekly international edition, p. 1.

26. Chae-Jin Lee, *China and Japan*, 116–19.

27. *Asahi Shimbun*, December 1, 1979; Chae-Jin Lee, *China and Japan*, 121.

28. Greg Story, *Japan's Official Development Assistance to China* (Canberra, Australia: Research School of Pacific Studies, Australian National University, 1987), 35.

29. *Asahi Evening News*, January 31, 1985, p. 1.

30. Nigel Holloway, "Aid in Search of a Policy," *Far Eastern Economic Review* (November 9, 1989): 64.

31. Masaji Takahashi, Japanese Consul General in Honolulu, interview with the author, Honolulu, July 17, 1990.

32. *Asahi Shimbun*, September 3, 4, and 9, 1979; also see Greg Story, *Japan's ODA to China*, 34; and Chae-Jin Lee, *China and Japan*, 118–19.

33. Swadesh De Roy, "Japan Image of China," *Daily Yomiuri*, January 14, 1985.

34. Allen Whiting, *China Eyes Japan*, 123.

35. *Japan Times*, October 14, 1985.

36. *Japan Times*, May 7, 1988, p. 7; and August 25, 1988, p. 1.

37. Amanda Bennett, "Japan Excels."

38. Jim Mann, "China and Japan: How They Buried Centuries of Hate," *International Herald Tribune*, May 6, 1985, p. 6.

39. *New York Times*, June 7, 1989, p. A8.

40. *Journal of Commerce*, November 30, 1989, p. 5A.

41. *Japan Times*, June 6, 1989, p. 12; and June 7, 1989, p. 10.

42. *Japan Times*, December 23, 1989, p. 9; and January 11, 1990, p. 1.

43. Henry Cutter, "Politicians Prepare to Restore China Aid," *Japan Times*, May 28–June 3, 1990, weekly international edition, p. 1.

44. *Japan Times*, June 6, 1989, p. 12; June 7, 1989, p. 10; and January 10, 1990, p. 1.

45. Susumu Awanohara, "No More Favors: U.S. Lawmakers Expected to Maintain Anti-China Stand," *Far Eastern Economic Review* (June 7, 1990): 56–57.

46. Henry Cutter, "Politicians Prepare."

47. U.S. Congress, *Legislation on Foreign Relations Through 1985* 1 (1985): 171.

48. Robert Orr, *The Emergence of Japanese Foreign Aid Power* (New York: Columbia University Press, 1990), 73.

49. Steven Weisman, "Foreign Aid Isn't Easy for Japan," *New York Times*, August 20, 1989, p. 3E.

50. *Sing Tao International*, May 11, 1990, p. 15.

51. *China Daily*, December 6, 1989, p. 1; also see *Japan Times*, November 29, 1989, p. 3.

52. *Japan Times*, July 5, 1989, p. 1; and December 15, 1989, p. 1.

53. *New York Times*, January 15, 1990, p. 5.

54. *Japan Times*, November 9, 1989, p. 12.

55. *Japan Times*, July 12, 1990, p. 1.

56. *Far Eastern Economic Review*, August 23, 1990, p. 32.

57. *Far Eastern Economic Review*, July 19, 1990, p. 57–58.

58. *Japan Times*, June 8, 1989, p. 1; June 25, 1989, p. 1; June 27, 1989, p. 3; and July 1, 1989, p. 3.

59. *Renmin Ribao* (People's Daily), May 19, 1990, p. 1; and May 21, 1990, p. 1.

60. *China Daily*, June 1, 1990, p. 1.

61. *Japan Times*, May 3, 1990, p. 7.

62. *Japan Times*, May 11, 1990, p. 1.

63. *Japan Times*, May 3, 1990, p. 7; and June 4, 1990, p. 20.

64. For a detailed account see "Sino-Japanese Relations Remain Far from Normal—Ties on Hold," *Far Eastern Economic Review* (May 10, 1990): 16–17.

65. *Japan Times*, May 10, 1990, p. 6.

66. Takashi Nagai and Tetsuro Taniuchi, director and staff member, Evaluation Division of the Ministry of Foreign Affairs, interview with the author, Tokyo, December 21, 1993.

67. Ministry of Foreign Affairs, *Japan's ODA 1992* (Tokyo: Association for Promotion of International Cooperation, 1993).

68. Yoshio Nomoto, director, China and Mongolia Division of the Ministry of Foreign Affairs, interview with the author, Tokyo, December 17, 1993.

69. Hisane Masaki, "Aid Policy toward China Comes under Review," *Japan Times*, November 22–28, 1993, weekly international edition, p. 3.

70. Michihiko Kunihiro, Japanese Ambassador to China, interview with the author, Tokyo, December 19, 1993; Reichiro Takahashi, deputy director, Technical Cooperation Division of the Ministry of Foreign Affairs, interview with the author, Tokyo, December 16, 1993.

71. Masato Kitera, director, Grant Aid Division of the Ministry of Foreign Affairs, and Kaoru Shimazaki, deputy director, Loan Aid Division of the Ministry of Foreign Affairs, interview with the author, Tokyo, December 21, 1993.

72. Akio Suzuki, staff director, Japan-China Economic Association, interview with the author, Tokyo, December 20, 1993.

73. Nobuo Maruyama, director, Economic Cooperation Department of the Institute of Developing Economics, interview with the author, Tokyo, December 17, 1993.

74. Michio Kanda, director, and Takumi Ueshima and Jitsuo Takasugi, staff members, Planning Department of the Japan International Cooperation Agency, interview with the author, Tokyo, December 22, 1993.

75. Chu Qimen, "Tokyo Seeks More Political Clout," *Beijing Review*, June 18–24, 1990, p. 17.

76. "Japan's New Gospel: Kaifu Signals Tokyo's Desire for Influence in Asia," *Far Eastern Economic Review* (May 17, 1990): 13.

# 12
## COMMUNITY NATURAL RESOURCE MANAGEMENT POLICIES IN COLOMBIA AND MEXICO

*William Ascher*

Over the past decade, there has been a remarkable turnabout in government policies toward natural resource management. Community management of forests, fisheries, irrigation systems, and general land use has become a credible strategy for resource conservation and sustainable development in many countries despite the strong, worldwide movement toward privatization. Although some governments have been slow to establish actual community control over lands that had previously been taken over by the state, the strategy of community management itself has become almost a new orthodoxy. Many governments publicize their efforts and, if they fail, suffer political embarrassment.

Community resource management is not just a modest shift from national to subnational government control. It typically entails recognizing the control of community groups that are defined by common social characteristics and interests rather than the control of the geographic community governed by subnational government units. Often the user groups are comprised of families that traditionally exploited resources under customary rights and that have continued to exploit them illegally under state restrictions. Often these groups are indigenous peoples who are still out of the economic, cultural, and political mainstreams.

This trend toward recognizing the resource management rights of traditional user groups has been widely applauded. What needs to be explained, however, is why governments have departed from previous strategies. The turnabout is surprising for four reasons. First, community resource management challenges the reputation, control, and discretion of the government. Relinquishing power is always difficult, but relinquishing control over natural resources has signifi-

cant economic costs for governments because natural resource rents are frequently a significant source of revenues. Moreover, because the state typically
took control of natural resources on the grounds that it could perform well,
giving up control often carries a strong implication of state failure.

Second, resource management by low-income, politically marginal, traditional resource users denies the government the opportunity to grant private
ownership rights to wealthier, more politically important interests. It would
seem that the privatization option—which for several decades was offered as
the solution to the "open access" problem that is often attributed, falsely, to
common property—better meets most governments' political agendas.[1] None
of the failures of state control over natural resources will discredit private
ownership any more than communal ownership. In other words, even if state
control were completely discredited, the choice of communal over private
resource ownership still would have to be explained.

Third, conventional wisdom perceived local resource exploiters as the problem not the solution. Saving natural resources was equated with excluding
traditional users. Because traditional natural resource users are typically low-
income, poorly educated ethnic minorities, their management capacity has been
widely discounted by both government officials and the higher-income, ethni-
cally dominant population in general. Changes in policy required a drastic
paradigm shift.

Fourth, recognizing the management authority of a subset of the community
rather than that of the entire geographical community leaves a policy vulnerable
to attack as undemocratic and slighting to local government. The natural
impulse of many national government officials is to think of communities as
administrative units (such as, districts, counties, and villages) controlled by local
officials. Even if popularly elected, these officials are often members of the local
elite and not the traditional natural resource users.

While the term *management* sounds mundane and even technical, it is
important to keep sight of the political issue of natural resource user rights in
almost all countries. It goes to the heart of critical issues: property ownership
and economic regulation. Insofar as community management puts control back
into the hands of relatively low-income community groups, it affects the
distribution of wealth and power.

This chapter explores these political issues in two Pacific Basin countries:
Colombia and Mexico. Each country has experienced a dramatic change in
community resource control policies. In Colombia, very large tracts of Amazonian land formerly under state control have been designated as protected
areas (*resguardos*) for indigenous groups. The policy was reinforced by important changes in property concepts introduced in the 1991 Constitution. The user
rights and authority of the indigenous groups have increased dramatically but
fall short of permitting the groups to sell the *resguardos*. In Mexico, some
community groups have also wrested control over forests and other natural

resources from state governments or from incursions by large, private resource exploiters, yet Mexico has also undergone a dramatically different transition— the dismantling of the long-standing *ejido* system of communal, inalienable landholding. The privatization of the *ejidos* has been a major blow to communal property even though the strategy of exposing *ejido* land to market forces could have been pursued by enhancing rather than reducing communal authority.

The success of policies promoting community management of natural resources depends on a complex combination of ideological and philosophical trends as well as pragmatic government problem solving in the face of specific challenges. As a consequence, this chapter pursues two paths: (1) it examines a few specific instances in which adopting a community management strategy was a politically and technically compelling option for the government, and (2) it assesses the evolution of thinking about community natural resource management that underlies the policy changes. The cases indicate that the greatest changes have been political. Community resource management has not just become a good strategy from a technical perspective; it has been advanced as a good technical solution for a long time. What has changed is the fact that it has become politically compelling for some governments to recognize the advantages of community resource management at the same time that some of the political obstacles, such as the dominance of business interests in the natural resources sector, have diminished. However, community resource management has been restricted even where the changes seem most dramatic. Indeed, an important element of the success—and limitation—of the communal resource management movement has been that governments have only partially incorporated into their policies the fundamental principles of community authority over natural resource exploitation. The obvious question would seem to be: How do governments hedge against risk when adopting such a nonincremental policy change? The megapolicies reviewed in this chapter address the governments' risks in two ways: (1) they are adopted in an attempt to shore up the governments' declining legitimacy, and (2) they are restricted in subtle ways.

Underlying this interpretation of policy change is a framework that recognizes the importance of two modes of problem solving: issue management and political management. It would be unnecessarily limiting to assume that governments' positions on natural resource management policy are driven strictly by political calculations. Government officials' deliberations on natural resource management and conservation usually take these problems at face value. The Colombian government has insisted on land inalienability, for example, not simply as a ploy to maintain ultimate control but as part of a genuine effort to cope with problems of deforestation and unsustainable migration. For a policy to be considered technically feasible, it has to be respectable within the relevant epistemic communities (that is, communities of knowledge) and relevant to the policy makers.[2] The technical feasibility filter is sensitive to the peculiar learning pattern of each country and sometimes leads to rather surprising differences in technically preferred options. Again, this is why tracking the intellectual history of natural resource property strategies within each country is so important. Respectable approaches to natural resource management are often derived from broader approaches, such as privatization, community empowerment, and decentralization.

Yet it would be naive to presume that political calculations play no part. This is particularly true for the two cases under examination. Both the Colombian and Mexican governments have been politically besieged by a host of guerrilla movements, defections from the mainstream parties, and periodic general unrest.

In short, an adequate framework for understanding why significant shifts in natural resource policy take place must examine the dual filters of technical and political feasibility. A satisfying explanation of the Mexican and Colombian policy changes must, at a minimum, show that the policy choices are consistent with government officials' perceptions of reasonable technical solutions and political necessities.

Moreover, the dynamics of community resource management policies in Colombia and Mexico are probably only applicable in situations of political crisis. The policy changes in both countries resulted largely from crises of legitimacy. They seem to be efforts not only to attack problems of inefficiency, inequality, or conservation but also to reduce the governments' political risks.

## POLICY CHANGES IN COLOMBIA

As in the governments of other states in Latin America, the Colombian government has steadily extended its formal control over the sparsely populated and heavily forested areas of its territory, particularly in the Amazon.[3] Over the years, various central governments have invoked the need for economic development, the importance of resource conservation, and the necessity for state control over areas theoretically vulnerable to Brazilian expansionism.[4]

Prior to the mid-1980s, state control over Amazonian lands facilitated migration into these areas. Unlike many other Latin American countries, however, Colombia never expunged the constitutional principle of indigenous claims to land. Yet, from independence to the late 1950s, the government did gradually decertify various legal designations of specific indigenous reserves (*reservas*). Spontaneous migration occurred because weak state control and the inability of indigenous groups to exclude outsiders rendered many of the areas formally controlled by the state into open access areas where newcomers could live, exploit resources, and sometimes eventually claim ownership by virtue of their extended presence on the land. The government also promoted migration by taking advantage of formal state control and the absence of indigenous peoples' legal user rights.

In theory, land reform could be confined to redistributing the large holdings of private owners, but in practice the occupation of "wilderness" met far less political resistance. The colonization of land that appeared superficially to be underutilized was often abetted by the lack of clear land titles for local groups who had enjoyed customary user rights. These lands—often designated as under state control for development or conservation purposes—were at the disposal of the government to reallocate for resettlement programs. In Colombia, violence in the Andean region pushed migrants into the Amazonian region where the roughly half-million indigenous, non-Hispanicized population had either been living for millennia or had found refuge from earlier Andean conflicts. Thus, in Colombia and, indeed, throughout Latin America, governmental land reform and colonization policies represented powerful threats to protected areas and to the user rights of indigenous peoples.

When the official Colombian land reform began in earnest in 1961 with the establishment of the Colombian Land Reform Institute (*Instituto Colombiano de la Reforma Agraria*, INCORA), the same law (Law 135) included provisions to reserve the lands of indigenous peoples. This was not a contradiction of land reform's basic thrust—which did indeed threaten indigenous peoples' lands— but allowed for setting limits on the degree to which land reforms would impinge on indigenous areas. Politically, it also served to offset the anti-indigenous and anticonservationist thrust of the colonization policy. The *reservas* allowed indigenous groups to continue to use the land in their traditional ways but did not fundamentally alter the government's claim to the land as state property.

The *resguardo* became the focus of the Colombian government's conservation and indigenous peoples policy beginning in the late 1960s. With no fixed legal definition, the *resguardo* designation has meant different degrees of community control according to specific laws and administrative rulings enacted since the nineteenth century.[5]

Unstable political conditions in 1980 prompted the government to enlist the support of indigenous groups by passing Law 89, which recognized the authority of indigenous leaders in the Cauca region in the Andes, but the general pattern was to weaken resource-use rights retained by indigenous groups. *Resguardos* came under siege. Sometimes they were replaced by the more restricted *reservas* that kept property in the hands of the state but granted temporary use to family, as opposed to community, activities.

In 1957, the Colombian government endorsed the Indigenous Rights Convention of the International Labour Organization, and in 1958, it announced the cessation of efforts to abolish *resguardos*. (Until 1958, the state tried to assimilate the indigenous groups by sponsoring missionaries and putting all Colombians under uniform national law.) It is significant that this date corresponds to the resolution of Colombia's decade of *La Violencia*, a period of dictatorship and bloody interparty warfare. The new coalition-backed civilian government sought to reduce all conflicts that could jeopardize its fragile legitimacy. Yet, the government did not then launch an expansion of the *resguardo* system, which could have provoked a confrontation with the nonindigenous groups still dislocated by Colombia's conflicts.

In the late 1970s, indigenous groups in the Andean region began pressing for government economic support for the remaining *resguardos*. The economic conditions of indigenous peoples, both within and outside the *reservas*, had been deteriorating. According to Bunyard, they began to organize themselves along the lines of peasant worker organizations.[6] This, in itself, must have seemed ominous to the government. In 1981, President Belisario Betancur initiated discussions with indigenous groups to expand the *resguardo* system. The land reform agency INCORA tried to respond by creating eighty more *reservas*, but some indigenous groups agitated to upgrade *reservas* to *resguardos*. However, it was President Virgilio Barco (1986–1990), responding to a new wave of guerrilla confrontations, who launched the massive expansion of *resguardo* territory. Between 1986 and 1989, Barco oversaw the establishment of *resguardos* that covered 18 million hectares for 156,000 indigenous people. This compares to only 8 million hectares (and 24,000 people) for the period from 1968 to the beginning of Barco's term in 1986. By 1989, approximately 365,000—or just over 80 percent of the 450,000 recognized indigenous people—had received some form of title.[7]

Since then, two important supporting developments have occurred. First, the government has made a commitment, albeit very slow in implementation, to buy the Andean land formally in indigenous peoples' possession that is actually occupied by nonindigenous settlers. Nearly half of the indigenous groups still reside in the Andean region, and much of their land is in dispute. Without compensation, few settlers would accede to losing their land. Indeed, more than 500 murders of Indian leaders have been reported since 1975, and most have been largely over land disputes.[8]

Second, the 1991 Constitution explicitly recognized the user rights and authority of indigenous peoples in indigenous territories. The constitution recognized the ultimate authority of the indigenous groups over the land within the *resguardo* and allowed user rights to be determined by the councils of the indigenous groups within them. In contrast, the *reservas* are state property assigned to indigenous peoples for the time being, but the government ultimately retains the constitutional authority to reassign the land. However, the constitution (though not the state) limits indigenous peoples' user rights by prohibiting the sale of the *resguardo* (*resguardo* land is "collective and inalienable property").[9] Thus, the 1991 Constitution assures the claims of the indigenous groups but does not fully embrace the essential principle of putting resource management entirely into the hands of the indigenous communities. Rather than relying on the wisdom of the indigenous people to pursue their own interests, the inalienability constraint limits the economic flexibility of indigenous governance. The rights of indigenous peoples within their territories are not equivalent to those of a nation. The indigenous peoples within indigenous territories—presumably including *resguardos*—are still under Colombian law. Although Article 246 of the 1991 Constitution states that "authorities of the indigenous peoples will be able to exercise jurisdictional functions within their territory, in conformity with their own norms and procedures," it qualifies the jurisdiction of the indigenous leaders by adding, "only if they are not contrary to the Constitution and laws of the Republic."

The 1991 Constitution can also be criticized for treating indigenous peoples as museum pieces. Explicitly, Article 330 of the constitution states that the "exploitation of natural resources in the indigenous territories will be undertaken without impairment to the cultural, social, and economic integrity of the indigenous communities. In the decisions that will be adopted with respect to such exploitation, the government will support the participation of the representatives of the respective communities." This would seem to give the government warrant to oppose actions of members of the indigenous communities if they threatened their cultural characteristics.

Implicitly, in dictating that *resguardos* cannot be sold or forfeited, the 1991 Constitution treats indigenous groups as if they will not or should not advance economically beyond their current modes of production to activities that would call for selling or mortgaging land. This may well backfire. When cash needs are high, indigenous peoples may resort to overharvesting trees, overfishing, and overexploiting other natural resources, especially if they are precluded from obtaining cash by collateralizing loans or selling land. To the degree that indigenous groups develop higher material aspirations and demand greater market rights, conflicts between the government and its current indigenous allies may increase as well. The long-term dilemma for the Colombian government is that the economic modernization of the indigenous peoples may threaten both the conservation strategy and the truce between the state and the indigenous groups which is based on the current congruence between resource conservation and their way of life.

### Changes in Process

The constitutional changes that culminated in the 1991 Constitution were also wrought by myriad private consultations among the government, the political parties, recently mainstreamed former guerrilla groups, business associations, labor organizations, and other organized sectors. The government essentially funneled the understandings developed through these consultations into the constitutional convention. The result was an elaborately orchestrated process dominated by the high-level representatives of social and economic sectors more than an exercise of mass participation. The rather poorly organized indigenous groups played, at best, a very minor role in this process.

In contrast, the process of making (as opposed to announcing the results of) the specific *resguardo* arrangements has been rather secretive, restricted largely to the indigenous leaders and the government. This is very much in keeping with the interpretation that the initiative was essentially a matter of political alliance building. Government officials consulted and negotiated with indigenous leaders in largely behind-closed-doors diplomacy, very much along the lines of treaty discussions. Nongovernmental organizations and the international community were loudly advocating the expansion of the *resguardos*, but the specifics were worked out with the indigenous groups and with sometimes surprising outcomes in terms of the magnitude and boundaries of the *resguardos*. For example, the huge magnitude of the areas granted to the *resguardos* that had been established in the late 1980s and early 1990s apparently was quite surprising to the actors outside of the government and to the indigenous groups themselves.

Even as a single case, the Colombian *resguardo* initiative has some simple but powerful lessons. First, the timing of policies recognizing the indigenous peoples' land rights—1890, 1957–1958, and 1986 to the present—reflects the strong connection between the government's need to bolster its legitimacy and its willingness to weaken the state's discretion. The Colombian strategy appears to be an effort to cement a political alliance with indigenous groups that occupy lands subject to incursions by guerrillas, drug traffickers, and possibly foreigners. It is true that indigenous peoples began agitating in the 1970s, nonetheless, the indigenous groups given *resguardos*, particularly in the Amazonian region, were not the major threat to the Colombian government. They were certainly less organized, mobilized, or armed than the guerrillas and the drug traffickers.[10] Nor are indigenous groups a serious challenge to the government's legitimacy; they are regarded as the potential bulwark against other challenges to the government's legitimacy.[11] Therefore, the political aim of the *resguardo* strategy is to mobilize the indigenous communities as defenders of their land and as allies of the government. The payoff to the indigenous peoples is greater recognition of their authority over land that the state would otherwise claim or perhaps cede to other groups it may feel compelled to win over.

It is also apparent that the observance of indigenous property rights—although certainly dramatic in the eyes of the Colombian government—is still significantly conditioned. The *resguardo* strategy has been infused with a strong conservationist rationale. The prevailing expectation may be that indigenous groups' rights are contingent on their pursuit of low-intensity resource uses deemed acceptable by the government. Ultimately, the state may be able to decertify particular *resguardos* by shifting to them the blame for environmental degradation.

This situation reflects two tensions. First, the willingness of government officials and the members of the constitutional assembly to grant authority to indigenous people was not as strong as the deep-seated presumption that the state is ultimately in charge. The 1991 Constitution makes this quite clear. The Colombian approach may be a political alliance strategy to gain the support of the indigenous groups, but it falls back on the strong *dirigiste* administrative option of reimposing state control through decertification.

Second, the *resguardo* strategy is not just a policy toward indigenous peoples or just a political strategy or just a resource conservation strategy. The conservationists who have backed the prohibitions on indigenous groups' discretion over the land reveal a pessimism about community control that presumes the government must hold the ultimate authority and are, thereby, forcing a conflict between indigenous rights and conservation. There are, in fact, two competing perspectives regarding the relationship between community resource control and sustainable development. The view reflected in Colombia's *resguardo* strategy is that full control by the community is risky because the community leaders or membership will abuse their authority. Therefore, the community must be protected from itself by restrictions that stand beyond the community's authority. Bunyard argues, for example, that "the *resguardo* belongs to the community in perpetuity. It cannot be sold, not even by the Indians themselves. *This system helps to maintain the integrity of the community and helps to prevent excessive exploitation of the natural wealth of the resguardo.*" [12]

The other perspective is that communities in full control of their natural resources will have enough incentive and capability to manage them effectively. Therefore, any infringement on the flexibility of the community to develop and exploit natural resources as the community leadership sees fit will reduce the value of resources in the eyes of the community and will increase the likelihood that community members will abuse them. It is striking how, as yet, only theoretical differences between these perspectives have led to such different policies. The choice of a policy allowing restrictions on indigenous peoples' user rights entails few short-term tradeoffs. Given the currently low economic aspirations of most indigenous groups in Colombia, it ignores, or at least postpones, dealing with the clash between community economic ambition and resource conservation.

Finally, the adoption of the *resguardo* policy during the 1980s involved a learning process that recognized the failure of a previous strategy, namely land reform. For many Colombian government leaders, the political unrest and guerrilla movements of the 1980s were shocking surprises. The government had pursued the orthodox strategy of the 1960s and 1970s: redistribute land where politically and fiscally possible; use colonization into low-density areas as a politically simple extension of the land reform effort; and restore liberal democratic practices. The recent incorporation of former guerrilla groups such as M-19 into mainstream political life acknowledged that liberal democratic practices per se are not enough; there must be changes in effective access to political power. The lesson regarding land reform is virtually the opposite: the prospect of effective access to land by all who want it was and is infeasible. Institutionally, this has meant that INCORA has been downgraded from an organization that represented the potential answer to the problem of rural unrest to an agency that is often an embarrassment in the now highly visible management of the Amazon. Of course, one could argue that the land reform was insufficient, or that it steered the landless to unproductive land while safeguarding the better assets of large landowners. But this was, indeed, part of the lesson learned: because land hunger cannot be satisfied in any politically feasible way, it must be blunted or rechanneled through political and economic transformations. The political transformation included the effort to recast the image of the Amazon from empty to sustainably populated and to elevate the indigenous groups to the status of political allies.

## POLICY CHANGES IN MEXICO

Until the 1980s, the customary rights of Mexicans traditionally involved in natural resource exploitation—particularly rural land and forests—received uneven treatment. In many areas, the governments of Mexico's thirty-one states, had appropriated lands that belonged to local groups by virtue of traditional use but not official titles. In other areas, these governments made arrangements, often in a heavy-handed fashion, for the private sector to gain access to the resources on lands formally held by traditional groups that often received only nominal income from the resources extracted from their lands. Even on the *ejidos* (explained in depth in the following section)—theoretically the most secure environments for communal resource control—outsiders had been able to gain access to resources with support from the state governments and by taking advantage of the typically weak economic capacities of local groups. These capacities had been limited not only by the standard obstacles (low savings and the lack of technical expertise facing all small, low-income communities) but also by the restrictions on using *ejido* land for collateral.

In the 1980s, the community groups in many states (especially in the poorer southern states such as Oaxaca, Chiapas, and Quintana Roo) began to protest these arrangements. Among the most visible protests were those directed against commercial logging concessions. In challenging the concessions, local groups were also challenging the wisdom and legality of the government's arrangements. Among the many specific episodes, a few cases may reveal why these efforts became markedly more successful in the 1980s.

Mexico has long recognized community resource management—70 percent of Mexico's forests are formally held by indigenous communities or in other communal arrangements.[13] Yet formal community jurisdiction had been severely compromised in reality by government practice. The movement toward effective community control appeared only in recent years. The key problem was that state governments had frequently been able to arrange for the assignment of user rights on *ejido* land. Especially in the 1950s, under the uncompromising progrowth policy of the central government, the state governments had arranged logging concessions for private timber firms on *ejido* lands. In many instances, the *ejido* leaders lacked the awareness, technical competence, or practical political clout to prevent or control these concessions even though the benèfits for the *ejidos* were minimal. In the southern state of Oaxaca, for example, the foreign-owned logging firm Fábricas de Papel Tuxtepec (FA-PATUX) secured a twenty-five-year concession over a 261,000 hectare area in 1956:

> Its concession failed to give FAPATUX absolute access to community forests, requiring the company to negotiate yearly contracts with the communities. In these negotiations, however, FAPATUX clearly had the upper hand, frequently with the collaboration of the secretary of agrarian reform, using its legal standing as concessionaire to suppress the communities' attempts to assert their right. Communities were denied the right to sell their timber to other buyers, for example, and one community that wanted to set up a woodworking shop was told it would have to buy back its own pine from FAPATUX.[14]

Similarly, in the southeastern state of Quintana Roo, the state government granted a concession to the state timber company Maderas Industrializados de Quintana Roo (MIQRO) in 1954. During its thirty-year concession, MIQRO and the private logging companies associated with it made deals with *ejidos* to harvest mahogany and cedar selectively. However, the *ejidos* received little in return because MIQRO brought in its own workers and shared little of the profits. Even worse, the company excluded local people from access to forest resources on their own land.[15]

The nationalization of FAPATUX in 1965 did little to alleviate the tensions between the enterprise and local groups. In 1968, fifteen communities boycotted the company by refusing to supply timber to the FAPATUX mills. The boycott lasted for five years but created only moderate problems for the company because of its ability to obtain timber from other communities. In 1981, the government of the state of Oaxaca tried to renew the FAPATUX concession, but this time a well-organized, multicommunity effort blocked the state and the company.[16] Outside help from Mexican nongovernment organizations (NGOs) enabled the communities to pursue legal claims against the infringement of *ejido* rights to determine the disposition of timber. FAPATUX failed to get the concession even though the community forestry operations, now organized on their own, still sell portions of their output to FAPATUX—on considerably better terms for the communities.[17]

MIQRO also failed to renew its concession in Quintana Roo. With the backing of the state governor, ten *ejidos* secured the rejection of MIQRO's request to continue its concession in 1983 and then received permission from the federal Secretariat of Agriculture and Water Resources to manage the forests in their area.[18] Once again, the *ejidos* could claim that the law was on their side. MIQRO proved to be a paper tiger; its political connections of an earlier era were ineffective in the 1980s.

Why did these actions, and scores like them in Mexico, succeed in the 1980s but not earlier? First, the local groups had developed new capabilities and gained confidence from the support of local, national, and international NGOs. They developed the potential to extract and market the resources themselves through cooperatives. Second, the state and national governments had been much less receptive to these claims before, largely because they were much more politically secure and saw little reason to jeopardize their alliances with the commercial business interests involved. But in the 1980s, the dominance of the ruling party, *Partido Revolucionario Institucional* (PRI), had become much more questionable. The potential of increasingly well-organized grassroots movements to challenge the legitimacy of the federal and state governments was becoming stronger than that of state-level business interests.

An extremely important aspect of these episodes is that they took place in many Mexican states and in many specific locales, but without a high-profile national confrontation with the federal government.[19] The pattern of community groups challenging previously ensconced business interests, invoking hitherto unenforced laws, and forcing state governments to come to terms with the new mobilization of communities was repeated time and time again. Yet, there was neither a high-profile national movement nor a need for a national decision nor an immediate threat to the legitimacy of the federal government. The result may have been a nationwide revolution in effective property rights, but it was conducted largely in a disaggregated, piecemeal fashion. It was certainly not lost on the federal government that these communities could have engaged in disruptive activities but typically eschewed them in favor of legal channels. The legitimacy of the state governments was often at stake, but the overt challenge to national authority, like that mounted in 1994 by the Zapatista Liberation Army in Chiapas state, was largely absent. It is telling that Chiapas has been different from most other southern Mexican states in that community-based forestry initiatives were brought to a standstill in 1987 by the decision of the state government to reject new applications for logging permits.[20]

### Macrochanges: The Privatization of the Mexican *Ejido*

The Mexican story told thus far involves the reclaiming of communal property rights from control by an alliance between the state and private commercial interests. In the 1990s, communal property itself has been challenged in a seemingly contradictory fashion.

Mexico had formally recognized community resource-use rights through the institution of the *ejido*, a communal property arrangement emerging out of the Mexican Revolution and its efforts to wrest land away from the large private landowners and the Catholic Church.²¹ Although inspired by precolonial communal land arrangements, the post-Revolutionary *ejido* arrangement left the state with considerable power. First, the state could enforce the inalienability of the *ejido*'s ownership because *ejidatarios* (property owners) were prohibited from selling, leasing, or mortgaging land. Prohibitions on land sales have even more serious consequences, inasmuch as they preclude using the land as collateral to obtain credit. Second, as noted earlier, the state has often dominated the allocation of concessions, particularly for noncrop land uses such as forest exploitation.

The *ejido* system is essentially the entire land reform sector in Mexico, comprising more than 60 percent of Mexico's agricultural land and 75 percent of its forests. While *ejido* lands are not typically the best agricultural lands in Mexico, the *ejido* system has been the most prevalent land-holding arrangement. By the late 1980s, it entailed more than three million households. In contrast to the Colombian *resguardo*, the *ejido* system clearly extends far beyond the refuges of remote indigenous peoples outside the Hispanicized economic and cultural mainstream.

Some *ejido* land is cultivated communally, and much of the forest land and grazing land is also for joint use. However, nearly 90 percent of *ejidatarios* had parceled out their high-quality cropland for individual household cultivation. Private user rights of these individuals (*ejidatarios*), which are critical for stimulating investment and sustainable development, had been limited by the possibilities of forfeit and penalties. Land left uncultivated would revert back to the *ejido*, and, in some instances, land too fragmented by inheritance could be reassigned by the *ejido* officials.

Improper cultivation, as defined by the state's interpretations of a large and inconsistent body of agricultural laws, could also warrant repossession or reassignment by state governments, although theoretically that required the approval of the Mexican presidency.²² The *ejido* arrangements appeared to grant secure property rights to the *ejido* members, but, in fact, several factors increased uncertainty. First, the constitutional provision that the state could ultimately reassign land rights persisted as a diffuse background risk. Second, and more directly ominous, was the risk of confiscation by either government or *ejido* officials for violating the unrealistic and often contradictory restrictions on the uses of *ejido* holdings, most particularly the prohibitions on leasing and the limitations on the size of parcels farmed by individual households. The risk of confiscation discourages not only the activities that are of questionable legality but also investments for improving the land.²³

In 1984, the Agrarian Reform Ministry complained that 86 percent of household *ejido* parcels were not legally titled.²⁴ This is a curious complaint because it implies that the absence of private titling is a problem rather than an expected characteristic of communally held land. It implies the possibility of injustices occurring when *ejidos* reassign land. In this interpretation, the *ejido* officials are cast as enemies of individual *ejidatarios* rather than as the community leaders of the *ejido* as a collectivity. The ministry could rightly worry that individual investment would be discouraged by the lack of private tenure, but communal investment would also be possible were it not for the state's restrictions on *ejidos*.

The Mexican government explicitly launched the *ejido* privatization initiative in 1990 by claiming that the *ejido* system was the cause of Mexico's agricultural stagnation. President Salinas asserted that the inefficiency of the *ejido* betrayed revolutionary aspirations to bring the Mexican peasant out of poverty. The president portrayed privatization as enhancing democracy in the countryside, thus equating democracy with individual economic freedom.[25] The *ejido* leadership and the state bureaucracies, by implication, were the obstacles. The *ejidatario* should be permitted to form whatever economic arrangements were in his interest. In 1992, Article 27 of the Mexican Constitution was amended to allow for the modernization of the *ejido*.

The reform essentially consisted of privatizing the *ejido* parcels already in the hands of households and of allowing the households currently enjoying the usufruct of the land to treat it as their private property. The old restrictions forbidding the sale, lease, or mortgaging of these parcels are being eliminated. The authority to manage or divest former *ejido* land would now be vested in the household rather than in the community.

In comparing the privatization of the *ejido* with the virtually simultaneous expansion of the Colombian *resguardo*, one is first struck by how the *ejido* reform recognizes the economic importance of giving landowners the full range of use options, including land selling, leasing, and mortgaging. However, this same flexibility could have been extended to the *ejido* as a collectivity by following the same economic logic. This option of strengthening or at least maintaining the authority of the community within the context of greater economic freedom now seems foreclosed. In many cases there is a strong likelihood that former *ejidatarios* will sell their land to larger landowners and that individually owned plots put up as collateral will be forfeited. By reducing the prospects for small landholder collectives, this may make it more difficult for small landholders to continue in agriculture. Some observers predict that privatization will yield a drastic reconcentration of Mexican farmland.[26] It is conceivable that the households of a privatized *ejido* could form a voluntary collective through a joint stock company or other arrangement of collective ownership. Yet, without the community as a collectivity with the authority to prevent defections from a collective enterprise, the obstacles and costs to the successful organization of such efforts may be fatal. John Heath notes the low level of success in setting up communal investment funds within *ejidos*.[27]

### Changes in Process

The *ejido* privatization initiative was promoted by the government through a series of presidential appearances and open just prior to the presentation of the Salinas legislative agenda in late 1991. Salinas announced on October 8, 1991, before the Permanent Agrarian Council (an umbrella organization of twelve large peasant associations) that "there will be modifications, by consensus, to the agrarian law."[28] Yet, the head of the orthodox National Peasant Confederation, also a PRI Senator from Durango state, publicly embraced all of the elements of the president's *ejido* reform. Leaders of many of the state-level *ejido* associations within the National Peasant Confederation openly stated their strong objections, couched as concerns that large landholdings would expand rapidly as individual *ejidatarios* sell their land or lose it upon defaulting on loans. These leaders had the opportunity to express their opposition, but consensus building was clearly not a high priority for the Salinas government, and the proposal proceeded to the Congress with little indication of willingness to modify it. In Congress, the support of the PRI and the center-right National Action Party ensured passage of the constitutional amendment and associated laws.

As a constitutional matter and a part of the broader issue of overall economic restructuring, this was clearly not business-as-usual governance but rather part of a new pattern of policy making and policy presentation that appeared in the economic crisis of the early 1980s. Prior to that time, important policy departures in Mexico were typically developed and portrayed as collective, consensual decisions reached in a corporatist fashion. There was a rhetorical commitment to pursuing the interests of all groups. In the heyday of the PRI, policy making on major issues was a rather closed process in which high-level government officials and their counterparts in the party huddled with officially sanctioned leaders of the remarkably broad range of economic groups within the PRI coalition. The leaders of urban organized labor and the peasantry were "representatives" of these sectors in a qualified sense—their status as leaders depended as much on their loyalty and acceptability to the PRI as on their standing among the members of these sectors. Business and large-scale landholding groups were more independently led, yet the proindustrial policies and the agricultural subsidies of the 1950s and 1960s kept most of these groups on relatively amicable terms with the government and the party. As a consequence, policy formulation was largely a matter of quiet consultation and negotiation. This was not unlike the constitutional discourse in Colombia.

Yet, in the 1980s, both the economic crisis and the legitimacy crisis of the PRI induced Presidents Lopez Portillo, de la Madrid, and Salinas—each more strongly than his predecessor—to adopt a new mode of unilateral, Draconian reformism without the presumption or fiction that everyone would be better off in the short term. Ironically, the newly open nature of the discourse corresponds to a process that was less democratic in one sense: a narrower range of interests is incorporated into each policy outcome. The losers express their objection more publicly, but they lose more completely. Since the launching of the privatization effort in the mid-1980s, these public encounters have been marked by the government's assertions of the necessity and urgency of the reforms, presenting the government's commitment to privatization as a fait accompli. This may be contrasted with the option of presenting the general problem and soliciting recommendations before the government position is formulated and announced.

The Mexican experiences of the 1980s and 1990s reveal an important principle of policy change. The several different imperatives driving the Mexican government led to quite different outcomes. The drive for economic efficiency propelled the privatization of the *ejidos* but had little to do with recognizing assertive community organizations pressing for the protection or restoration of their customary user rights. The reduction of confrontation seems to have been preeminent in this recognition, but not in the *ejido* privatization. Perhaps the government's overall legitimacy was a superordinate goal for both, but the point is that different, more proximate objectives resulted in very different stances on community resource management.

The timing of the *ejido* privatization reflects the importance of the political filter. The Mexican *ejido* system persisted for several decades even after it became strongly linked to the crisis of agricultural stagnation. There was a widespread view that the *ejido* system was an economic failure, but as a high-profile, historically prominent provision of the constitution, the *ejido* arrangement was sacrosanct. Many debates over reforming agricultural and forestry policy came up against the communal property constraint but had to take it as a given. Yet, in the 1980s, the nation's economic situation and the PRI's political position became precarious. A crisis in the rather closed political system arose largely from the failure of the economy, which had grown rapidly from the 1940s through the 1960s. As the import substitution and industrialization models faltered during the 1970s, economic stagnation was accompanied by a deterioration in the distribution of income that seemed to raise the specter of widespread political disintegration. In the early 1980s, a very severe financial and economic crisis led to the halving of real incomes for many Mexicans. The economic contraction undermined the PRI's remarkable capacity to coopt potential political opposition by providing moderately better economic benefits to groups cooperating with the government and party. This cooptation model had included the *ejido* leadership. Only when the general cooptation model—which had also favored the business interests pursuing logging until the 1980s—was acknowledged as a failure, did the abolition of the *ejido* arrangement become thinkable. Bowing to the wishes of the organized peasant sector within the PRI, which for decades has represented the interests of the *ejido* leadership, became less important than winning the direct support of would-be peasant individualists and entrepreneurs who otherwise may have abandoned the PRI in the increasingly contested elections. These changes were initiated a full half decade after the inception of general economic liberalization policies.

Privatization of the *ejido* system also became thinkable as a means of reducing the state's role in the economy. In an important sense, the privatization of the *ejido* reduces state control in that rules restricting uses of *ejido* land were formulated and implemented by the state. In short, the Mexican strategy is to substitute the old administrative-based, constitutional control mechanism with a market mechanism that simultaneously relieves the state of demands to control land uses and restricts the state's opportunity to do so in the future. Thus, the market strategy reduces the extent of government control, but it also reduces the demands on government while allowing the government to appear to be taking an active role in reform. The irony is that the Mexican government has adopted an activist reform strategy—and an activist image—to reduce the scope of the government's activist intervention.

The longer-term problem with the market strategy from a political economy perspective is that the government will have less leverage in responding to future demands for resource management. Without reopening the question of state intervention—which may well be a risky step—the government will be limited in reassigning property rights or regulating user rights. In essence, the Mexican government is counting on the general economic improvements expected from exposing farming and other elements of the economy to market forces to provide legitimacy in spite of these risks.

## BROAD LESSONS: THE NATURE OF LEARNING AND COPING

Colombia and Mexico are embedded in a world system in which policy makers are all exposed to essentially the same currents of international thinking about common policy problems. Colombians and Mexicans attend most of the same international conferences, and they are pressured by the same international advocacy groups concerned with indigenous rights, conservation, cultural survival, and related issues. They participate in and are pressured by official organizations on the global level, such as the World Bank, and by such regional institutions as the Inter-American Development Bank and the United Nations Economic Commission on Latin America and the Caribbean. Colombian and Mexican policy analysts are trained at essentially the same international universities in the United States, Europe, and Latin America; they identify with essentially the same epistemic communities of like-minded experts sharing the same outlooks, professional values, and general diagnoses of policy problems.

It is, therefore, worth exploring the degree to which these international currents and their domestic counterparts might account for policy changes in Colombia and Mexico. Yet we also see highly significant differences in the policy approaches of the two countries with respect to the key issues of inalienability and communal versus private authority. This section speculates on the interplay between learning from international intellectual currents and learning to cope with specific domestic challenges.

### Global Patterns

Several global changes in thinking about natural resource management are reflected in both Colombia and Mexico. First, the image of poor, rural people (whether or not indigenous in the sense of cultural and economic isolation) as potential resource conservers has risen dramatically. For this to happen, the alternative formulation—namely that the state is wiser and better at husbanding the nation's resources than are the ignorant, undisciplined local people—had to be discredited. This has happened on the global level with the mutually reinforcing movements of decentralization and privatization.

The ideological acceptability of community resource management is embedded in the broader issue of the legitimation of decentralization and local governance. As Vernon Ruttan has pointed out, community development was an intellectual precursor to the strategy of integrated rural development that was pushed strongly by international donors during the 1960s and 1970s.[29] The theme of fiscal decentralization arose strongly in the 1970s and 1980s, partially as a response to the fiscal crisis of central governments. The deregulation component of liberalization programs indirectly endorses the idea of community control inasmuch as deregulation in most countries has largely meant the dismantling of central government regulations and left more space for subnational, including community, control. In a rather curious convergence of right and left ideological positions, the libertarian strain within rightist thought calls for alternatives to big, centralized government. Because anarchy is rejected, the alternative of community empowerment—an idea long congenial to many leftists—becomes attractive to some rightists as well.

Privatization is similarly associated with the failure of the state in the economic sphere. Whereas this critique of the expanded state has emphasized the failures in general economic management, it has clear sectoral parallels in natural resource management where state control has been diagnosed as ineffective in trying to prevent deforestation, the decline of wetlands, and the destruction of biodiversity. It would be hard to find a country anywhere in the developing world where state intervention in natural resources is regarded as highly effective. In most countries, the full indictment of state intervention is quite plausible. In many developing countries, the gradual empowerment and mobilization of rural populations has finally reached the level at which their dissatisfaction has become an important political liability for the government.

The national parallels to these patterns are found in the crises of legitimacy of the Colombian and Mexican states. The crisis in legitimacy does not necessarily mean that the populace is actually disposed to oust the current government or even to reduce its compliance with government directives. The key question is whether high government officials—and often high officials of the governing party, the military, or both—perceive a significant danger to the government's legitimacy. The prevailing interpretation of why a given government faces a crisis of legitimacy is crucial. In both Colombia and Mexico, a widespread interpretation has been that the government loses its legitimacy when the state apparatus becomes pervasive, invasive, and ineffective.

Until the 1980s, the governments in both Colombia and Mexico had strong incentives to expand. "Expectant peoples" often concurred with government officials that the state had the right and the responsibility to be the central institution of control and change. Inactive governments were often perceived as failures.[30] Government officials also had strong incentives on behalf of their own institutions to expand the scope of the state, insofar as that meant adding to the government's control and fiscal capacity. The state expanded not only into the billion dollar, concentrated sectors of oil and mining but also into the more dispersed exploitation of forest products, fisheries, and even agriculture. Yet, state expansion reached its point of diminishing or even negative political returns when the Colombian and Mexican economies contracted in the 1970s and 1980s.

When it comes to such highly concentrated sectors as petroleum and hard minerals where huge natural resource rents are still available, the Colombian and Mexican governments have been reluctant to withdraw state control. But with respect to natural resources that could have widespread private or communal ownership, the potential for huge profits is generally lacking, and the number of people who may be resentful if their user rights are denied by the government is huge. Therefore, when government may be held responsible for natural resource failures—whether in terms of efficiency, conservation, or equity—community control may be the option of least political risk for the government. State control of the resource may fail to prevent overexploitation. If the government assigns user rights to private actors, they may misuse the resource, or the government may be blamed for putting resources into the hands of the wealthy.

## Contrasts between Colombia and Mexico

If the global currents of decentralization, privatization, respect for local resource exploiters, and the contraction of the state are common, what accounts for the differences between Colombia and Mexico? In light of the demonstrated pervasiveness of incremental policy making, it is reasonable to expect that megapolicy changes would typically require a dramatic rejection of past policy approaches.[31] In such sweeping rejections, it is often the case that the apparently defining characteristic of the old policy will be singled out as the problem. Thus, in an agricultural system in which the *ejido* was the predominant form of property ownership, the *ejido* itself—rather than the conditions within which it had to operate—would end up as the target of dismantling. This occurred even though there is considerable doubt about whether the *ejido* structure per se is associated with lower agricultural productivity.[32] Reinforcing this learning process—in which the *ejido* as the defining characteristic of the land-holding system was taken as the source of stagnation in agricultural production—was the fact that political leaders such as former Mexico City Mayor Hank Gonzalez, who were put in charge of the *ejido* privatization, were probably neither disposed nor equipped to tease out the seemingly subtle distinctions between the liberalization of communally and privately controlled property.

In Colombia, communal resource control on a massive scale is a rather novel idea. It is not subject to the disillusionment and fatigue that many Mexican policy makers and intellectuals feel toward the *ejido*. The Colombians have discovered the *ejido* system just when the Mexicans were abandoning it. Whereas in Mexico the inalienability of *ejido* land has been viewed as a very significant part of the policy problem, inalienability in Colombia seems to have been discovered as a "win-win" principle for both conservation and safeguarding the rights of indigenous peoples. This may be a delusion, but it is widespread nonetheless. In Colombia, the rejected principle is the sustainability of resource use by autonomous individuals (that is, the settlers) who ironically are the heroes of the Mexican *ejido* reform.

Thus, the Colombian and Mexican patterns also differ in that the concept of community has been elevated in Colombia, while the Mexican *ejido* privatization reflects a downgrading of the respect for the community structures that have run the *ejidos*. The speeches defending privatization (for example, by President Salinas) come close to equating *ejido* officials with the state itself. Again, defenders of the *ejido* might argue that the restrictions on *ejido* economic activities, imposed by both the state and the constitution, were more to blame than the *ejido* leadership. Yet this point is not of great relevance to Mexican policy makers who associate privatization with individual freedom rather than communal solidarity.

## CONCLUSIONS

Political crises, rural mobilization, and the delegitimation of the expansive state go a long way in accounting for the shift to community resource management in both Colombia and Mexico, which otherwise would seem politically inconvenient. These conditions were reinforced by the growing global respectability of self-governance and privatization. Given the three broad alternatives of natural resource management—state control, communal control, and private control—the movement away from a strong state role has increased the standing of communal and private resource management to different degrees in each country depending on its particular history and political challenges. None of the three alternatives have become paramount. State restrictions remain important even though weaker than restrictions of a decade ago.

Rather than thinking of these megapolicy changes as dramatic departures, what can be seen from all of these developments is that, first, the new policies had precursors, and, second, the new policies themselves were more hedged than the image of radical departure would imply. The precursors in both cases were the formal rights extended to local communities, whether through the older conceptions of *resguardos* in Colombia or the *ejidos* in Mexico. These preexisting policies or principles may have become vestigial—or at least relatively unimportant—at various times and reflect the strategy of partial incorporation that accepts a principle, restricts its effective applicability, and deflects criticism because the principle is not openly rejected. Yet this restriction through partial incorporation can have the ironic result of facilitating the later, fuller incorporation of the same principles. Legal precedents are important. Principles of community resource management became more relevant than when they had first been formulated, as conditions enabling their fuller implementation came to pass.

The hedged nature of the Colombian and Mexican policies is apparent when it is seen that the Colombian *resguardo* initiative and the Mexican *ejido* privatization both limit the role of community authority. In adopting the inalienability principle, the Colombians, although glorifying the indigenous communities as today's defenders of the environment, express faith only in economically primitive communities. The Mexican policy expresses belief in the *ejidatarios* as individuals but not in the *ejido* and its governance. The *ejidatarios* as private economic actors can be managed through conventional economic policy, over which the Mexican government believes it has a high level of competence and control. In short, the governments have been able to accommodate the risks that dramatic changes in resource management might entail.

Nevertheless, the changes in Colombia and Mexico represent very significant departures from the perspectives and institutions that prevailed in the early 1980s. The connections between these developments in the natural resource sector and the more general changes in the role of the state, community control, and privatization provide rather clear explanations for the directions and limitations of these changes.

## NOTES

1. "Open access" refers to the situation in which no one is effectively excluded from exploiting a resource.

2. See E. Adler and P. Haas, "Epistemic Communities, World-Order, and the Creation of a Reflective Research Program," *International Organization* 46, no. 1 (Winter 1992): 367–90.

3. An excellent summary of the historical patterns and existing legal status of indigenous user-rights in Colombia can be found in Raul Arango Ochoa, "Situacion territorial y tratamiento legal de las areas indigenas del litoral pacifico y la Amazonia de Colombia" (Territorial Situation and Legal Treatment of the Indigenous Areas of the Columbian Pacific Coast and Amazonia), in *Derechos territoriales indigenas y ecologia en las selvas tropicales del America Latina* (Territorial Rights and Ecology in the Tropical Forests of Latin America), ed.

Martha Cardenas, Hernan Dario Correa, and Mauricio Gomez Baron (Bogota, Colombia: Gaia Foundation, 1992), 223–60.

4. William Ascher, "Brazil's Future Foreign Relations," in *The Future of Brazil*, ed. William H. Overholt (Boulder, Colo.: Westview Press, 1978), 49–70.

5. See Ochoa, "Situacion territorial," for a more detailed explanation.

6. Peter Bunyard, *The Colombian Amazon: Policies for the Protection of its Indigenous Peoples and their Environment* (Cornwall, England: The Ecological Press, 1989).

7. Ibid., 5.

8. Ted Moses, "Commentary," *The Montreal Gazette*, December 28, 1992, p. B3.

9. Republica de Colombia, *Constitucion de la Republica de Colombia*, 1991, Article 329.

10. Carmen Alicia Fernandez, "Environment: Latin America Spearheads Movement to Conserve Nature," *Inter Press Service*, January 27, 1992.

11. Bunyard, *The Colombian Amazon*, 1–2, writes, "The Colombian Amazon has its share of guerrillas and army, particularly in the western part of the Amazon. . . . In addition, some guerrilla activity is to be found around the gold mining operation on the Colombia/Brazilian border. . . . Drug-related activity appears to have dwindled in the Colombian Amazon . . . , although some processing laboratories are still operating in the depths of the jungle. . . . Overall, the Colombian Indians seem to be enjoying their most tranquil period for nearly a century; for them it has become a time of recovery and reestablishing their tribal traditions. In all this they have the support of the Colombian government, which in any case sees their allegiance as important in the struggle against counter-government forces."

12. Peter Bunyard, "Guardians of the Amazon," *New Scientist*, no. 1695 (December 16, 1989): 38–41, quote at 39 (emphasis added).

13. David Bray, "The Forests of Mexico: Moving from Concessions to Communities," *Grassroots Development* 15, no. 3 (1991): 16–17.

14. David Bray, "The Struggle for the Forest: Conservation and Development in the Sierra Juarez," *Grassroots Development* 15, no. 3 (1991): 13–24, quote at 14–15.

15. David Bray et al., "On the Road to Sustainable Forestry," *Cultural Survival Quarterly* 17, no. 1 (1993): 38–42.

16. See Bray, "Struggle for the Forest," 15–16.

17. Ibid., 18.

18. E. M. Richards, "Plan Piloto Forestal," *Commonwealth Forestry Review* 70, no. 4 (1991): 290–311.

19. Bray, "Forests of Mexico," 16, lists efforts in Chihuahua, Durango, Guerrero, Michoacan, Oaxaca, and Quintana Roo.

20. Ibid., 16.

21. For a history of the *ejido* in Mexican land reform, see Susan Sanderson, *Land Reform in Mexico: 1910–1980* (Orlando, Fla.: Academic Press, 1984).

22. John R. Heath, "Contradictions in Current Mexican Food Policy," in *Politics in Mexico*, ed. G. Philip (London: Croom Helm, 1985), 97–136.

23. A solid assessment of Mexico's agricultural problems can be found in Paul Lamartine Yates, *Mexico's Agricultural Dilemma* (Tucson: University of Arizona Press, 1981).

24. See Heath, "Contradictions," 117.

25. Guillermo Correa, "El ejido sobrevive de nombre, per se acerca la privatizacion" (The Ejido Survives in Name, but Privatization Nears), *Proceso* 783 (November 4, 1991): 13–15.

26. Fred Rosen, "The Fate of the *Ejido*," *NACLA Report on the Americas* 36, no. 5 (May 1993): 3.

27. John R. Heath, "Evaluating the Impact of Mexico's Land Reform on Agricultural Productivity," *World Development* 20, no. 5 (May 1992): 695–711.

28. Correa, "El ejido," 13–14.

29. Vernon Ruttan, "Integrated Rural Development Programmes: A Historical Perspective," *World Development* 12, no. 4 (1984): 393–401.

30. Kalman Silvert, *Expectant Peoples: Nationalism and Development* (New York: Random House, 1963), used the term "expectant peoples," referring particularly to Latin Americans.

31. See Charles Lindblom, "The Science of Muddling Through," *Public Administration Review* (Spring 1959): 79–88; and David Braybrooke and Charles Lindblom, *A Strategy of Decision: Policy Evaluation as a Special Process* (New York: Free Press, 1963).

32. Heath in "Evaluating the Impact of Mexico's Land Reform on Agricultural Productivity" demonstrates that private land and *ejido* land did not differ significantly in crop productivity, partly because *ejidatarios* actually ignored some of the restrictions that might have reduced the production on their assigned parcels. On the other hand, Paul Wilson and Gary Thompson, "Common Property and Uncertainty: Compensating Coalitions by Mexico's Pastoral *Ejidos*," *Economic Development and Cultural Change* 41, no. 2 (1993): 299–318, argue that *ejido* livestock raising is less productive than private livestock raising. However, the relevance to Mexico's huge staple deficit is not very high, and the differences in productivity may be explained precisely by the fact that *ejidos* had lacked the economic opportunities that could have stimulated greater efforts to produce efficiently.

# 13

# PROCESSES OF STRATEGIC INNOVATION: THE DYNAMICS OF DECISION MAKING IN THE EVOLUTION OF GREAT POLICIES

*Dennis A. Rondinelli*

Megapolicies, by definition, are innovative ways of dealing with critical problems and opportunities. To the extent that they transcend sectoral boundaries, depart significantly from conventional procedures, create new institutional structures or interactions, and require new forms of behavior, these great policies have substantial impacts on society.

The cases examined in this book offer a wide array of experiences with extraordinary policies in Asia and the Pacific Basin and offer a rich source for comparative policy analysis. There is a strong tendency for those who assess great policies, however, to focus primarily on their substance and outcomes, which is necessary but not sufficient for comprehensive analysis. The most fascinating aspects of these cases are the underlying processes through which great policies emerge. Comparative analysis depends on the ability to identify patterns of decision making and to derive lessons from the dynamics of policy evolution that provide greater insight into how and why the policies evolved as they did.

Although most policy analysts recognize the importance of process, it is often far more difficult to gather information about how policies evolved than about their substance or impact. This chapter offers a framework for identifying and comparing different stages of strategic innovation that have shaped great policies. Not all of the cases address all of the stages of the policy-making process. But to the degree that examples can be culled from the cases to illustrate various dimensions of the policy-making process they can both verify the utility of the framework developed here and provide greater insights into the evolution of decisions about strategic innovation across cultures and political systems in Asia and the Pacific Basin.

## CHARACTERISTICS OF STRATEGIC INNOVATION

Most great policies are strategic in the sense that they fundamentally change the course of action of governments or other institutions in society in more than an incremental way. They are innovative in the sense that they introduce new ideas or ways of doing things that strongly depart from convention or that require new or unfamiliar forms of behavior and interaction.[1] Few policy innovations are pure invention; they are more often discoveries combining ideas that have been tried elsewhere that are recast to meet new circumstances.[2]

Most often, innovations are motivated by dissatisfaction with existing conditions or conventions. Whatever the sources of policy innovations, they require both the introduction of new ideas and their translation into specific courses of action. The transformation of new ideas into action usually requires wider recognition in society of the problems and opportunities that inspired a much smaller group of policy innovators. Some degree of social learning must take place in order for innovations to be widely accepted.[3] Some degree of consensus must develop in society that new problems or opportunities are important, that old ways are no longer effective, or that conventional approaches are too costly in economic, political, or social terms.

Once significant problems and opportunities are identified and recognized among a large enough segment of society to stimulate action, innovative ideas must be transformed into specific courses of action and new policies must be proposed to undertake them.[4] In nearly all political systems, strategic innovations must be legitimized before they can be implemented. A large enough portion of society must approve, or at least not strongly oppose, the changes in order for them to be adopted formally and implemented effectively. Policies must be enacted by a unit of governance within society, usually a government institution, with the authority to impose changes on society. Great policies must be made acceptable through any of a number of means, including persuasion, bargaining and negotiation, coalition building, authoritative command, or force.[5] Usually strategic innovations are legitimized and implemented through one or more of six major methods: enactment into law; administrative decrees; creation of new bureaucratic structures; reorganization of social, political, or economic institutions; procedural or regulatory changes; or the imposition of new norms or conventions that govern behavior.

Finally, the assessment of innovations must take into account their results, outcomes, and disposition. Some strategic innovations are applied successfully and largely achieve their objectives. Others undergo substantial adjustment through experimentation or are revised and reformulated during implementation. They may achieve some but not all of their goals and generate unexpected or unintended consequences that either displace original problems with new ones or alter the original intent of policies. Still others are unsuccessful; they are either terminated after they have been tried or simply disappear after unsuccessful attempts have been made to implement them. Whatever their disposition, innovations may set in motion fundamental and profound changes that were never intended.

At each stage of the process of strategic innovation, key actors play crucial roles in identifying problems and opportunities, disseminating knowledge, building awareness among relevant segments of the public, and translating ideas into policy proposals. Other actors must take part in mobilizing support for alternative courses of action, legitimizing the policies that are adopted, implementing new courses of action, and assessing their outcomes and results. The processes seem to be similar in both democratic and authoritarian political systems although there are substantial differences in the ways in which the process is organized and decisions are made. Differences may arise from: (1) variations in how open and participatory the process is, (2) the institutional structures through which decisions are made, (3) whether politics, the market, or authoritarian controls are used to allocate resources and resolve conflicts among interests in society, and (4) the degree to which decision making is visible to the public. Most frequently the key actors are formal and informal political leaders or bureaucratic officials. But sometimes, depending on the characteristics of the political system, they are leaders of nongovernment organizations, representatives of special interest groups, the media, private business leaders, personnel in international organizations, technical experts, and others. Usually different sets and combinations of actors enter and leave the decision-making process at different stages.

Figure 13.1 summarizes this description of the process of strategic innovation and policy making. Although the conceptual framework simplifies the process by making it appear sequential and linear, policy making is rarely, if ever, simply a linear progression through the stages depicted in Figure 13.1. Strategic innovations usually follow several indirect and complex "loops" through the process and can be redefined, refined, or modified substantially at each stage.

## THE PROCESS OF STRATEGIC INNOVATION

The great policies described in this book illustrate the dynamics of strategic innovation in public policy making in different political and economic systems. Analysis of the cases can answer many of the questions implied in the framework depicted in Figure 13.1. How were strategic innovations initiated? How were problems and opportunities identified? Who were the critical actors involved at various stages of strategic innovation? Why did society come to understand the importance of problems and opportunities requiring new policy solutions? How were the innovations transformed into policy proposals? How did governments or other institutions in society obtain the legitimacy needed to enact the policies? By what means were policies enacted and implemented? How did outcomes or results affect the ultimate disposition of the policies?

**Figure 13.1**
**The Dynamics of Strategic Innovation**

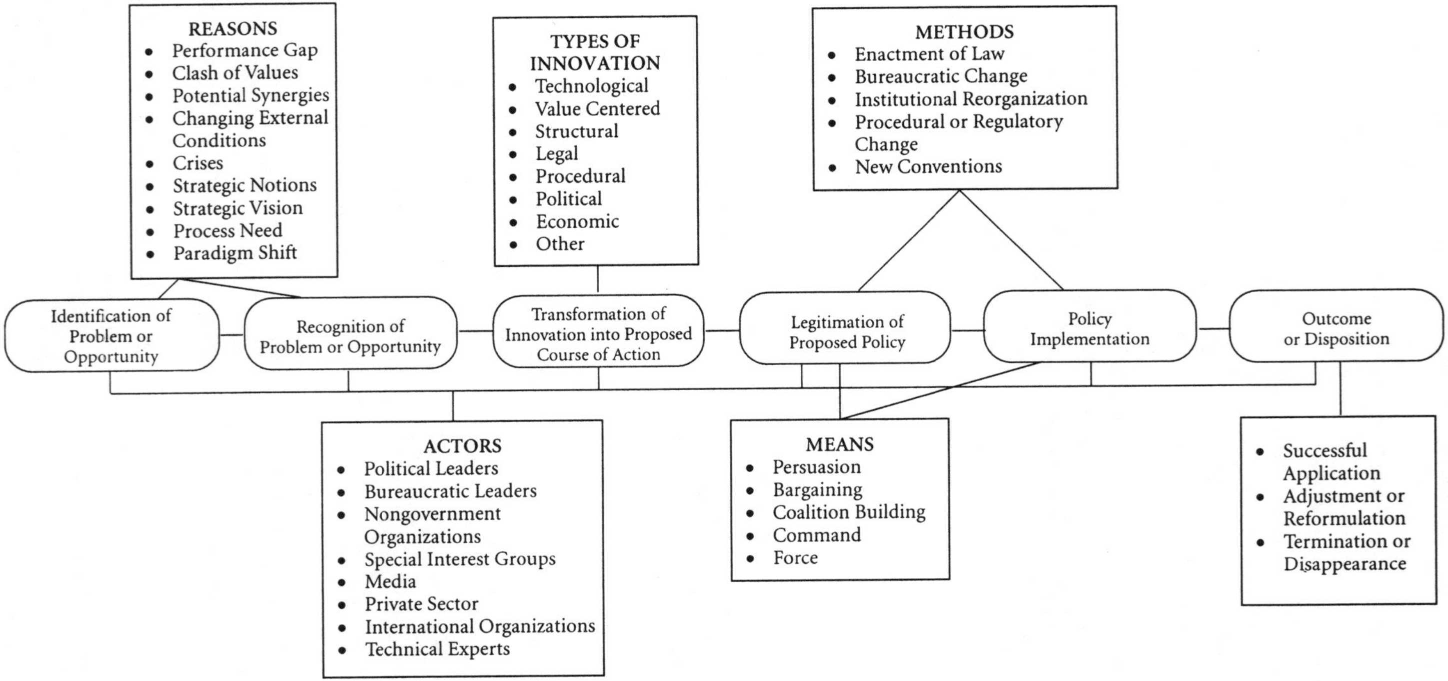

**REASONS**
- Performance Gap
- Clash of Values
- Potential Synergies
- Changing External Conditions
- Crises
- Strategic Notions
- Strategic Vision
- Process Need
- Paradigm Shift

**TYPES OF INNOVATION**
- Technological
- Value Centered
- Structural
- Legal
- Procedural
- Political
- Economic
- Other

**METHODS**
- Enactment of Law
- Bureaucratic Change
- Institutional Reorganization
- Procedural or Regulatory Change
- New Conventions

**ACTORS**
- Political Leaders
- Bureaucratic Leaders
- Nongovernment Organizations
- Special Interest Groups
- Media
- Private Sector
- International Organizations
- Technical Experts

**MEANS**
- Persuasion
- Bargaining
- Coalition Building
- Command
- Force

- Successful Application
- Adjustment or Reformulation
- Termination or Disappearance

Identification of Problem or Opportunity

Recognition of Problem or Opportunity

Transformation of Innovation into Proposed Course of Action

Legitimation of Proposed Policy

Policy Implementation

Outcome or Disposition

## The Origins of Megapolicies

Great policies evolved because individuals or small groups of people identified critical problems or opportunities that had to be dealt with in new ways. The ways in which strategic innovations were initiated, were spread within society, and were transformed into policy proposals were critical to their survival and emergence as great policies. In most of the cases in this book, a combination of factors were at work.

### Performance Gaps

Performance gaps are disjunctions between public expectations and institutional performance. The recognition that conventional policies were no longer doing the job—first by a small group of discontented people and later by larger numbers within an organization or a society—brought forth innovative changes that set them on new paths. Ascher pointed out in Chapter 12, for example, that in Colombia and Mexico changes in natural resource management policies came about in part because of worldwide assessments of governments' ineffectiveness and inefficiency in managing land, timber, mineral, and other resources. The proposals for local management by indigenous groups in Colombia and for privatization of resource management in Mexico, were shaped by people who saw increasing evidence that central government agencies were not capable of making decisions about natural resources more effectively than those who occupied the land and had to survive on it. Nor could they make more efficient choices than private owners with an economic stake in conserving and sustaining the resources from which they derived their income.

The adoption of energy conservation policies in China, as Zhao noted in Chapter 11, also was driven in part by performance gaps. After the government adopted an open door policy and economic reforms in the early 1980s, government agencies could no longer keep up with the demand for energy supplies. The assumptions underlying China's self-reliance policies for energy production during the 1960s proved to be unrealistic in the 1980s when shortages of energy became a critical bottleneck in China's push for rapid economic development and modernization. Although some political factions in China attempted to close the gap by urging heavier investments in energy production facilities, the adoption of energy conservation policies was an official recognition that increased production alone was insufficient and that unless serious energy conservation measures were enacted, conventional approaches would undermine the objectives of both economic development and environmental protection.

### Strategic Notions

Strategic notions are strongly held beliefs by important people about how situations can be improved through drastic changes in policy. Such beliefs can emerge only gradually. In Chapter 2, Orme credited junior officials in the U.S. State Department who knew intimately the political and economic conditions in post–World War II Europe, for example, with the original ideas that eventually evolved into the Marshall Plan. The megapolicy described by McConnell in Chapter 5, was born of a provincial education official in Japan who thought that foreign English teachers could help improve the conversational learning and cross-cultural awareness of Japanese middle- and high-school students and thereby change Japan's image as an inward-looking culture. Other ideas came from a governor of Taiwan and a leader of the Sino-American Joint Commission on Rural Reconstruction (JCRR) who believed that land reform was crucial to the survival of an occupying regime on Formosa; the same governor and a few key economic advisors later advocated changing Taiwan's import substitution policy to an export-oriented strategy that eventually created the "economic miracle" in Taiwan. A new paramount leader in China, Deng Xiaoping, and a small group of advisors realized that the Communist Party in the post-Mao era would have to depart dramatically from the ideology of self-sufficiency and adopt an open door policy in order to save the economy—and Communist Party rule—from collapse. A small group of environmental protection advocates in China interjected energy conservation and environmental protection values into that country's energy policies.

Johnston and Park described in Chapter 4 policies in Taiwan that were initiated with only a dim perception by policy makers of the scope, direction, and magnitude of the changes that were needed. But these notions—formed by a combination of the innovators' personal experiences, interpretations of others' experience, their own perceptions of problems and opportunities, influential arguments made or written by people with similar ideas, and the subtle processes by which thinking is influenced by education and analysis—were powerful sources of new ideas. The cases of Taiwan, Colombia, and Mexico indicated that strategic notions were often shared among people who had been exposed to similar experiences or educational backgrounds, or who moved in the same intellectual or professional circles.

Individuals with strategic notions initiated great policies by advocating fundamental changes in organizations, procedures, or behavior to address problems or opportunities in new ways. It was the strategic notion of Sun Yat-sen that land reform and income redistribution were crucial to building a strong political base in China. Although Sun's notion was not implemented on the mainland, the concepts were not lost. The strategic notion of land reform was later revived by Chen Cheng when he was appointed governor of Taiwan by the Chinese Nationalist Party (Kuomintang, or KMT), and by Chiang Monlin, the chairman of the Joint Commission on Rural Reconstruction; its adoption during the late 1940s in Taiwan set the country on a new path to economic development.

## Strategic Vision

Often, great policies have emerged from strategic visions that set a whole new direction and agenda based on the innovative notions of individuals and groups. Japan's agricultural development policies in Korea during a forty-year colonial period, as Ramachandran observed in Chapter 8, were driven by the strategic vision of creating in Korea a source of food that was badly needed by Japan. All of the policies were calculated to make Korea an efficient and productive source of agricultural products that would be exported to Japan. The strategic notions of Chen Cheng, K. T. Yin, and others in Taiwan about a new export-oriented direction for the economy were eventually incorporated into a strategic vision: the 19-Point Program for economic development. The 19-Point Program provided a framework for a new economic development strategy that departed drastically from the conventional import substitution approach and gave the bureaucracy, the KMT, and the military a new set of principles by which to manage economic development during the 1960s and 1970s.

Although Japan's strategy was not described in a formal plan, there was a strong strategic vision shared by leaders of succeeding governments about the aims of its overseas development assistance to China. Underlying its offer of aid was a vision of Japan exerting its political influence on another country (one that Napoleon had referred to as "a sleeping giant") through economic assistance and trade. Gan implied in Chapter 10 that Japan's selection of projects to fund through concessional loans evinced a well-defined strategy that would provide new and more stable energy supplies to Japan, build infrastructure needed to generate economic growth in China that would fuel trade with Japan, and avoid supporting projects that would compete with Japan's other worldwide economic interests. Japan's goals for aid to China remained consistent for more than a decade and reflected an articulate if not official vision of a broader strategy.

## Changing Environmental Conditions

Changes in external economic, political, social, or technological conditions often generated ideas that became great policies. In Chapter 6, Englesberg attributed China's willingness to send students and scholars to capitalist countries in the 1980s—after closing off opportunities for more than two decades—to a realization by some political leaders of the need for China to catch up with and become familiar with changing economic, scientific, and technological conditions in the West. External conditions also shaped China's policy of accepting foreign loans from Japan and international organizations in the 1980s, after repeatedly rejecting them previously. The decisions evolved, to some degree, from the need for government agencies and state enterprises to adjust to the changing global economy in order to achieve the Four Modernizations. Learning from the experience of Hong Kong, Singapore, and Taiwan, China's leaders saw that these countries achieved high levels of economic growth by switching from an inward-looking, import substitution strategy to an outward-looking, export-driven approach that integrated their economies into the mainstream of international trade and investment. Once domestic economic changes were accepted, China needed concessional loans and grants from other countries such as Japan to meet its enormous infrastructure development needs and to strengthen trade relationships that could bring the foreign exchange and hard currency income it needed to promote domestic economic growth.[6]

Other rapidly changing political and economic conditions in Asia during the past half century also generated innovations that became great policies in several Asian countries. The diplomatic and political efforts of the United States were decisive in convincing the leadership in Taiwan to accept outward-looking, export-oriented economic policies during the early 1960s. By providing financial aid and military support, the U.S. State Department pushed, prodded, and induced KMT leaders and the government bureaucrats who were comfortable with conventional import substitution policies to accept the export-oriented approach needed to sustain economic development in a rapidly changing global economy.

### Crises

Emergencies or threats to the survival of a government or other institution often forced leaders to seek new ways of dealing with problems or opportunities. The crisis situation in which the KMT found itself when it resettled in Taiwan during the late 1940s prompted the search for new economic and social policies that would reduce the political resistance of and build support among poor and landless indigenous Taiwanese.

Clearly, the changes in natural resources management policies in both Colombia and Mexico arose from what Ascher calls the "crisis of political legitimacy." In both countries the dominant political parties were under strong pressures to find a new constituency in order to build and sustain a majority coalition. The political leaders in both countries began to see indigenous groups that occupied forest or agricultural lands as potential new allies if their land-use rights were recognized by law. The crisis of legitimacy forced political leaders to recognize changing paradigms about effective natural resource management, not so much because of the compelling technical logic of the new ideas but because of the compelling need to neutralize political opposition among indigenous land users and to obtain their political support.

The perceived threats to the government of Thailand from communist insurgency during the 1960s clearly motivated political leaders to adopt the accelerated rural development program. Whether the threats were real or imaginary, political leaders' fear of insurgency and spread of civil war from Vietnam created an atmosphere in which they were willing to adopt a rural development policy focused primarily on suppressing communist insurgency.

*Synergies*

Strategic innovations sometimes emerged from perceptions that multiple objectives could be achieved by taking a new course of action or that a new objective could be attained by combining several courses of action at the same time. All of the policies described in this book sought to create synergies among sectoral objectives. As Wei noted in Chapter 9, China's economic reforms in the 1980s benefited from packaging and sequencing components of policy change in ways that reinforced each other. The overall reform policy was strengthened by pursuing the open door policy of foreign trade and domestic economic restructuring simultaneously. Japan's official development assistance (ODA) to China, on the other hand, offered opportunities to accomplish several strategic goals in different sectors through a single change in policy. Through concessional lending and grants to China, Japan could satisfy the strong emotional feelings of many of its citizens that they owed reparations to China for the behavior of Japanese soldiers during World War II—reparations that two of China's leaders had earlier rejected as a gesture of goodwill. At the same time, ODA to China met Japan's strategic goals of extending its influence in Asia through economic means, of developing strong trade relationships in a country with a vast potential market, of acquiring new sources of energy and natural resources, and of developing better political and diplomatic relationships with a large and potentially influential Asian nation, while leading the way for Western industrial countries to reestablish political and economic ties with China.

The land reform policies proposed in Taiwan during the late 1940s and early 1950s also depended on important cross-sectoral synergies. Land reform policies turned out to be a multipurpose solution to urgent economic, political, and social problems and achieved important goals in all three sectors. Not only did the land reforms offer a large number of Taiwanese tenant farmers hope for economic and social improvements but, as Orme pointed out in Chapter 3, they also provided the government with a means of extracting large amounts of capital from agricultural and rural development for industrialization, shifted the capital of former landowners into the industrial sector, stimulated the development of an important food processing industry, and increased the demand for consumer goods among farmers whose incomes had risen as the result of land redistribution. Moreover, the land reforms reduced the attractiveness of communism to poor landless farmers in Taiwan, built domestic and foreign political support for the KMT, and was essential for privatizing large numbers of corporations that had been nationalized under the Japanese occupation.

*Paradigm Shifts*

Great policy innovations often emerged only after fundamental shifts in concepts and assumptions allowed new ways of doing things to become thinkable. A paradigm shift is a change in conceptual framework that allows large numbers of people to perceive problems and opportunities in very different ways than they had done in the past or to conceive of responses to problems and opportunities in a new context.

The rapid spread of the domino theory of communist insurrection in Southeast Asia during the 1960s, for example, led many policy makers to believe that a successful communist revolution in any one country would spread rapidly and inevitably to all the surrounding countries. Existing regimes would fall like dominoes once the process was set in motion. As von der Mehden noted in Chapter 7, this paradigm played an important role in shaping Thailand's accelerated rural development policies. The widespread belief that programs to win the hearts and minds of poor peasants could help stem the tide of social and political discontent that was being exploited by insurgent communist groups in Malaysia, Indonesia, and the Philippines in the 1950s and in Vietnam, Cambodia, Laos, and Thailand in the 1960s brought about the dominant school of thought within which the accelerated rural development policies emerged in Thailand and in other Southeast Asian nations.[7]

Natural resource management policies in Colombia and Mexico changed after political crises established a conducive environment for reform. But community resource management and privatization were accepted in large part because the technical personnel in ministries and agencies dealing with natural resources had been exposed to changing paradigms. Ascher noted that ministry officials in both countries attended the same international meetings, were pressured by the same types of nongovernment organizations and international assistance agencies, and largely read the same literature on natural resources management. The dominant ideas about the most effective means of managing natural resources for environmental sustainability changed drastically in the 1980s from one that assumed that only governments could manage resources effectively to one that placed far greater emphasis on privatization of state property and on decentralization of authority to local governments and nongovernment organizations as well as to indigenous land-users. Without fundamental changes in thinking about decentralization, privatization, and community participation during the previous decade, the emergence of community resource management policies would have remained unthinkable in Colombia or would have been far more difficult to justify politically.

A fundamental set of changes in the political-economy paradigm in China in 1979 set in motion forces that led to the adoption of several megapolicies, including China's willingness to accept foreign aid and engage in trade with noncommunist countries and its shift from an energy production to an energy conservation and environmental management policy. The open-door and Four Modernizations policies announced by Deng Xiaoping in 1978 and the policies adopted for foreign economic relations during the 1980s produced a drastic shift in thinking from the Maoist self-reliance paradigm. Accepting loans from

Japan and from international financial institutions or sending Chinese students and scholars to study in capitalist countries were unthinkable under Maoist ideology. The Four Modernizations paradigm justified acceptance of foreign loans and economic interactions as instruments for achieving development on China's terms and created a foundation for even more dramatic market-oriented reforms to be implemented more than a decade later. Under the socialist market economy paradigm not only foreign loans but foreign direct investment became acceptable policies to party officials and government leaders in China.

Paradigm shifts also created new perceptions among government policy makers in China of the relationships between economic development and environmental protection that helped to advance energy conservation policies. The emergence of the sustainable development paradigm during the 1980s and its culmination in the United Nations-sponsored Summit Meeting on the Environment and Development in Brazil in 1992 provided a conceptual framework for China's advocates of energy conservation and environmental protection. The Rio de Janeiro meeting had a strong influence on the thinking of environmental advisors in China. Gan contended in Chapter 10 that the development of China's version of Agenda 21 recommendations reinforced the position of those government leaders who saw the harmony between economic development and environmental sustainability and hastened adjustments in China's energy policies in the early 1990s.[8]

*Process Needs*

Finally, Drucker contends that, in many organizations, innovation emerges from process needs, that is, from the realization that the organization must change what it does in order to conform more realistically to the needs and characteristics of its clientele or to broader and more encompassing processes in which it must operate.[9] The internationalization of the Japanese English-teaching program in middle and high schools, for example, was accepted in part because many school officials at the national, provincial, and local levels believed that they were not effectively serving their clientele—students who took English classes but could not effectively converse in English—with conventional methods of teaching. National ministry officials attempted to adjust the educational system by bringing in foreign teachers of English who used different and presumably more effective methods of meeting student needs.

The strategic notions of Chen Cheng and Industrial Development Commission chairman K. T. Yin also played a critical role in replacing Taiwan's import substitution strategy with an export-oriented approach that better suited the rapidly emerging process of global trade. They understood that the conventional import substitution strategies on which Taiwan's development plans had initially been based would no longer serve the country well in the future. Their persistent efforts to change policies to conform to global trade patterns spurred the evolution of a great policy in Taiwan.

## Transformation, Legitimation, and Implementation

The transformation of ideas into action defines the characteristics of an innovation. The most common types of innovations are technological, value-oriented, organizational, legal, procedural, political, or economic. In most of the cases reviewed in this book, a combination of means was used to transform ideas into action and to implement great policies. China's energy conservation policies, for example, focused primarily on legal, administrative, and technological innovations to promote research and development on energy-saving approaches. The policies emphasized setting up demonstration projects for new technologies and creating incentives both for the science and technology institutions in China to develop domestic energy-saving equipment and products and for industries to adapt and apply energy-saving technology. The policies also introduced new regulations and institutions to monitor energy use and assess new technologies.

The adoption of community resource management policies in Colombia came primarily through constitutional and legal changes that altered the formal status of land ownership for indigenous communities, as did the privatization of *ejidos* in Mexico. Changes in the scope and direction of economic development plans and the restructuring of government agencies were the vehicles through which Taiwan shifted from an import substitution to an export-oriented economic strategy in the early 1960s. The Japan Exchange and Teaching (JET) program introduced innovations in both procedures and values by inviting foreign teachers of English who would use team-teaching methods that were unfamiliar to most Japanese teachers and instill new values of cross-cultural tolerance among teachers and students.

Generally, policies are legitimated within society and implemented through one or a combination of five major means: (1) persuasion, (2) bargaining, (3) coalition building, (4) command and authority, and (5) force. None of the great policies examined here were legitimized or implemented through overt force, although the agricultural policies imposed on Korea during the Japanese occupation and the brutal repression of Taiwanese landowners by the KMT in 1947 may come close. Generally, a combination of the other means were used by governments and interest groups to implement innovative ideas.

The impact of persuasion can be seen in the role that scientists in research and development institutions in China played during the 1970s and early 1980s in convincing government leaders of the need to shift from an energy supply to an energy conservation policy. Once the Chinese government adopted a more energy-conserving approach, it used demonstration projects, incentives, and propaganda to convince state enterprises to adopt energy-saving technology.

Clearly, the United States leveraged its bargaining power by providing incentives to the government of Taiwan to adopt land reform in the 1950s and an export-oriented policy in the 1960s. It used a combination of incentives and threats in Thailand to get the government to use the Accelerated Rural Development (ARD) program as a counterinsurgency tool. The incentives were financial and technical aid; the threats were the perceived consequences of Thailand's failure to stem communist influence in the northeastern region of the country. Threats of punishment focused on withholding or appropriating valued resources if agreed-upon actions were not taken. Japan withheld foreign aid to China after the Tiananmen incident in order to achieve concessions in the form of more liberal domestic political policies in China, release of some political prisoners, and changes in the way in which foreign loans were provided.

The governments of Mexico and Colombia used implicit and explicit bargains with community groups and landowners in those countries to form a larger political coalition that not only changed the way in which natural resources were managed but also provided desperately needed support for the regime. In return for constitutional and legal changes in natural resource and land use management, indigenous land users worked within the political system rather than subverting, undermining, or revolting against it.

When it became clear in China that many study-abroad program students were not returning home as quickly as anticipated, the government enacted a set of rules and regulations that would bring the policy under their authority and control. In addition, it created incentives that would make retuning home desirable, such as preferred housing, better job assurances, and so on. It was the combination of restrictions and incentives that reversed the brain drain. China also relied heavily on rules and regulations to carry out its environmental policies.[10]

### Outcomes and Consequences

Finally, these great policies developed in three different ways during their implementation. First, some policies were carried out largely as they were conceived. Japan's official development assistance to China largely achieved the objectives of both countries during the 1980s until the Tiananmen incident disrupted and changed the nature of the aid relationship. Natural resource management policies in Colombia and Mexico achieved the governments' objectives of building a stronger and broader political coalition and overcame the crisis of legitimacy, although the policies did not necessarily solve the problems of land tenure and ownership of indigenous resource users. Taiwan's land reform programs were quite successful in attaining the intended goals for which they were designed; later, in the 1960s, its export-oriented policies far exceeded expectations, making Taiwan one of the most successful "newly industrializing countries" in Asia.

Second, policies were modified during implementation, either deliberately by the government in response to changing circumstances or as the result of compromise with or reactions to opposing forces. Great policies also generated unintended or unanticipated consequences to which governments had to re-spond. These unanticipated consequences often required implementors to carry out policies in different ways than the initiators intended.

Although the JET program in Japan was successful in infusing large numbers of foreign teachers of English into middle schools and high schools, it was never implemented as its advocates and proponents had intended because the pro-gram could not change social values as quickly as necessary for the foreign English teachers or their teaching methods to be fully accepted. Conventional Japanese values and pedagogical methods were reinforced by Japanese teachers in ways that undermined the practices and values that foreign English teachers were attempting to instill. In many subtle ways, the message was given to Japanese students that what the foreign teachers were doing was neither impor-tant nor a lasting part of the curriculum. The educational system at the provin-cial and local levels marginalized many of the foreign English teachers and weakened the impacts of the national program.

China's foreign study program was successful in placing large numbers of Chinese students and scholars in foreign universities to accelerate the modern-ization of China's economy but had to be modified when it began to generate the opposite effects of those intended—draining China of educated scientists rather than adding to their numbers. The accelerated rural development policies in Thailand focused on activities that were not fully intended by either their Thai or American proponents. Although promoted as a poverty alleviation and rural economic development program, ARD was buffeted by changing U.S. policies and Thai government priorities. Instead of focusing on rural poverty alleviation, it emerged in its early years as a counterinsurgency program con-cerned primarily with neutralizing the influence of communist factions in northeastern Thailand and, in its later years, as a road-building program. Although ARD had significant impacts on the economies of the areas in which roads were built and on local government operations where the program operated, its major accomplishment remained rural road building.

The colonial agricultural policies in Korea were successful, but not in achiev-ing the goals Japan had set for them of establishing a food supply source for land-scarce Japan. Instead, the policies had the unintended consequences of creating a strong agricultural base for Korea's industrialization after inde-pendence. Japan inadvertently created a model of agriculturally driven eco-nomic development that could generate surpluses for industrial development, and that was adopted by many other Asian countries later.

Finally, some policies fail to be implemented at all, or are implemented ineffectively, or quietly disappear from the policy-making agenda. None of the great policies examined in this book were complete failures and therefore provide little information about why innovations sometimes fail. But the pol-icy-making literature indicates that all policy innovations are experiments and that some never advance beyond the status of interesting ideas.[11]

CONCLUSIONS

Analysis of the processes underlying great policies in Asia and the Pacific highlight important lessons about this genre of strategic innovations.

First, the great policies described in this book were significant disjunctions from the way things were done in the past. They were decisions that set in motion a set of activities that were more than incremental improvements or changes in previous policies. All of these policies, for reasons noted earlier, changed interactions, organizations, and behavior and sent governments and other social institutions in new or different directions. Unlike incremental policies, great policies emerged from macroeconomic and macropolitical conditions and not from microlevel adjustments in legal, economic, political, or bureaucratic conventions.

Second, unlike incremental policies, megapolicies transcended sectoral boundaries and usually involved the interaction of two or more sectoral organizations. All of the policies examined here emerged from the need to deal with multiple problems in different sectors; they built upon and yielded synergies that would not have occurred through more routine policy changes. In several cases, it was synergies among sectoral objectives that allowed disjunctive innovations to evolve or be accepted.

Third, an examination of the processes through which great policies emerged confirms Johnston and Park's observation in Chapter 4 that great policies can only be adopted at "strategic moments" in history when there is a confluence of factors that creates an environment conducive to change. The process of policy making must play out in an economic, political, or social environment that allows innovators to reach beyond incremental changes. A close examination of megapolicies lends credence to the theory and indicates that this confluence of factors is the result of a complex combination of happenstance and the deliberate and persistent efforts of individuals and groups to bring about change.

Fourth, despite the fact that they created noteworthy changes in government activities, most of the innovations underlying megapolicies were discoveries rather than inventions. Their acceptance in a new setting depended heavily on proper timing and sequencing as well as the creation or emergence of a conducive political and economic environment. Strategic notions or visions may attract little or no interest at one period in time and, at another, are hailed as great innovations that change the direction of history. Japan's ODA policy toward China was rebuffed until economic, political, and social forces changed drastically in China at the end of the 1970s. Community resource management was a fully developed idea long before it was used by Colombian political leaders to build a new supporting coalition in the late 1980s and early 1990s. Team-teaching and conversational games had been used to teach languages in the United States and in other countries for many years before Japanese officials invited foreign English teachers to introduce them in Japan's schools. Agricultural-led economic development policies were pioneered by the Japanese in Japan and Korea before they were adopted widely in East and Southeast Asia. Energy-saving technologies had been developed in the West before they were recognized as useful or important in China. The theory of export-oriented economic development was discussed widely before either Taiwan adopted it in the 1960s or China tried it in the 1980s.

Finally, because they emerged from macroeconomic or macropolitical conditions, most of the policies examined here seemed to be influenced or made primarily by national political leaders and bureaucratic officials, with some participation by technical experts and foreign advisors. Little participation was seen by the media, community organizations, public interest groups, and nongovernment organizations that have initiated or supported innovations in the United States and Western Europe.[12] This may be explained by the different degrees of openness in political systems and government structures, but it also may reflect the fact that many of the megapolicies described here emerged at a time when public participation in policy making was less widespread, even in Western democracies.

In sum, the policy-making process described here and depicted in Figure 13.1 offers a conceptual framework for comparing and assessing what remains a rare phenomenon in public decision making: the adoption of strategic innovations that change the course of history. The cases described in this book provide a glimpse into the processes through which great policies in Asia and the Pacific were made and carried out.

## NOTES

1. For a discussion of the characteristics and processes of innovation see Everett M. Rogers, *Diffusion of Innovations*, 3rd ed. (New York: Free Press, 1983); James Utterback, "The Process of Technological Innovation Within the Firm," *Academy of Management Journal* 14, no. 1 (1971): 75–88; G. Zoltman, R. Duncan, and J. Holbek, *Innovation and Organizations* (John Wiley and Sons, 1973); Chris Argyris, *Organization and Innovation* (Homewood, Ill.: Dorsey Press, 1965); Anthony Downs, *Inside Bureaucracy* (Boston: Little Brown, 1966).

2. See the discussion of public sector innovations in the United States by Alan Altshuler and Marc Zegans, "Innovation and Creativity: Comparisons Between Public Management and Private Enterprise," *Cities* 7, no. 1 (1990): 16–24.

3. See Howard Goldstein, *Social Learning and Change: A Cognitive Approach to Human Services* (New York: Tavistock, 1981).

4. For a discussion of the dynamics of policy formulation, legitimation, and implementation see Charles O. Jones, *An Introduction to the Study of Public Policy* (Belmont, Calif.: Wadsworth Publishing Company, 1970).

5. See Charles E. Lindblom, *The Intelligence of Democracy: Decision Making Through Mutual Adjustment* (New York: Free Press, 1965); and Charles E. Lindblom, *Politics and Markets: The World's Political-Economic Systems* (New York: Basic Books, 1977) for a discussion of how policies are legitimized and implemented in different types of political and economic systems.

6. See Dennis A. Rondinelli, ed., *Expanding Sino-American Business and Trade: China's Economic Transition* (Westport, Conn.: Quorum Books, 1994).

7. This same paradigm provided the conceptual basis for U.S.-sponsored rural development programs in Vietnam during the 1960s and early 1970s. See, for example, Dennis A. Rondinelli, "Community Development and American Pacification Policy in Vietnam," *Philippine Journal of Public Administration* 15, no. 2 (1971): 162–74.

8. Feng Jing, "Harmony Between Economy and Environment," *Beijing Review* (May 30– June 4, 1994): 8–13.

9. Peter F. Drucker, *Innovation and Entrepreneurship: Practice and Principles* (New York: Harper and Row, 1985).

10. See Lindblom, *Politics and Markets.* The exercise of authority through mandates can also create or reinforce an adversarial relationship among conflicting parties. In order to work effectively, the parties wishing to establish authority and control must be able to punish those not complying with rules and regulations. Effective control requires the creation of specific conditions: first, those being punished cannot avoid the punishment; second, the punishment must be severe enough to deter undesired behavior in the future; and, third, the punishment must be administered on a continuous schedule of reinforcement immediately after undesired behavior occurs. See Albert Merabian, *Tactics of Social Influence* (Englewood Cliffs, N.J.: Prentice-Hall, 1970).

11. For a more extensive discussion of policies as experiments, see Dennis A. Rondinelli, *Development Projects as Policy Experiments*, 2nd ed. (New York: Rutledge, 1993).

12. See Dennis O. Grady and Keon S. Chi, "Formulating and Implementing Public Sector Innovations: The Political Environment of State Government Innovations," *Public Administration Quarterly* 17, no. 4 (1994): 468–84.

# INDEX

# ABOUT THE CONTRIBUTORS

WILLIAM ASCHER is Professor of Public Policy Studies and Political Science at Duke University, and Director of Duke's Sanford Institute of Public Policy. His research covers policy making in developing countries, natural-resource policy making, Latin American political economy, and forecasting. His books include *Scheming for the Poor: The Politics of Redistribution in Latin America* (1984), *Natural Resource Policymaking in Developing Countries* (1990), and two books on political-economic forecasting. He was the project director of the International Commission for Central American Recovery and Development. He is currently writing a book on the political economy of policy failures in managing the entire range of natural resources.

PAUL ENGLESBERG is Assistant Professor of Education at Pacific University, Forest Grove, Oregon. Professor Englesberg taught at several universities in Taiwan and China between 1981 and 1992. His research on Chinese education has included studies of college student culture and the 1978 reforms in higher education.

LIN GAN is a lecturer at the Research Policy Institute, University of Lund, Sweden, and a Research Fellow at the Institute of Social Science, Danish Technical University, Denmark. In the past few years, Mr. Gan has conducted intensive field work and research for the World Bank, United Nations Development Programme (UNDP), United Nations Environmental Programme (UNEP), and in China, especially on the Global Environment Facility (GEF) policies and the financial transfer mechanism and its influence on environmental policy in China.

BRUCE F. JOHNSTON is Professor Emeritus at Stanford Food Research Institute. He served in the occupation of Japan, and as consultant to the European Office of the Marshall Plan, the World Bank, and the Food and Agriculture Organization. He is coauthor of *Redesigning Rural Development* (1982), *Agricultural Change in Tropical Africa* (1979), and *Agriculture and Structural Transformation* (1975).

DAVID L. MCCONNELL is Assistant Professor of Anthropology at the College of Wooster. He was a Fulbright scholar at Kyoto University from 1988–1990 and an Advanced Research Fellow at the Program on U.S.-Japan Relations at Harvard University from 1991–1992. He is currently working on a book about the JET Program tentatively titled, *Japan Jets International: Coping with Diversity in Public Education.*

JOHN D. MONTGOMERY is Ford Foundation Professor of International Studies, Emeritus, at Harvard University, and Director of the Pacific Basin Research Center of Soka University of America and the Center for Science and International Affairs, Harvard. He is author of *Forced to be Free* (1957), *The Politics of Foreign Aid* (1962), *Technology and Civic Life* (1974), *Aftermath* (1986), and *Bureaucrats and People* (1988).

JOHN ORME is author of *Political Instability and American Foreign Policy* (1989) and *Deterrence, Reputation and Cold War Cycles* (1992) and has published articles on topics such as deterrence theory and the future of European security in the journals *International Security*, the *Washington Quarterly*, and the *Political Science Quarterly*. He is currently at work on *The Paradox of Peace*, an investigation into the origins of negotiated peace between international rivals. Orme was a research fellow at the Pacific Basin Research Center and the Center for Science and International Affairs in 1991–1992 and is currently Associate Professor of Politics at Oglethorpe University in Atlanta, Georgia.

ALBERT PARK is a doctoral candidate at Stanford University. He is coauthor with Bruce Johnston of several chapters dealing with agricultural development.

VIJAYA RAMACHANDRAN is a development economist and Deputy Director of the Center for International Development Research at Duke University. Her research interests include the role of agriculture in economic development, technology licensing to developing countries, and linkages between agricultural growth and industrialization in East Asia.

DENNIS A. RONDINELLI is the Glaxo Distinguished International Professor of Management at the Kenan-Flagler Business School and Director of the

Center for Global Business Research in the Kenan Institute of Private Enterprise at the University of North Carolina at Chapel Hill. He has done applied research on public policy for private enterprise development, privatization, the environmental industry, urban and regional development, economic reform policies in emerging market economies, employment generation policies in developing countries, international trade and investment, and program and project management for economic development. He has carried out research in Asia, Central Europe, Latin America, and Africa. Dr. Rondinelli has published 15 books and more than 150 monographs, book chapters, and articles in scholarly and professional journals. In addition, he has served as an advisor, consultant, or expert to the U.S. State Department's Agency for International Development, the World Bank, the Asian Development Bank, the Canadian International Development Agency, and several United Nations agencies.

FRED R. VON DER MEHDEN is Albert Thomas Professor of Political Science at Rice University. Professor von der Mehden has done extensive research on accelerated rural development and other economic and social development programs in Northeast Thailand. He has served as a consultant to the U.S. Agency for International Development, the U.S. Information Agency, the State Department, various agencies of the Thai Government, and several U.S. corporations. He is author of *Politics of the Developing Nations*, *Religion and Modernization in Southeast Asia*, and *Two Worlds of Islam*, as well as other books, monographs, and articles on the politics of Southeast Asia.

SHANG-JIN WEI is Assistant Professor of Public Policy, Kennedy School of Government, Harvard University, and Faculty Research Fellow, National Bureau of Economic Research. His areas of research are international finance, political economy, and economic reforms in transition economies. He has been a visiting lecturer at the Central European University in Prague, Czech Republic, and a visiting scholar at the International Monetary Fund, Board of Governors of the Federal Reserve System, and the Federal Reserve Bank of San Francisco.

QUANSHENG ZHAO is Director of the Institute of Asian Studies and Associate Professor of Political Science at Old Dominion University, Norfolk, Virginia. He has taught or conducted research at the United States Institute of Peace, the East-West Center, Cleveland State University, University of California at Berkeley, University of Tokyo, Oxford University, and Fletcher School at Tufts University. His books include *Japanese Policymaking: The Politics Behind Politics* (1993), *Politics of Divided Nations: China, Korea, Germany, and Vietnam* (co-editor, 1991), and *Interpreting Chinese Foreign Policy* (forthcoming). Dr. Zhao's research interests are in East Asian international relations and the domestic politics and foreign politics of Japan and China.

ISBN 0-275-95050-6

90000>

EAN

9 780275 950507

HARDCOVER BAR CODE